OFFICIAL PARTNER

D1343476

ILES

ESOME

CONGRATULATIONS TO ALL TRIATHLETES WHO COMPETED IN KONA

FOREWORD

Running has been a part of my life since my school teacher asked her class of lively 11-year-olds to run two laps of a sloping grass track. To my surprise she seemed pleased with how it went and I was asked to join a running club. I have been running ever since. After enjoying some success as a junior I carried on to become a senior athlete, representing Great Britain at the Olympics and World Championships. To have run for so many years I have relied on good training and nutrition advice, and plenty of support and motivation.

Runner's World magazine offers all of these things to its readers each month. The science of running and the running scene are continually developing and having an up-to-date source of authoritative information is why I originally started reading the magazine. The *Complete Guide to Running* brings together years of knowledge and experience from the *Runner's World* team, giving you all the information you need to run successfully. It will help you to train and eat well, avoid injury and motivate you to get the most out of your running. I hope you enjoy reading it as much as I did.

JO PAVEY British Olympian and former Commonwealth Games Silver Medallist

RUNNER'S WORLD
COMPLETE GUIDE TO RUNNING

Editor-in-Chief **Andy Dixon**
Editor **Matt Gilbert**
Associate Editor **Michael Donlevy**
Art Direction **Saxty Design**
Sub Editor **Anna Downing**
Group Editorial Director **Morgan Rees**
Group Publishing Director **Alun Williams**
Production Manager **Katie Allen**
Production Controller **Alison Kenehan**
Advertising Director **Jason Elson**
Senior Sales Executive **Gary Chambers**
Sales Executive **Gemma Taylor**
Classified Sales Executive **Jamie Fricker**
Marketing Director **Claire Matthews**

NATMAG RODALE LIMITED JOINT BOARD OF DIRECTORS
Chief Executive Officer, The National Magazine Company
Arnaud de Puyfontaine
President and CEO, Hearst Magazines International
Duncan Edwards
General Manager & Finance Director,
The National Magazine Company **Simon Horne**
Executive Vice President, Publishing Director, Hearst Magazines
Michael Clinton

THE NATIONAL MAGAZINE COMPANY
Director of Consumer Sales & Marketing **Sharon Douglas**
Head of Newstrade Marketing **Jennifer Caughey**
Business Manager **Paul Matias**

RUNNER'S WORLD Published by NatMag Rodale Ltd, 33 Broadwick Street, London W1F 0DQ Tel 020 7339 4400 Fax 020 7339 4420 For annual subscription rates for the UK, please call our enquiry line on 0844 848 5203. Back issues, customer enquiries, change of address and orders to: Runner's World, The National Magazine Company Ltd, Tower House, Sovereign Park, Lathkill Street, Market Harborough, Leics LE16 9EF (0844 848 5203; Mon to Fri, 8am to 9:30pm and Saturday, 8am to 4pm). Credit card hotline: 0844 848 1601 Runner's World is published in the UK by NatMag Rodale Limited, a joint venture by The National Magazine Company, a wholly owned subsidiary of The Hearst Corporation, and Rodale International, a division of Rodale Inc. Runner's World is a trademark of, and is used under license from, Rodale International. ISSN 1350-7745 Copyright © 2010. All rights reserved. Runner's World is printed and bound by Polestar Chantry, Wakefield. Repro by Wyndeham Argent Ltd, London.

♻ recycle

FROM THE EDITOR

Do you really need a complete guide to running? After all, just about anyone can plonk one foot in front of the other at speeds upwards of walking pace – that's one of the inherent joys of our sport. But like most of the fun things in life, you (and I) can do it better.

That's where this hefty 300-page tome comes in – a *Runner's World* "best of", with more than 1,000 top tips from experts and the editors of the world's best-selling running magazine. You'll also find easy-to-follow training schedules, proven weight-loss plans and inspirational real-life stories.

Whether you're a beginner or chasing down a PB, this book can help you do it better – which according to Reasons to Love Running (p34) might well help you out with some of life's other fun things.

MATT GILBERT
Editor

CONTENTS

3 NUTRITION

4 HEALTH & INJURY

5 MIND

CONTENTS

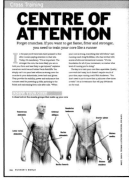

244 TWO FOR THE ROAD
How to keep going when you're with child

9 THE GREAT OUTDOORS

250 OFF THE BEATEN TRACK
Get off the road and up a mountain!

256 PEAK PRACTICE
The joys of running an Alpine race

262 COLD COMFORTS
25 reasons to ignore winter and get outside

266 BEAT THE HEAT
How to run in summertime without wilting

10 RACING

270 NATURAL SELECTION
Find out which distance is best-suited
to you: 5K, middle distance or marathon

RAVE RUN

Brecon Beacons, Wales

IMAGE: IAN ALDERMAN

1 Getting Started

A FRESH START

Our guide to becoming a runner – whether you're new to the sport or you just want to know more

Anybody can be a runner

The sport's inclusiveness is part of its appeal. But how do you actually become a runner? Tie your shoes and go? In essence, running is that simple. That's also part of its appeal. But as you get going, questions arise: should I run for 20 minutes or 30?

Is walking okay? If I've run before, do I need to start right back at the beginning? Over the following pages, you'll find the answers, along with everything else you need to get started on a running programme.

1 BEFORE TAKING YOUR FIRST STEP

Make sure you're well prepared for your first run

Many new runners are reluctant to spend money or time on the sport before they get started because they don't know if they'll stick with it. But getting started will be easier if you commit some time and do a bit of planning first. It may be overwhelming to begin with – thoughts of new shoes, training plans and races can get too much, so we've made it really simple for you to get started.

GET A CHECK-UP

You may feel fine, but if you're a man over 45 or a woman over 55, and especially if you have risk factors for heart disease (obesity, family history, hypertension, high cholesterol), get your doctor's clearance to start exercising. If you have cardiovascular disease, which you may not know about, you could be at greater risk of suffering a

heart attack. A plan to start running is a good excuse to get a check-up scheduled.

SET A GOAL

"Your goals become incentives," says coach Nick Anderson (fullpotential.co.uk). "If you don't set a target, you'll get bored. A target might be to run for 30 minutes continuously, or it might be a 5K race that you want to do without having to walk." Choose a realistic goal while you build your base levels of fitness.

TAKE IT EASY

Beginners can be enthusiastic, but don't push too hard. "I always start new runners gently," says coach Richard Holt (momentumsports.co.uk). "It's vital not to let eagerness lead to early injuries through over-training, but to build a platform from which to progress later."

BUY RUNNING SHOES

"Often beginners are reluctant to buy a pair of running shoes in case they decide not to keep it up," says Ben Noad, runner and marketing manager for specialist shop Runner's Need. "Shoes are the most important piece of kit – you can start in any clothes, but you must wear decent trainers. They'll pay for themselves in keeping you injury-free." Cross-trainers, tennis shoes and other athletic footwear don't have enough cushioning to handle running's impact – nor does the pair of shoes you wore two years ago, so buy new ones. We'll tell you how later in the chapter.

2 HOW TO START

Taking you through your first three weeks of running

First-run horror stories are common, but avoidable. "Starting or returning to a sport is going to be a little uncomfortable because you're not conditioned to it," says coach Greg McMillan. Having been a runner before or being fit doesn't exempt you from this reality. Elizabeth Hufton, 29, who recently returned to running after more than a year out, says, "At first my legs gave out with a few minutes' jogging. I'd cross-trained, but it was a shock to find how much running fitness I'd lost."

Minimise discomfort by taking walk breaks and keeping your pace slow. Use the following guidelines to make running a positive experience.

WALK FIRST

Start with three 30-minute walks a week for two to three weeks.

THEN RUN/WALK

Interspersing walk breaks into your running lets you catch your breath and protects your joints and muscles. "Even if you've run before, and especially if you're returning from an injury, walk breaks are smart," says top coach Jeff Galloway.

GO FOR TIME OVER DISTANCE

Runners love ticking off the miles, but don't worry about that at first. Running by time de-emphasises pace, and allows you to adjust to how you feel that day.

TAP THE POWER OF THREE

"People who do not run regularly are more likely to quit," says Galloway. Run three days a week: you can only achieve running fitness if you do it consistently.

GET TO THE NINTH RUN

The end of the third week is the turning point for many new and returning runners. "Your metabolism's changed, you've got more energy, you've probably improved your diet – everything starts happening for you," says Anderson. "But you start to feel unfulfilled, so you need a new target."

ENDURANCE OVER SPEED

Fast running puts a greater demand on your muscles, connective tissues and cardiovascular system than jogging. Build to 30 continuous minutes before you work on speed.

3 MAKING IT STICK

Avoid the guilt of missing a session any way you can

SEEK PEER PRESSURE

Having a running date, whether it's with one person or a group, is a strong motivator. Ask about groups at your local running store, or check in with the forumites at runnersworld.co.uk.

RACE

A race is a great way to focus the mind and help runners plan ahead, says Holt. "You need to know what you are aiming for, whether it be to complete a race or simply to measure progress through your weight loss."

REWARD YOURSELF

When you hit a milestone – that ninth run, running three days a week for a month or completing your first race – give yourself a treat. "Whether it's the medal for finishing a race, a cake or a trip to the Bahamas, it doesn't really matter. It is the carrot dangling at the end of the race that can help people achieve," says Holt. Rewards don't need to be physical, either. "We set new targets as a reward," says Anderson. "Once a runner has achieved their first target, they feel euphoric – 'I've become a runner' – and want to do more."

ENLIST FAMILY

Support from your family and friends is vital if you're to keep it up. If you are being nagged by a partner every time you go for a run it can soon become a chore, says Holt, but "most runners' families and friends can see the benefits in terms of both health and enjoyment". They may need a crash course when you start though. "Educate your family so they understand what you do," says Anderson.

ADD VARIETY

A new route can enliven your running regime. Find a trail, a different area to try, or if you normally run a loop do it in reverse.

ACCEPT BAD RUNS

If you acknowledge that every run is not going to feel great, you will reduce your frustration. On tough days, slow your pace, take walk breaks or shorten your run. "Runners think that once they've built up, they can't go back," says Galloway. "You can."

ACCENTUATE THE POSITIVE

McMillan wishes all new and returning runners would stop comparing themselves to others. "Don't put added pressure on yourself," says McMillan. "Instead, focus on the accomplishment of every workout."

FLEX PLAN Stretches for runners

It's likely that you'll wake up after your first run with sore, stiff muscles. You can minimise the 'morning after' effect by walking for a few minutes and stretching after your run. As well as improving flexibility, it flushes the muscles with blood and oxygen, which promotes recovery. At the very least, focus on these three areas...

➔ HAMSTRINGS

WHY They're your main propulsion muscles.
HOW Place your heel on a step or any elevated surface and bend slowly at the waist until you feel a stretch in the back of your thigh (you may also feel it in your calves). Avoid rounding your back. Hold for 30 to 60 seconds. Release and repeat four or five times. Change sides.

➔ CALVES

WHY They help propel you and absorb impact.
HOW Place both hands on a wall and take a step back with one leg. Keep your heel on the ground and lean into the wall until you feel a stretch. Hold and repeat four times. Change sides. Repeat, but bend the knee of the extended leg slightly, so you feel the stretch in the lower calf.

➔ QUADS

WHY They are your legs' shock absorbers, cotrolling your movement every time you land.
HOW Stand up straight, bend one leg behind you, and grab your foot; pull it towards your bottom and push the hip of the same leg forwards until you feel the stretch in the front of your leg. Hold for 30 to 60 seconds. Release and repeat four times. Change sides.

FITTING IT IN

You have the motivation to run but find you don't have the time – or so you think. These 25 tips will help you squeeze running into the busiest of schedules

With so much to do in everyday life, from shopping to putting the children to bed, running can get squeezed out. Lack of time – whether actual or perceived – is the biggest barrier to getting in a run or running as much as you might like. We're here to help.

The way we see it, time problems fall into the three categories below: making time (questions of when, where and how); saving time (little dos and don'ts that add up to serious savings); and re-thinking time (adjusting the relationship between your running and the time you need to do it).

Here's the plan: below are 25 time-management tips in these three categories. Pick any three of the strategies – one from each section – and try them for a month. If any work, great; if not, pick three more. If you try them all and still can't find time to run, you probably don't really want to. Which is a shame. Chances are, however, you'll find some that work every time. So stop making excuses and get your kit on!

MAKING TIME

You can do it for yourself, *and* rope in a little help from those around you.

1 PLAN YOUR WEEK
Sit down with your diary on a Sunday night and draw up a realistic training schedule, before the blank spaces start filling up with other priorities.

2 THINK QUALITY, NOT QUANTITY
Take the most out of what you have. Finding time for a 20-minute run is easy. Just make every minute count. Alternate one minute a little faster than your normal pace with one-minute recoveries. Do a two- to four-minute warm-up first and a similar cool-down afterwards.

3 GET UP 30 MINUTES EARLIER
Run before anyone else is even out of bed, because there are no appointments to get in the way of an early morning run, and it will invigorate you for the day ahead.

4 GET YOURSELF A DOG
There's no way to ignore a wet snout in your face telling you, "now, now, NOW!" Having to exercise the dog will literally drag you out of the door.

5 SWAP YOUR DUTIES
One morning, afternoon or evening, let your other half look after the children while you run. The next day, reverse the roles. Or…

6 TAKE THE KIDS WITH YOU
Many gyms now offer in-house nurseries. In 90 minutes, you can squeeze in an hour on the treadmill and a 20-minute circuit-training session on the weight machines – an excellent all-round workout that will improve strength and endurance. And your kids should get a bit of exercise into the bargain.

7 GIVE 'EM THE RUNAROUND
While the children are playing football (or whatever), run loops around the outside of the field. "I do this twice a week," says mother-of-two Judie Simpson. "Once as a steady one-hour run. The second time I'll pick it up on the long side of the field and jog the short side for 45 minutes or so."

8 BEAT THE RUSH HOUR
Take your kit to work and run home while everyone else is stuck in gridlock or squashed on a train. By the time you're home you'll be de-stressed from the rigours of the day and can allow yourself to feel ever so slightly smug.

IMAGES: GETTY

BUDDY UP
Owning a dog gives you
no excuse to stay indoors

9 SET SHORT-TERM GOALS
Too many runners think too far ahead – a six-month or year-long plan – when laying out their training. "That vision can be lost pretty quickly when you're feeling bad," warns Dave Scott, six-time Ironman Hawaii winner. "Instead, set a fortnightly goal, and make it specific: run three times a week for the next two weeks." Then set another, and so on.

10 PLACE YOUR BETS
People who bet £25 that they could stick with their training programme for six months had a 97 per cent success rate in a study at Michigan State University in the USA. Less than 20 per cent of those who didn't place a bet stuck it out. Bet against a friend, and the first to give up pays up.

11 THINK LITTLE AND OFTEN
If you're new to it, aim for frequency, not duration, to make running a regular part of your life. Instead of trying to find time for a 45-minute run two or three times a week, do shorter sessions of 15-20 minutes, but run most days. A few small steps are more likely to keep you on your feet that one giant leap.

12 GO LONGER TO GET STRONGER
Veteran runners should focus on two "key" runs every week, sessions where they really push. Try a one-hour interval, fartlek or hill run during the week and then a weekend long run. Fill in around them with short, easy runs, cross-training and rest days. Two very tough runs will make you faster and stronger than five or six so-so weekly runs with little rest between them.

13 FIND A FRIEND
Recruit a regular training partner and agree on time, place and distance. If someone is expecting you to show up, you're less likely to make excuses.

SAVING TIME
Fifteen seconds here, a minute there. It doesn't seem like much, but watch how fast it all adds up.

14 THINK AHEAD
Get your kit ready the night before. Even loosen your laces so your feet slide straight into your shoes. That way, you sit down and dress for battle quickly. No back-and-forth from bedroom to laundry and back to bedroom, tracking down something clean to wear.

BEAT THE TRAFFIC
Running to work saves time and money

15 GET READY FOR BREKKIE
Plop your smoothie ingredients in a blender the night before an early morning run and put it in the fridge. After your run, hit the switch and eight seconds later... breakfast is served. We tried this ourselves: assembling from scratch in the morning took 1:53, meaning we saved a grand total of 1:45.

16 HOLD OFF ON THE STRETCHES
Don't spend time stretching cold muscles before you train. Instead, walk briskly for a few minutes, then jog slowly to start your run.

17 RUN BEFORE YOU TALK
You meet your running partners and start talking while doing some lame trunk twists as a warm-up. Don't do it. Say hello (it's only polite), and start jogging slowly into your run. Talk then, before the pace picks up. Do all four of these tips from 14 to 17 and you save from seven to 10 minutes – enough time to turn your usual five-mile run into a six-miler.

a study at the University of Northern Iowa in the USA. More isn't always better, so don't scramble to find time for miles simply to pad out your weekly total.

21 THE 10-MINUTE MIRACLE

"Run faster-than-normal training pace (but don't sprint) for 10 footfalls of your right foot. When you reach 10, do 10 more steps of easy jogging," says exercise physiologist Jack Daniels. Then do 20-20 and so on up to 60-60. Then work back to 10-10. This is a good way to warm up, cool down and throw in some intensity in a short space of time.

RE-THINKING TIME

Some time barriers to running are external – work, picking up the children, doing the shopping, and so on. But equally restrictive are internal roadblocks – attitudes toward running and/or ourselves that stop us working out.

22 BE REALISTIC

Cut back on your running if you need to. But don't throw in the towel because life gets busy. Ride these periods out, and fit in a run of some kind – 15 minutes, 10 minutes – every second or third day. Then resume a more intense routine when you can. When your schedule implodes, short-term changes can stop you fretting your way into sofa sloth.

23 BE A BIT SELFISH

By giving your run a high priority, you boost your physical and emotional health, and live up to your obligation to your family to be healthy and happy.

24 BE FLEXIBLE

If circumstances change, don't make excuses. If a surprise meeting cancels the lunchtime run, do it after work. If you miss the alarm, take your kit to work and run at lunch. And "I don't feel like it" doesn't wash. "If you really want to run, you'll find time," says former 2:09 marathoner Ron Hill. "It's really no different than finding time to shave, eat or read the paper."

25 HAVE FUN!

Enjoying a run greatly increases the likelihood that you'll want to – and will – find time for the next one. Run a new route; run an old one backwards. If you usually run on roads, head for the park and run through the trees. Variety really is the spice of life.

Over the course of a working week, you net at least 35 minutes of extra running time.

18 KEEP YOUR SHORTS ON

"Wear running shorts as underwear," says US running guru Jeff Galloway, so you're run-ready the instant your antennae pick up a 10-minute block of free time. "Accumulate enough short runs and they add up," he says. A Stanford University study found that multiple bouts of moderate-intensity exercise produce significant training effects. Leading us to...

19 DIVIDE AND CONQUER

On busy days, beat the clock by breaking up your run into two shorter sessions. Instead of a single 40-minute run, maybe do 20 in the morning and the same at lunchtime, or whatever fits your schedule.

20 TURN DOWN THE VOLUME

Runners clocking up 50 miles a week had marathon times no faster than those who logged 40, in

Our doctors and scientists have contributed to 19 of the top 20 drugs used to treat cancer patients worldwide

Cancer Research UK are entirely funded by the public, so please join our team in a running event and help beat cancer.

Together *we will beat cancer*

For more information and a wide range of events visit:
http://running.cancerresearchuk.org
Tel: **0871 641 2403**

Reg. Charity No. 1089464

CANCER RESEARCH UK

IT'S GOOD TO WALK

There's no shame in adding a little walking to your running, reckons 1968 Boston Marathon winner Amby Burfoot

Shhhh. I have a secret to share with you. You see, I used to be a fairly fast runner. In fact, I won the Boston Marathon in the USA at the age of 21. And there's a certain amount of honour among Boston winners – a sort of "pain is my friend" ethic – that we're sworn to uphold. Now, about that secret. I wouldn't want anyone to think I've gone soft or anything but... this is hard to get out... I often take walking breaks during my daily runs.

There, that feels much better. Though I don't know why it was hard to say in the first place. After all, it makes perfect sense to mix running and walking. Think about it: when new runners start off, they often follow a run-walk routine; they run for maybe 30 seconds, walk until they feel recovered, then repeat the process for 20-30 minutes. This system has proved successful a thousand times over.

When world-class runners peak for the Olympics, they concentrate on "interval" training – the still-unsurpassed method for achieving maximum results. They run hard for one to five minutes, then walk or jog very slowly until they're ready to run hard again.

When ultra-distance runners participate in those seemingly crazy races of 100 miles or more, they inevitably alternate running and walking. It's hard to imagine any other way to cover the mega-mile distances. You, on the other hand, probably view walking as the enemy. The thinking is that you run, and this is good. You are proving and improving yourself; you are determined; you are a moral person. Whereas when you walk, it is bad. You are lazy; you are a loser; you don't deserve to be loved (not even by your mother).

Mental-health therapists have many words for this sort of inflexible, perfectionist thinking, and I have one, too. I call it "stupid". (None too elegant, but it has the benefit of clarity.) The goal of a session is not to

BIG STRIDES
Walking breaks can push your running to new heights

avoid walking. The goals are to feel better, get in better shape, reduce tension, lose weight, train for an upcoming race and so on. Take your pick. They're all worthwhile goals.

Run/walk training (R/W training) is a simple, common-sense approach to conditioning. It can help you train more (for better marathon preparation and calorie-burning); it can help you to train healthier (who needs injuries and burnout?); and it can even help you to get faster (through interval training).

Enough talk. Let's be more specific.

THE GALLOWAY MARATHON

Olympic marathon runner Jeff Galloway has pioneered the idea of walking breaks during marathons. He advocates this programme not only for many first-timers, but also for those who have previously hit the wall and experienced the crushing fatigue and depression of those last few miles. By walking early and often, Galloway has found, most runners survive the final miles in much better shape. They feel better, and often run faster as a result.

You can run/walk a marathon any way you want, but the simplest is to run the first mile, then walk for 60 seconds. Run the second mile, then walk for 60 seconds (and have a sports drink). Repeat 24 more times, then hold your head high and sprint like a hare.

The method has been used successfully by thousands of marathoners. Several have dipped below 3:30 this way, but fast times aren't the point. The point is that you can finish the marathon, feel good, run strong to the end, and admire that gleaming finisher's medal for the rest of your life.

THE NEXT STEP

The Galloway programme has many converts, and I'm one of them. I've now run four marathons with walking breaks, in times ranging from 3:45 to 4:30. I'm a modest trainer these days, averaging 20-30 miles a week, so the marathon can easily intimidate me. A few years ago, I was beginning to dread the thought of running 26.2-milers. Now, I don't even think of the marathon that way. I think of it as a one-mile run that I just happen to repeat 26 times. Piece of cake.

R/W training has also made my daily training easier. It used to be that, much as I love running, I sometimes felt too tired to get through the door. I talked myself out of many sessions: when you're already tired, why drag yourself out on the roads for 40 minutes? I don't have this problem any more, because I don't run for

TOP TIPS

→ If you want to call yourself a runner, walking's out, isn't it? Not really. Running is good, but so is walking. It's a valid form of interval training employed even by elite runners.

→ R/W training can allow you to run longer, healthier and, yes, faster – even on marathon day.

→ Try this marathon day plan: run a mile, walk 60 seconds. Repeat 26 times until complete in good time and with no walls hit.

→ Incorporating walking into your routine reduces your chances of injury and assists injury recovery.

→ Ease the pain of those long runs with an R/W strategy that will deliver near-full endurance benefits.

40 minutes. I run for four minutes, then walk for a minute, then repeat the process until I've completed 40 minutes. All I care about is getting into the session and feeling energised afterwards, which I always do.

A STEP BACKWARDS

Let's pause for a moment to consider some of the differences between running and walking. Some are small, others more significant. Running and walking have much in common, with one big difference. Runners "jump" from foot to foot, walkers don't. When you run, the knee flexes more than in walking, the quadriceps contract, and you "toe-off" in more or less the same way as a long jumper leaps.

Because you toe-off and jump, you come down forcefully on the other foot. This is the "impact shock" of running – said to be two to three times your body weight – that can lead to over-use injuries. Walkers don't jump, so they are less likely to get injured.

Because you jump when running, you can cover ground much faster than a walker and burn many more calories per minute (because moving faster requires you to consume more oxygen). In other words, you get a superior session in less time, which is one of the major benefits of running.

Unfortunately, many potential runners never get into the rhythm of running. They set out to run around the block a few times, but find themselves breathless at the first corner, so they repair to the sofa and never leave it again. These are the people who need to learn about

one minute, run hard for two minutes and jog for one minute. Then do the one-minute walk. Repeat this eight times, and you've come reasonably close to the 8 x 400m torture my college coach loved to inflict on us.

On the topic of intervals, exercise physiologist Jack Daniels had two groups of women run three times a week, either continuously or with walking breaks. After 12 weeks, the run/walk group was more fit. Why? "In effect, the walking breaks turned the sessions into one big interval session," says Daniels. "It allowed the women to go faster overall."

Fewer injuries Walking doesn't cause as many injuries as running, so R/W training shouldn't either. Walking uses the leg muscles and connective tissues in a different way to running so it should reduce over-use injuries. Walk with a slow, elongated stride to feel other muscles coming into play.

More sightseeing What's the point of running in some beautiful location if all you see are the rocks and gnarly roots on the trail in front of you? Yet that's all many trail runners see, because they're concentrating so hard on avoiding falls and twisted ankles. With R/W you can drink in the views during your walking breaks.

More effective recovery days Some days you need to run slow, particularly if you ran long or fast the previous day, or if you're busy at work or home.

Faster comebacks You've had a sore knee, a bad Achilles or a nasty cold. You're ready to get back into your training routine but don't want to overdo it and suffer a setback. Listen to your body, and don't run further or faster than what feels right.

FINAL THOUGHTS

The aspect of R/W training I find most appealing – the mental breaks provided by the brief walking periods – won't prove equally compelling to all runners. Many will staunchly resist. "I didn't start running to become a walker," they'll snort derisively. Old habits die hard, and R/W training isn't for everyone. Or for every session. I do it a couple of times a week, usually when I run by myself and often as a long run.

However – and this is the most surprising thing about it – I've found that it has motivated me to do more speedwork. In fact, you say that R/W training is classic interval training that's been liberated from the track and allowed to roam wherever you want to take it. You just might discover an entirely new, enjoyable (and effective) way to run. It's worth a try, isn't it?

R/W training. You won't get exhausted and frustrated (thanks to the walking breaks), and you'll get all the benefits that vigorous exercise brings (thanks to the running). There are many reasons for R/W training. Some are physical, some mental, but all will change (and probably improve) your running. Here are a few...

Running further, easier All runners, from beginners to veterans, would like to run longer and easier. The R/W system gives you a new tool to help achieve this. Does it come at a cost? Sure. Your overall session is slower, so you get slightly less training effect, but most of the time you do long runs to build overall endurance and increase your body's ability to burn fat and calories in general.

Increased variety Far too many runners do the same session at the same pace every time they run. It's boring, and it's not a smart way to train. An R/W session naturally has many small segments, which encourages you to experiment.

Better speedwork An R/W session is an offshoot of the classic interval session, so it's easy to make it a real gut-buster. Here's one of my favourites: jog for

A SHOE THING

There's no such thing as the "best shoe" – everyone has different needs. Biomechanics, bodyweight, the surfaces you run on and the shape of your feet mean one person's ideal is someone else's nightmare. Here's how to avoid the pitfalls

SHOEPAEDIA An A-Z of running shoe jargon busting

Making your first trip to your local running specialist to choose a pair of shoes can be a daunting prospect. A reputable shop will always try and make sure they sell you the best shoes for you, rather than the most expensive ones, but in order to understand your needs, you have to be able to communicate them. Check out our jargon-busting guide to the technical talk before you make your purchase.

⊙ ARCH LOCK
A reinforced mesh that tightly wraps the midfoot and supports the arch. If it's not snug, the foot will move inside the shoe, causing blisters.

⊙ BIOMECHANICALLY EFFICIENT
A runner with a foot which follows the natural gait cycle, with no excessive inward or outward rolling. Does not need added stability features in a shoe. Also called "neutral" or "efficient".

⊙ BLOWN RUBBER
The lightest, most-cushioned and least-durable form of rubber on the outsole. Made by injecting air into the rubber.

⊙ CARBON RUBBER
A harder, more durable outsole, made from solid rubber with carbon additives.

⊙ COLLAR
Made out of a soft material, the collar should wrap just below the ankle and supply a snug, gap-free fit.

Shoes can be divided into four main categories – neutral cushioned, motion-control, stability and performance – which, for all the bright colours and crazily named hi-tech features, are basically designed to suit different people's biomechanical needs.

The first step in finding your ideal shoe needs is to try our "wet test" (see the panel on your right). This works on the basis that the shape of your wet footprint roughly correlates with the amount of stability you might need in your shoe. "Roughly" is the key word here, though: it's a handy starting point, but no more than that.

Secondly, read our section on shoe categories over the page for a greater understanding of the four types on offer. And once you've done that, and got at least some idea of what type of shoe will best suit you, visit a biomechanics expert or, more realistically, an experienced specialist running shop to get a "gait analysis" done. This is a more scientifically advanced version of the wet test, where a specialist will look at how your foot strikes the ground to help choose a shoe with the right levels of support.

ONE FIT NEVER FITS ALL

Most runners will find it relatively easy to find at least a nearly ideal shoe with the right advice. Once you've determined which category you fall into, you have a wide range of shoes to choose from. All you have to do is decide which shoe within your category provides the best comfort, fit and performance for your needs – although that can be a daunting prospect for a beginner. Try out a range of shoes, listen to the advice and don't rush into a decision if you're unsure.

Some people, however, have problems finding a comfortable shoe at all. A minority of runners have very specific needs, which can make shoe buying an altogether more frustrating business. Over the page we will outline the most common "minority" biomechanical problems, such as heel striking, underpronation – bear with us here. All will be explained in due course – to help you get ready... set... to go shopping.

THE WET TEST

Dip the bottom of your foot in water, step straight onto a brown paper bag, and match the imprint with the arch types below.

HIGH, RIGID ARCHES need more impact protection and are best suited to neutral-cushioned shoes.

NORMAL ARCH runners can wear shoes from all categories, depending on their weight.

LOW, FLEXIBLE ARCHES are often found on overpronating runners. They should wear stability or motion-control shoes.

CUSHIONED SHOE
A shoe without added stability features, for biomechanically neutral runners.

CUSHIONING
The ability of a shoe to absorb the forces of footstrike. Except at the extremes, there's no right or wrong level of cushioning, but heavier runners tend to do better with firmer shoes.

DUAL-DENSITY MIDSOLE
A mechanism, usually a firmer wedge of foam on the medial (inner) side of the shoe, used to correct overpronation.

EYELETS
The laces run through these to tighten the shoe. If you feel pressure under a pair of eyelets, you don't have to use those ones to tie your shoe.

FLEX GROOVES
Indentations moulded into the midsole and outsole to make a shoe more flexible.

FLEXIBILITY
The ability of a shoe's forefoot to bend under the ball of the foot. If the shoe does not flex easily under your weight, your foot and leg muscles have to work harder, which saps energy and can cause injuries such as shin splints.

FOREFOOT
The broad, front section of the shoe or foot. This is the point from which you propel yourself forward, so the shoe

SHOE CATEGORIES

There are four types of shoe, so work out which one fits your need before parting with your hard-earned cash

Running shoes come in four main categories: neutral cushioned, motion control, stability and performance. Heavier runners (women over 11st 6lb, men over 13st 3lb) usually need a stability or motion-control shoe, but your arch type and how much you pronate (the inward roll of the foot that helps the body dissipate shock) will help determine which category best fits your feet. Match up these characteristics to the categories below to find the perfect pair for you.

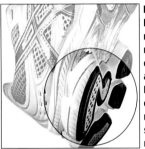

NEUTRAL CUSHIONED
Recommended for runners who need maximum midsole cushioning and minimum arch support. These are best for biomechanically efficient runners and midfoot or forefoot strikers with high or normal arches.

MOTION CONTROL
Recommended for runners with low arches who are moderate to severe overpronators and who need maximum stability and support on the medial side of their shoes. Best suited for bigger runners who need plenty of support.

STABILITY
Recommended for runners who are mild to moderate overpronators and have low to normal arches. These runners tend to need a shoe that has a combination of good support and midsole cushioning.

PERFORMANCE
Recommended either for racing or, if you're biomechanically efficient, for training. They have varying degrees of support and cushioning but they're light (most weigh around 250-300g) and fit like a glove.

SHOEPAEDIA An A-Z of running shoe jargon busting

should be protective yet responsive. Some runners land on the fronts of their feet, and need maximum cushioning in the forefoot of their shoes. They're called, appropriately, forefoot strikers.

➜ GAIT CYCLE
The natural movement of the foot against the ground when you walk or run. The rear, outer part of the heel hits the ground first: the foot then rolls forwards and inwards (pronates) as the arch collapses to absorb shock; then it moves on to the inner and front part of the forefoot as the foot stiffens and pushes away from the ground (toe-off).

➜ HEEL COUNTER
An internal support feature in the rear of the shoe that sits around your heel, and usually has a notch cut in the top to prevent irritating the Achilles tendon. The fit of the shoe isn't perfect unless the heel sits flush against this stiff backing. Tapping the foot back into the heel will lock it into position.

➜ INSOLE
The foot-shaped insert, usually removable, which sits between your foot and the shoe. Also known as a "sockliner".

➜ LACES
Used to pull the upper around the arch. If you can feel your laces, either they or the tongue are too thin.

IF YOU'RE A FOREFOOT STRIKER...

You... land and push off from your toes when you run, rather than following the normal pattern of landing on the outside edge of your heel and rolling through to push off from your toes.

You need shoes that... have excellent forefoot cushioning, flexibility and stability. However, you need to have an expert assess precisely why you're a forefoot striker. If it's because you have a high arch and a rigid ankle, you need a neutral, relatively curved shoe to encourage foot motion, with a flexible forefoot and a high arch support.

If you're a forefoot striker simply because you have tight calves, you should address this problem with stretching and/or physiotherapy rather than trying to compensate via your shoes.

Finally, some runners favour the forefoot simply because they run quickly; they need light, responsive shoes, with an emphasis on forefoot cushioning and stability.

IF YOU'RE A HEEL STRIKER...

You... prematurely destroy the outsole rubber (and probably the cushioning) on the outside heel of your shoes. This is usually because you land in an exaggerated way, though if you're heavy, that could also contribute.

You need shoes that... have thick, durable outsoles and resilient midsole foam. Because the composition of the outsole compound is at least as important as its thickness, you need to know about a shoe's reputation before you buy. Ask your local specialist retailer, or check out *Runner's World* for regular shoe tests and expert opinion on the latest ranges.

IF YOU UNDERPRONATE...

Your... feet and ankles don't roll inwards enough when you run, a movement that would normally help to absorb shock every time your feet strike the ground. This is a rare condition, and certainly less common than excessive roll (overpronation) but there are shoes to help overcome the problem.

You need shoes that... encourage the inward movement of the foot (pronation). Look for a soft midsole, and a curved "last" (the shape around which the shoe is built).

Avoid shoes with added stability features, such as medial posts. These are firm sections on the arch side of the midsole, designed to limit lateral movement for those runners who overpronate.

IF YOU WEAR ORTHOSES...

You... have custom-made insoles designed to correct biomechanical imbalances. They are usually – but not always – built to provide additional stability.

You need shoes that... fit your orthoses, and work with them in the way that your podiatrist intended. Usually, if your orthoses provide all the correction you need, your podiatrist is likely to recommend using them in a neutral but supportive shoe. Extreme overpronators may be recommended a motion-control shoe, especially as, in the view of many leading podiatrists, the chance of having too much stability is slim.

In either case, look for shoes that are roomy enough to accommodate orthoses comfortably. Look particularly for a deep heel counter, as built-up orthoses can compromise stability and comfort in shallow-fitting shoes.

LATERAL
The outside (little-toe) edge.

LUGS
Deep, rubber tread on the underside of the shoe to provide grip in off-road conditions.

MEDIAL
The inside (big-toe and arch) edge.

MEDIAL POST
A firmer density of foam, sometimes with an additional plastic device, inserted into the rear, arch-side section of the midsole to add support or control excessive rear motion.

MIDSOLE
The material (usually EVA or Polyurethane foam) that sits below the upper and above the outsole, protecting you from impact and often encasing other technologies, such as gel pouches or air pockets, for extra durability and protection.

OUTSOLE
The durable part of the shoe that makes contact with the ground, providing traction.

OVERLAYS
These leather strips over the top of the upper work with the laces and eyestays to make the shoe conform to the shape of the foot.

OVERPRONATION
Excessive inward rolling of the foot,

IF YOU HAVE WIDE FEET...

You... are not alone. As more runners get specialist advice and gait analysis, so more manufacturers now offer a growing range of shoes to cater for the specific needs of those with wide feet.

You need shoes that... keep pressure off the sides of your feet, and allow the recommended thumb's width of space between your longest toe and the end of the shoe.

Beware, though. Finding the right shoe isn't simply a matter of reaching for the nearest available option in a wide fit. It actually depends on *why* your feet are wide relative to their length (it also has to meet your stability and cushioning needs). If you have short toes, you'll need a shoe that flexes further forward than normal because relatively speaking, that's what your feet do. You retailer will look for the position of the flex grooves on the underside of the shoe to help you avoid a retail blunder here.

IF YOU HAVE NARROW FEET...

You... need to do more than just lace up normal shoes tightly.

You need shoes that... don't allow your feet to slip inside. Not only will over-wide shoes feel less responsive, you'll also be more at risk of blisters in the areas where your feet do touch the shoe, because you'll be sliding around. As with the wider fits, most manufacturers have woken up to the fact that not everyone has standard size of shaped feet, and they now offer narrow options.

It may be coincidence, but you could turn out to be really fast, because often the best narrow-fit running shoes fall into the performance category...

TOP TIP

Loop-lacing lock

This is a great way for anyone to create a secure, tight fit. Just put each lace end back into the same hole it just exited, leaving a small loop on the top side of the shoe; now thread each loose end through the loop on the opposite side; then pull to create a super-tight closure.

➡ **PROBLEM** Narrow foot
SOLUTION Using the loop-lacing lock halfway up the shoe doubles the laces over your midfoot, ensuring a tight fit.

➡ **PROBLEM** Heel slipping in your shoe
SOLUTION Lace the shoe using the normal criss-cross technique, then tie a loop-lacing lock on the last eyelet.

➡ **PROBLEM** High instep
SOLUTION Start with normal criss-cross lacing, but over the midfoot feed the laces up each side of the shoe. Finish with the criss-cross technique at the top.

➡ **PROBLEM** Wide forefoot
SOLUTION Over the width of your foot just feed the laces up each side of the shoe, again using the criss-cross technique at the top.

SHOEPAEDIA An A-Z of running shoe jargon busting

which prevents normal toe-off and can expose you to a host of injury problems, particularly in the knees.

➡ **PRONATION**
The inward rolling of the foot, which is a natural part of the gait cycle.

➡ **SUPINATION**
The opposite of overpronation, the foot rolls outwards on impact, and needs to be corrected with appropriate footwear.

➡ **TOE-BOX**
The front part of the fabric upper surrounding the toes.

➡ **TOE-OFF**
The final stage of the gait cycle, which propels you forward as your foot pushes off from the ground.

➡ **TONGUE**
The tongue should be pulled up tight and lined up straight. You should use a tongue's lace keeper to hold it in place.

➡ **UNDERPRONATION**
Too little inward rolling of the foot to dissipate the force of the footstrike.

➡ **UPPER**
The fabric section of the shoe at the top of the foot that holds the laces.

➡ **VAMP**
A part of the upper that surrounds the toebox. If you can pinch a quarter inch, the vamp is too baggy. If you can't wiggle your toes, it's too tight.

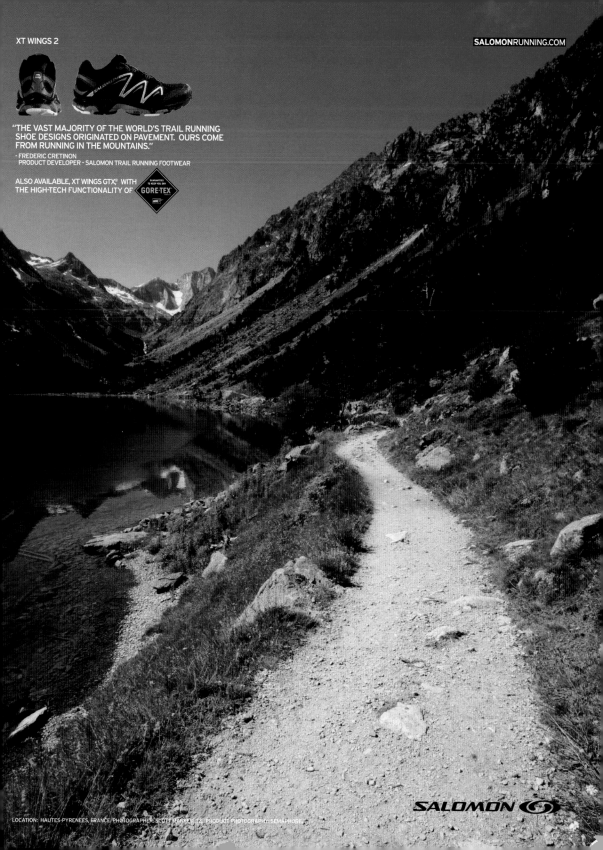

TWO RIGHT FEET

Make sure you buy the right running shoes by following our seven steps to sensible shopping

Arch locks? Medial posts? Decoupled SRC impact zones, anyone? There's enough shoe-related jargon out there to make buying a new pair of trainers a baffling experience. It's no wonder so many of us part with our hard-earned cash only to end up disappointed.

Before heading out on your quest for your ideal running shoes, here is our step-by-step guide – from experts with years of experience in specialist shops – to help you avoid the kind of pitfalls that can befall even the most experienced of shoe shoppers.

1 DON'T BE A FASHION VICTIM

"The most common error is that people pick a shoe off the display and ask for it because of its looks, particularly the colour. People go for dark colours, which are the trail shoes, when what they might really need is a high-mileage road shoe. Runners should start by looking at the way they run, get a gait analysis and use that to decide which shoe they end up with."
David Newman, Runner's Need, London

2 BE FLEXIBLE ON SIZE

"Most people who are new to running ask for a size smaller than they actually need, especially women who are used to wearing fashion shoes and swear blind that they've been a size five all their life. Shoes that are too small can cause problems from black toenails and blisters to shin splints, so it's vital to be properly fitted."
Gareth Long, The Derby Runner, Derby

3 STEER CLEAR OF THE INTERNET

"Sure, you can save loads of money by heading online, but the bargains you can find on certain internet sites might not seem like quite such a good idea when you start to get physiotherapy bills for twice the cost of the trainers. We had one customer who had bought completely the wrong pair of shoes online after a knee operation. They could have done some serious damage to themselves, because the shoes gave too much support. Always get your shoes physically fitted at a specialist running shop whenever you need a new pair."
Jamie Halliday, Up and Running, London

4 JOIN A CLUB TO CUT THE BILL

"Some people don't know that they can get a discount on shoes if they are a member of a running club. Obviously, the stores can't ask every single customer, but a lot of returning customers say they didn't realise they could have saved money. We offer 10 per cent off for members of an AAA affiliated club, as long as they bring along a club card or a fixtures list that proves membership."
Dipika Smith, Run and Become, London

5 KEEP AN OPEN MIND

"People shouldn't get too hung up on well meaning advice from friends and seemingly "expert" websites. Customers who have asked friends for guidance often come to us and request a particular

OFF THE SHELF
Use our expert tips to
make sure you pick up
the best pair for you

brand of shoe, just because it worked for someone else. That doesn't mean it will be the best shoe for them – it could cause discomfort or injury. And websites confuse people by using terms without explaining their meaning. I would say stick to a few trusted sources of advice, and be aware that you can always phone up a specialist shop."
Simon Royle, Sole Obsession, Salisbury

6 KNOW YOUR CONVERSION RATES

"The conversion rates between US and UK sizes can vary quite a lot between brands. Customers often come in to our store expecting a uniform size six, but

these different conversion rates mean that an Asics six will not be quite the same as a Nike six. Customers should be aware of that when they're getting fitted out and trust the expert."
Jamie Smith, Sweatshop, Reading

7 WATCH THE TIME

"The foot expands towards the end of the day, so shoes you buy in the morning can start to feel too tight later on. We recommend that you leave a gap of between half a millimetre to a full millimetre around the foot to allow for this, or go shopping at the end of the day."
Steven Curtis, Running Bath, Bath

GET YOUR KIT ON

You've got the shoes. Here's what else to look for – and why

T-SHIRTS

The best ones have...

- Flatback seams for comfort
- Wicking material to transfer away sweat
- A UV protective coating for running in the sun
- Anti-odour technology

SHORTS

The best ones have...
- An elasticated waistband for comfort
- Flourescent piping for night running
- Small pocket for change, keys, etc
- Webbing inside to hold everything in place

JACKETS

The best ones have...
- Adjustable waistband and cuffs
- Strong weather-resistant material
- Soft non-rubbing fabric
- An ergonomic design

LEGGINGS

The best ones have...
- An elasticated waistband for comfort
- Flourescent piping for night running
- Small pocket for change, keys, etc
- Panelling for an ergonomic fit

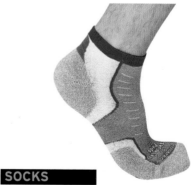

SOCKS

The best ones have...
- Elasticated arch lock
- Padded soles
- Seam-free toe section
- Breathable, anti-chafe material

49 REASONS TO LOVE RUNNING

You shouldn't need an excuse to get out there, but there are plenty of very good reasons to slip those shoes on right now

1 SAY GOODBYE TO YOUR BELLY
Dublin University researchers report that a 10-stone adult burns 391 calories in 30 minutes of running, compared with 277 calories while cycling, and 272 calories while playing tennis. Translation? You blitz your belly up to 40 per cent faster.

2 BULLET-PROOF BONES
Fifteen minutes of light jogging three times a week is all it takes to reduce your risk of developing osteoporosis in later life by up to 40 per cent, according to the National Osteoporosis Society.

3 HIT THE MARK
Some runners set distance or time goals, many focus on health or weight; others run simply to relax. It can help you achieve any goal you set your mind to.

4 IT'S THE ALL-WEATHER ACTIVITY
Rain, cold, sun, wind – there's no excuse not to get out there. Just strip off or layer up and see it as another challenge. It's an activity made bespoke for the unpredictable weather in this country!

5 GET H-A-P-P-Y
"Mild to moderate exercise releases natural feel-good endorphins that help counter stress and literally make you happy," explains Andrew McCulloch, chief executive of the Mental Health Foundation.

6 TAKE OVER THE WORLD!
Early-morning runs present truly beautiful experiences worth cherishing – while the rest of the world sleeps, you're the first to break the virgin snow over that field, the deserted streets are yours and yours alone, you see the glory of the sunrise and you don't have to share it with anyone. How smug do you feel?

7 JOIN THE ZZZ-LIST
Stanford University School of Medicine researchers asked sedentary insomnia sufferers to jog for just 20-30 minutes every other day. The result? The time required to fall asleep was reduced by half, and sleep time increased by almost one hour.

8 MEDALS ARE COOL
Silverware isn't just for Olympians. Enter a race, finish it, and you'll have your own to line up on your mantelpiece as proof of what you've managed to achieve.

9 ENJOY GUILT-FREE SNACKING
Upping your salt intake is seldom a doctor's advice, but in the last few days before a marathon that's exactly what you should do – giving you the

perfect excuse to munch on crisps. The salt in them helps protect against hyponatraemia, a condition caused by drinking too much water without enough sodium that can lead to disorientation, illness and, in rare cases, death.

10 GET REGULAR

According to experts from Bristol University, the benefits of running extend right to your bottom. "Physical activity helps decrease the time it takes food to move through the large intestine, thus limiting the amount of water absorbed back into your body, leaving you with softer stools that are easier to pass," explains gastroenterologist Dr Ken Heaton.

11 KEEP THE DOCTOR AT BAY

"Moderate exercise makes immune cells more active, so they're ready to fight off infection," says Cath Collins, chief dietician at St George's Hospital in London. In studies at the University of North Carolina, people who jogged for 15 minutes five days a week took half as many sick days as couch potatoes.

12 SEE THE WORLD

What other sport is there where you get the chance to travel to all four corners of the earth in the name of fitness? From the New York to Rio de Janeiro marathons all the way to seeing parts of our own sceptred isle you never even knew existed, it's a veritable ticket to ride.

13 YOU DON'T NEED AN INSTRUCTION MANUAL

If you can walk, you can run. Think back to being a child and you will realise that running is one of the most natural instincts to humankind.

14 PROTECT YOUR TICKER

Studies from Purdue University in the US have shown that regular running can cut your risk of heart disease by 50 per cent.

15 GET TIME BACK ON YOUR SIDE

Whether loosely lodged in your mental schedule or typed into your BlackBerry, your daily workout should be a focal point of your day. It helps you organise everything else you need to do, often into B.R. (Before Run) and A.R. (After Run) time frames, as well as giving you time to absorb and ponder your daily itinerary.

16 REACH CREATIVE BREAKTHROUGHS

Writers, musicians, artists and all other kinds of creative professionals use running to solve mental blocks and make must-do-it-today decisions. For this we can credit the flow of oxygen to your grey matter when it matters most, sparking your brain's neurons and giving you breathing space away from the muddle of 'real life'.

17 THINK FASTER

Researchers from Illinois University found that an improvement of only five per cent in cardio-respiratory fitness from running led to an improvement of up to 15 per cent in mental tests.

18 YOU CAN BE AN ALL-ROUNDER

Whether you want to keep in prime shape like F1 champion Jenson Button, or go 12 hard rounds like boxer Amir Khan, running is *the* place to begin.

19 HILLS: THE ULTIMATE CALORIE-KILLER

Find a decent incline, take a deep breath (at the bottom, not the top) and incorporate it into your running programme. You'll burn up to 40 per cent more calories – the average 150lb runner will burn 1,299 calories running a 10 per cent incline for an hour, compared with 922 on the flat.

20 MAKE A DIFFERENCE

Millions of runners worldwide turn their determination to get fitter and healthier into fund-raising efforts for the less fortunate. The Flora London Marathon is the single largest annual fundraising event in the world, having brought over £400 million into the coffers of good causes to date. If that doesn't give you a warm glow, what will?

found men over 50 who run at least three hours a week have a 30 per cent lower risk of impotence than those who do little or no exercise.

22 IT CAN REPLACE A HARMFUL DEPENDENCY...

...such as smoking, alcoholism, or overeating, says William Glasser, author of *Positive Addiction* (HarperPerennial Books). Result: you're a happier, healthier person getting the kind of fix that adds to, rather than detracts from, the good things in life.

23 END BOREDOM

The most mundane errand can be transformed into a training run, from returning DVDs to Blockbuster to taking the dog for a walk. Suddenly every journey has a double purpose – and, most importantly, one you'll love.

24 THAT NEW-SHOE SMELL

You've read the reviews in *Runner's World* (haven't you?), chatted to fellow runners, tried on and sampled your top three and made your choice. Now they're here, in your hands. It's the start of a beautiful relationship.

25 THE JOY OF FINDING A NEW ROUTE

Today you took a left rather than a right and suddenly found amazing views and a piece of solitude you never knew existed before now. Then you imagine how many more runs there are out there just waiting to be discovered...

26 THAT KNOWING NOD FROM A FELLOW COMPETITOR

The race is about to start and you see the same face from the last meet. Out of mutual respect and an acknowledgement of the challenge to come, you both nod. Nobody else knows it, but the gauntlet has been thrown down.

21 BOOST YOUR SEX LIFE

A study from Cornell University in the US concluded that male runners have the sexual prowess of men two to five years younger, while females can delay the menopause by a similar amount of time. Meanwhile, research carried out at Harvard University

27 INDULGE YOUR WANDER-LUST

There's simply no better way of getting to know a new city than pulling on your trainers and hitting the streets. As well as giving you necessary orientation, it'll energise you after your journey, reset your biological clock to any new time zone and give you the chance to meet locals in half the time. As well as giving you necessary orientation, it will energise you after your journey, reset your biological clock to any new time zone and give you the chance to meet locals quicker.

28 GET (A LEGAL) HIGH

Comparing the pre- and post-run scans of runners, neurologists from the University of Bonn, Germany, found evidence of more opiate binding of the happy hormone endorphin in the frontal and limbic regions of the brain, areas known to be involved in processing emotions and stress.

29 YOU'VE GOT A REAL FRIEND

We all go through phases in our lives, including times when we run less. You may get a job that demands more of your time. You may have to spend more time having and caring for a new baby. Maybe you simply go on holiday or take a sabbatical. That's fine. Running adapts itself easily to your ebbs and flows. Best of all, running is always there to take the strain when you need it most.

30 NUMBERS DON'T LIE

There's no leeway for dishonesty with running, from distances to times. You get back what you put in.

31 A RUNNING CLUB CAN SAVE YOUR LIFE

A nine-year study from Harvard Medical School found those with the most friends cut their risk of death by more than 60 per cent, reducing blood pressure and strengthening their immune system.

32 BLITZ BODY BLEMISHES

"Running tones the buttocks and thighs quicker than any other exercise, which literally squeezes out the lingering fat," according to Dr James Fleming, author of *Beat Cellulite Forever* (Piatkus).

33 BOOST YOUR BELLOWS

When running, an adult uses about 10 times the oxygen they would need when sitting in front of the television for the same period. Over time, regular jogging will strengthen the cardiovascular system, enabling your heart and lungs to work more efficiently, getting more oxygen where it's needed,

quicker. This means you can do more exercise for less effort. How good does that sound?

34 BURN MORE FAT

"Even after running for 20 minutes or half an hour, you could be burning a higher amount of total calories for a few hours after you stop," says sports physiologist Mark Simpson of Loughborough University's School of Sports Science.

36 THAT PB FEELING

Note the 'P' here, being 'personal' – you set the goals, you put the work in, you get the results. Savour it.

37 SPEND QUALITY TIME AS A FAMILY

It's one of the few activities that the whole family can do together. The smallest tyke can clamber into his jogging buggy, fit parents and grandparents can take turns pushing, and Junior can follow along on his new two-wheeler. Hundreds of races include events for everyone in the family.

38 OUTRUN THE REAPER

Kings College London researchers compared more than 2,400 identical twins, and found that those who did the equivalent of just three 30-minute jogs a week were nine years 'biologically younger', even after discounting other influences including body mass index (BMI) and smoking.

39 TEACH YOURSELF DISCIPLINE

Practise makes perfect, in running and in life. The most successful people are the ones with a modest amount of talent and a huge amount of discipline.

40 IT'S NOT ELITIST

You're struggling in last in the race but get the biggest cheer. You deserve it. After all, you've been running for longer than anyone else. What other sports are there where the laggards are applauded as much as the winners? Running's there for everyone, regardless of talent.

41 SIZE DOESN'T MATTER

Running is a great activity for every body type. There are no barriers to giving it a go.

42 YOU'RE IN CONTROL

Whatever the pressures of your job or personal life, you have the final say in how much or little running you do. Squeeze in a pre-dawn blast, a lunchtime refresher or an evening stress-buster. It's your call.

35 APPRECIATE THE ENVIRONMENT

The days of Bush Junior's denial are long gone, and with Barack Obama's new era comes a dawn of awakening – the world needs your help. You crave fresh, clean air when you run. You long for soft trails, towering trees, pure water. You have plenty of time to ponder the big questions. You resolve: save the earth. You've got a vested interest.

43 HELP BABY

Mums-to-be who regularly exercise during pregnancy have an easier, less complicated labour, a quicker recovery and better overall mood throughout the nine months, say researchers at Michigan University in the US. Just ask Paula Radcliffe.

44 EXCUSE FOR A MASSAGE

Post-race, nothing quite beats the indulgence of a massage and the relaxed, floaty feeling as you walk back to real life.

45 IRON OUT THE CREASES

Regular running can reduce the signs of ageing. "Increased circulation delivers oxygen and nutrients to skin cells more effectively, while flushing harmful toxins out," explains Dr Christopher Rowland Payne (thelondonclinic. co.uk). "Exercise creates the ideal environment within the body to optimise collagen production to support the skin, helping reduce the appearance of wrinkles," he adds.

46 YOU CAN KEEP ON GOING FOREVER

While other sports have a limited shelf-life, runners don't have to throw the towel in. Just look at 71-year-old legend Ron Hill, who hasn't missed a day's running since December 1964.

47 TAKE A JOURNEY

You never know what you'll find. You don't know whom or what you'll see. Even more interesting, who knows what thoughts might flash into your mind. Today's run could change your life in a way that you could never have imagined when you laced up your shoes.

48 YOUR PERSONAL THERAPIST

There's no greater escape from the pressures and stresses of modern life than slipping on your trainers and just getting out there. It's just you and the road – giving you time to organise your life, think things through and invariably finish in a better place than when you set off.

49 IT'S FREE

All you need are shoes, shorts and a shirt.

THEY DID IT...
SO CAN YOU

These four runners had very different reasons for taking up the sport. But they are united by one common belief – that everyone can benefit from following in their footsteps

'I lost six stone by taking up running'
Dan Watkins, 33

The first time I began to think about running was in 2006. I was admitted to hospital with chest pains, and the paramedic said to me: "You have a suspected heart attack. Things have got to change." Less than a year before I had been diagnosed with Type 2 diabetes caused by my poor diet and sedentary lifestyle – and I was faced with having to take tablets for the rest of my life. I was 30 years old and weighed 24 stone.

One morning it came to me in a flash: "What are you doing to yourself? You've got to do something." It was as if someone flicked a switch in my head.

I gave myself a fresh start. I left a relationship that I wasn't happy in, moved to Norwich and joined a gym.

'I had to ease myself into an exercise programme. I started off by walking on the treadmill'

Even the first meal in my new flat was a healthy one.

Being so overweight, I had to ease myself into an exercise programme. I just couldn't run at that stage. I started off by walking for 10 minutes on the treadmill. As I lost more weight, I was able to increase my speed, until eventually I was running for a minute at a time.

By December 2007, I had lost six stone. But I was just aimlessly running on the treadmill. I needed a goal to motivate me. I entered the Breckland 10K on May 4, and started a 10K training programme.

It was four weeks before that I ran non-stop for half an hour. My first ever run outside was the Sport Relief

5K in March. I finished in under 30 minutes, and running became real for me. I wanted to finish the 10K in 60 minutes, and this was a significant stepping-stone towards achieving that goal.

I was terrified in the weeks leading up to the race, worried that I would come in last or make myself look stupid. I turned up alone on the day, and was really nervous. I felt like a rabbit in headlights. But I thought to myself: "You're here now, you've got to do it." I positioned myself near the back of the 300 runners and started slowly. I latched on to a couple of runners for the first half, but decided to go for it once I'd hit 5K.

The course was a loop, so the front-runners were coming back past us. They were shouting words of encouragement, as were the marshals. Then I saw the finish line. I realised that I was going to achieve my goal. I ran as fast as I could for that last 500m.

I'm not an emotional person. But there was something about crossing that finish line that set me off and I felt a euphoric wave of emotion. There are runners and there are non-runners – I went from being one to being the other as I crossed that line.

My doctor is happy with me these days. The diabetes will never go away, but it doesn't need to be managed by medicine anymore. And my first 10K was a milestone for me: I'm a lot happier; I'm a positive person; and my family and friends say that I'm a much nicer person to be around, too.

'I raised money in memory of my mum'
Catherine Robertson-Ross, 50

The only reason I started running was because of my mum, Jean Robertson. She was a great inspiration to me, even when she was spending her last weeks of life in Strathcarron Hospice in Denny Stirlingshire in 2003.

She suffered greatly before she died but never complained. That's the way she was. She couldn't speak because of cancer so she wrote me notes. In one, she said: "I want to give you one last piece of advice as your mother. You are wasting your very precious life and I want you to do something about it."

That was the last thing she wrote to me. At the time I was overweight, probably four stone heavier than I am now. I was also on betablockers to try to ease migraines, which could put me in bed for three days.

I didn't do anything right away, but one day I woke up and I decided I was going to do something for my mum. I vowed to complete the Great Scottish Run 10K in Glasgow in September 2006. I started running in the July. I'd never exercised before – never been to a gym or an aerobics class – but I got some shoes and jogged to the end of the road. It nearly killed me! I was holding onto the wall thinking, "I'm not sure I can do this." But I stuck at it and every time I ran I realised that

'The first race was meant to be a one-off, but people seemed glad to give me their money'

I could go a wee bit further. Still, race day came around quickly. My husband Graham took a picture of me standing at the start with my shoulders down and a lost look on my face. The one thing that I was determined not to do was walk – and I didn't.

I'd written, "I'm supporting Strathcarron Hospice in memory of my mum" on my T-shirt, and when I started to tire a woman patted me on the back and said, "Come on, you're nearly there. Your mum would be proud." When I came into Glasgow Green towards the finish,

I was done. Then as I came around the corner I could hear a voice shout out, "That's my mum!" It was one of my sons, Barry, who had turned up without me knowing. He was crying. It lifted me, and I managed to smile and run to the end, finishing in 1:01:39.

That race was supposed to be a one-off, but for me to do it was a big deal and people were glad to give me their money, so that's kept me going. It is the first time in my life that I've ever done anything for me. I've never had a career or been a great achiever and my claim to fame is that I hope to have been a good mum. But this year I beat my 10K PB with a time of 49:47.

Life is so much different since I started running. I've become a happy and confident person and I've found friends by running throughout Britain. It's never too late to change, and you can have a different and healthier life.

Now I run in my mum's memory. She shared my happiness and wiped away my tears and the very last thing she did for me was to put me on the right path. In her last days on this earth she thought of me rather than herself and she saved me.

I was 50 recently and to celebrate I ran my first half-marathon at Inverness. That was my birthday present to myself.

'Running is a pressure valve to beat stress'
Pauline Munro, 40

I only really started running when I was at uni to keep fit and to break the long days of study. I guess I've had the bug since then. I've got a 10K PB of 35:54, and have won a variety of medals at Northern and Yorkshire levels with Bingley Harriers (bingleyharriers.org.uk), and have had County and England vests on the fells.

I'm married with two young daughters, with all that involves, as well as working as a partner at an international commercial law firm, so every minute is precious. With work, I often defend major global corporations and can be called away last minute for meetings all over the country, which makes balancing life's demands tricky. With kids, you don't have the luxury of staying late in the office to get things done,

'Home life gets muddied with working late into the night after finishing all the family stuff'

which means home life gets muddied with working late into the night after finishing all the family stuff.

This makes my running that much more important as a pressure valve – some time for me to unwind, relax and get my thoughts together. But as these other pressures started mounted up, I was running tired all the time simply from trying to do too much.

Through guidance from Sarah Rowell (former Olympic marathon runner) I came to understand the concept of quality over quantity. I'd been approaching my running on the basis of fitting in as much as I could in between working, rather than thinking about how I could improve my game in the time I had available, taking into account the increasing demands of my job.

My weekly mileage has gone down from around 70 to 50 miles, but I still compete at a senior level on a serious basis when time permits. I have always had to be creative about when I run, but even more so now. At the weekend my husband and I have to tag-team run in the mornings so that someone's always at home.

When I come back from a run I'm focused and raring to go. I ran through both my pregnancies and even with the girls, pushing a buggy. Running is part of my life – my working life and my family life.

'I was addicted to heroin but found the right path'

John Catchpole, 42

I was born in 1967 in Glasgow. I come from a big family and we lived in an area that had a bit of a reputation. I started sniffing glue around 1974 and for years I was hooked on heroin, plus whatever else I could get my hands on. Through my teens, I was shoplifting and stealing cars – anything to subsidise my addiction. By 1997, I had no life left. I'd spent time in prison, lost my family and ended up homeless, selling *The Big Issue*.

I finally decided to contact my family, and I went home. I was happy to be there but I was beat – I just curled up and went to sleep. When I woke up I decided I had to do something. I got onto a methadone programme and came off heroin. But I wasn't getting better, so I went back to the doctor to get off the methadone. I was told it would take three to four years.

I started attending New Horizons, a day centre for recovering addicts. I told them I wasn't sporty, but that I liked to do a bit of running. It was meant as a joke – the other people at the centre and I had been running

'My chemist saw an article about me and hung it on the wall as inspiration to addicts'

from the authorities all our lives. We decided to see if we could turn this into a positive and become real runners. In 2000 we put on our trainers for the first time and ran around the block. Soon we were running 5K, then 10. We were buzzing. It was great being sore for good reasons, rather than from withdrawal.

To understand addiction you have to realise that you're comatose for much of the time. Suddenly I was energised. I was productive. Running was helping me take control of my life and we set up our own running club: Team Horizon. I was training three times a week, and going to the gym four times a week. Now I had structure and discipline that I'd never had before.

In 2002 we were discussing personal goals at the day centre. I mentioned I'd never been on an aeroplane, never had a holiday and never run a marathon before. One of the coaches told me: "We can make that happen – just keep up your running." At the start of 2003, I was booked to go and take part in that year's New York City Marathon. The centre had secured funding for me, and I was being sent there for 10 days. I couldn't believe it, and running through New York City was surreal. It was

a place I'd only seen on TV. Crossing Brooklyn Bridge, with spectators shouting, waving and giving high fives, was pure adrenaline. When I took the final turn into Central Park, I caught a glimpse of the finish line, with the crowd and the banners, and I slowed right down so that I could really savour the moment. My time was 4:10:52. The sense of achievement was overwhelming, and the emotion was written all over my face. And without running that never would have happened.

The story was covered in the local paper back home. My chemist saw the article and hung it on the wall as inspiration for other addicts. What I've done and where I am now *has* inspired other people. They come up to me and ask if I'm still running. People used to approach me to ask if I knew where they could get drugs. But now they know me as a runner.

RAVE RUN

Elgol, Isle of Skye

IMAGE: JOCHEN PFSCHER

2 Training

THE 12 TRAINING ESSENTIALS

Running doesn't have to be complicated: arm yourself with some basic knowledge and you can start training with confidence. Here's how to make it through your first effort with flying colours

1 WELCOME TO THE START LINE

This might be your first try at running, or a return visit, or an attempt to improve on what you already do. The less running you've done recently, the more you can expect to improve your distances and speeds in the first 10 weeks. On the other hand, the less you've run lately, the more likely you are to hurt yourself by doing too much, too soon. That's why it's so important to set two related goals as you start or restart your running programme – to maximise improvements, and to minimise injuries.

2 MAKE A PLAN

As for finding places to run, anywhere that's safe for walking is also fine for running. Off-road routes (parks, bike paths, playing fields) are better than busy streets, while soft surfaces (grass and dirt) are better than paved ones, but any choice is better than staying at home. Map out the best courses in your immediate neighbourhood. That saves time, solves the "place" issue and makes it much more likely you'll execute your planned runs.

3 EAT AND DRINK THE RIGHT FOODS

Sports nutrition is a big topic, but, in general, the rules for good nutrition and fluid consumption are the same for runners as for everyone else. Three areas of special interest to runners: (1) control your weight, as extra pounds will slow you down; (2) eat lightly after training and racing; (3) drink 250-500ml of water or a carbohydrate drink an hour before running, as dehydration can be a dangerous enemy.

4 GET F.I.T.

Kenneth Cooper, a giant in the fitness field, long ago devised a simple formula for improving as a runner. Run two to three miles, three to five days a week at a comfortable pace. It's easier to remember as the F.I.T. formula: frequency (at least every other day); intensity (comfortable pace); and time (about 30 minutes). Even with some walking breaks thrown in if you tire, you can cover two miles in 30 minutes, and you might soon be running three miles in that time. It's important to run these efforts at an easy, comfortable pace. Think of yourself as the Tortoise, not the Hare. Make haste slowly.

5 FIND YOUR PACE

We've told you to make it comfortable, which sounds simple. But the problem is that most novice runners don't actually know what a comfortable pace feels like, so they push too hard. As a result,

ON YOUR MARKS
Follow these tips and
you're ready to go...

they get overly fatigued and discouraged, or even injured, so either give up almost before they've started or face an injury lay-off.

Here are some more guidelines: a comfortable pace is one to two minutes per mile slower than your optimum mile time. Or you can use a heart-rate monitor and run at 65 per cent of your working heart rate. (To calculate effort based on your WHR, see the heart-rate training section). Finally, as an alternative, listen to your breathing. If you aren't gasping for air, and you can talk while you're running, your pace is about right.

6 REMEMBER TO WARM UP AND COOL DOWN FIRST

Don't confuse a little light stretching with a good warm-up. Stretching exercises generally don't make you sweat or raise your heart rate, which is what you really want from a warm-up. A proper warm-up begins with walking or running very slowly to ease your body into the session. Try walking briskly for five minutes (about a quarter of a mile), and then breaking into your comfortable running pace.

(Don't count the warm-up as part of your run time or distance – that's cheating.)

When you finish your run, resist the urge to stop. Instead, walk another five minutes to cool down more gradually. After you've cooled down is the best time for stretching – when your muscles are warm and ready to be stretched a little.

7 RUN SAFELY AT ALL TIMES

The biggest threat you'll face as a runner on the road, by far, is traffic. Cars, lorries and bikes zip past you. A moment's lapse in attention from either you or them can result in, at the very least, a bad case of road rage. The best way to lower this risk is to avoid running near roads, but for many of us this is a near impossibility, or it's an approach that adds time and complexity to our routine (if we have to and from drive to a park, for example).

So most of us adapt and learn to be extremely cautious on the roads. Try to find quiet roads with wide pavements; if there is no pavement, run on the right side of the road, facing the oncoming traffic; obey traffic signs and signals; and follow every road

rule your parents taught you. If you look out for cars, lorries and bikes, they won't have to look out for you.

8 USE PAIN AS YOUR GUIDE

Runners get hurt. We rarely hurt ourselves as seriously as skiers or rugby players, but injuries do happen. Most are musculoskeletal, meaning we recover rapidly when we take days off or other appropriate action (such as ice treatment), and most are self-inflicted – we bring them on by running too far, too fast, too soon or too often.

Prevention is more often than not as simple as a change of routine. If you can't run steadily without pain, mix walking and running. If you can't run-walk, simply walk. If you can't walk, cycle. If you can't cycle, swim. As you recover, climb back up this fitness ladder until you can run again.

9 TAKE THE MILE TRIAL

Friends who hear that you've begun running will soon ask what your best mile time is – so you might as well get used to it. Before long, you'll be calculating your pace per mile on longer runs, but you should begin with a simple one-mile test run (four laps on a standard track) to determine your starting point.

Think of this run as a pace test, not a race. Run at a pace a little beyond easy, but less than a struggle, and count on improving your mile time in later tests as your fitness improves.

10 STRETCHING AND STRENGTHENING

Running is a specialised activity, working mainly the legs. If you're seeking total-body fitness, you need to supplement your running with other exercises. These should aim to strengthen the muscles that running neglects, and stretch those that running tightens, which means strengthening the upper body and stretching the legs. Add a few minutes of strengthening and stretching after your runs, because that's when these exercises tend to have the greatest benefit.

11 FOLLOW THE HARD DAY/EASY DAY TRAINING SYSTEM

Most runs need to be easy. This is true whether you're a beginner or an elite athlete. (Of course, the definition of easy varies hugely; an easy mile for an elite runner would be impossible for many beginners

STRETCH YOURSELF Stretching after a run is better than doing it before you set off

or even experienced runners.) As a new runner, make sure you limit yourself to one hard day a week. Run longer and slower than normal, or shorter and faster than normal, or enter a short (5K) race and maintain your best pace for the entire distance.

12 CONGRATULATE YOURSELF

One of the great beauties of running is that it gives everyone a chance to win. Winning isn't automatic; you still have to work for success and risk failure, but in running, unlike in other sports, there's no need to beat an opponent or an arbitrary standard (such as "par" in golf). Runners measure themselves against their own standards.

When you improve a time or increase a distance, or set a personal best in a race, you win – no matter what anyone else has done on the same day. You can win even more simply by keeping at it for the long haul, for years and decades. You don't have to run very far or fast to outrun people who have dropped out. It's the Tortoise and the Hare all over again. Slow and steady always wins the most important race.

LONG MAY YOU RUN

If you manage them right, your long runs will help you run better from 10K to marathons and beyond

Compared with other training sessions, the long run is fairly simple – put one foot in front of the other and stop when you've done 20 miles – but its simplicity is deceptive. "The long run is the single most important workout you can do," says coach Jeff Galloway, who ran the 10,000m for the USA in the 1972 Olympics, "but it's more complex than you'd think, and most runners don't do it right."

There are many questions about the long run, including the big four: Why? How long? How fast? How often? We'll answer those, and take a look at related issues such as nutrition, rest and recovery. So put your feet up and read on at a comfortable pace.

WHY DO IT?

Long runs give you endurance – the ability to run further. Yet they can help 10K runners as well as marathoners. Long runs do several things...
- They strengthen the heart.
- They open capillaries, speeding energy to working muscles and flushing away waste from tired ones.
- They strengthen leg muscles and ligaments.
- They recruit fast-twitch muscle fibres to assist slow-twitch tasks – such as marathon running.
- They help burn fat as fuel.
- They boost confidence. "If you know you can go that far in training, it gives you the confidence that with the adrenalin of the race, you can do that too," says Danielle Sanderson, former European 50K champion.
- They make you faster. "Increase your long run from six miles to 12 – change nothing else – and you will improve your 10K time," says Galloway.

HOW LONG SHOULD YOU GO?

It's not an exact science but there are two general rules:
TIME IS A BETTER GAUGE THAN DISTANCE "The duration of the long run will vary depending on the athlete's age, fitness and the competitive distance they're training for," explains Norman Brook, Britain's former national endurance coach. "The run should usually be for at least 45 minutes and can extend up to three hours for elite athletes and those preparing for the marathon or ultra-distance events."

Measure your long runs by all means, if it helps, but for the most part, the goal of a long run is not covering a certain distance, but quality time spent on your feet.
RUN FOR ONE-AND-A-HALF TO TWO HOURS That's the minimum – roughly 10-16 miles – needed to maintain a high endurance level. Increase your long runs by no more than 15 minutes at a time. "Build up to the long run gradually," Brook advises. "If the longest you're running for in training is 30 minutes, gradually build up to an hour by adding five minutes to your run each week." Just a few minutes of extra running make a difference – but do too much and you're setting yourself up for injury or illness.

HOW FAST?

You want to run a marathon in 3:30, which is eight-minute mile pace, so you do your long runs at that pace. Sounds logical, right? Wrong. "Running isn't always logical," says Benji Durden, a 2:09 marathoner who now coaches both elite and recreational runners. There are reasons for going easy on your 20-milers:
- Long runs at race pace may be training sessions in your mind, but they're races to your body. That can lead to overtraining, injury or illness. "Running long runs fast causes more problems than any other mistake," says Galloway. Marian Sutton, winner of many marathons, agrees: "There's no point pushing too hard. Run at a pace that feels comfortable."
- Fast, long runs miss the point. "Long runs are for endurance," says Sanderson. "It's amazing how quickly they reduce your resting heart rate, making your heart more efficient."

THE LONG ROAD
Increase your
distance gradually to
avoid burning out

⊙ The ideal pace for long runs is at least one minute per mile slower than your marathon pace. "The intensity of effort is low, and you should ensure a steady state is maintained," says Brook. You should be able to conduct a conversation during the run without discomfort."

⊙ You might even walk at points during longer runs – it works for Sanderson. "It's good to just plod round, walk a bit if you need to, or even stop for a break," she advises.

HOW OFTEN?

Don't run long more than once a week. It is, after all, a hard session, requiring rest or easy days before and after. The other end of the scale is debatable. Some runners have no problem going two or three weeks between long runs. Others will come back with a midweek long run if a shorter race precludes the weekend session.

Galloway recommends a simple formula: roughly one day's gap per mile of your long run. For example, if your long run is 12-17 miles, you can go two weeks between long runs without losing endurance; if it's 18-23 miles, three weeks. "That is, if you're running at

least 30 minutes every other day in between," he adds. This rule can also be used to taper before a marathon. For instance, if your last long run is 22 miles, you'd run it three weeks before race day. If it's 16 miles, you get a two-week rest before the race.

WHICH DAY IS BEST?

Sunday is traditional, because that's when most people have most free time. Also, most marathons are at weekends, so why not set your body clock in advance? There's no need to stick to a set day. "I'm not rigid about the day I do my long run," says world marathon record holder Paula Radcliffe, "because I never know when I'll be racing." Sanderson also plans her schedule around events. "I do my long run on a Sunday, unless I'm racing," she says.

DON'T GO SOLO

Contrary to popular opinion, long runs aren't boring. You just have to know how to run them – that is, with friends. Find a Saturday or Sunday morning group, or arrange to meet a training partner regularly. "I do some of my runs with friends," says Sanderson, "and the time always goes so much faster."

SPEEDWORK FOR EVERY RUNNER

It may be a cliché, but that's because it's true: the only way to run faster is... to run faster

Most of us can come up with plenty of reasons to avoid speedwork: it hurts; it increases our chances of picking up an injury; it makes us too tired for our other runs; we don't need it for running marathons... the list is endless. The thing is, they're all unnecessary fears. What's more, whether you want to beat an ancient 800m best set on the grass track at school, or out-kick the runner who always sprints past you in the local 10K, adding speedwork to your regime will be immensely rewarding.

Speedwork doesn't just make you run faster. It makes you fitter, increases the range of movement in your joints, makes you more comfortable at all speeds, and it will ultimately help you to run harder for longer. If you've already added a speed session or two to your schedule then you'll know all of this already. If you haven't, then here are a few things to remember.

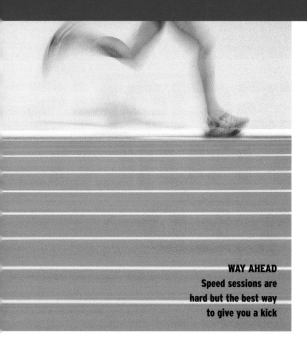

**WAY AHEAD
Speed sessions are
hard but the best way
to give you a kick**

EASE INTO IT

When you started running, you ran for just a couple of miles every other day, and gradually built up to your current mileage. You didn't suddenly start running 35 miles a week, so adopt the same approach to speedwork. Put at least three months of steady running behind you, then start with just one session every 10 days or so. Then go on from there.

NOT TOO HARD

Speed sessions aren't about sprinting flat out until you're sick by the side of the track. They're about controlling hard efforts and spreading your energy evenly over a set distance or time, just like you would in a perfect race.

PACE YOURSELF

When you first start speedwork you may find monitoring your pace difficult. If you've run a 5K race you'll know how that pace feels, but don't panic if you haven't – you'll find the right pace through trial and error. Don't be afraid to make mistakes, but don't worry about being over-cautious at first – it's better to build up gradually than fail and hate speedwork.

WARM UP AND WARM DOWN

Before each session, jog for at least 8-10 minutes to raise your blood temperature, increase blood-flow to the muscles and psyche yourself up for the fast running ahead. Follow that with some gentle stretching and then run a few fast strides before getting down to the tough stuff. Afterwards, jog for another 5-10 minutes, before stretching once again.

FIND A PARTNER

Speedwork takes more effort and willpower than going out for a gentle jog. It's much easier and more fun to train with someone else – and if you really want to improve, try running with someone just a bit quicker than you are.

QUALITY NOT QUANTITY

Speed training should not account for more than 15 per cent of your total mileage. So slot in your speed sessions around the regular work you've been doing all along.

TYPES OF SPEEDWORK

● REPETITIONS/INTERVALS Periods of hard running at 5K pace or faster, between 200m and 1200m in length, or 30 seconds and five minutes. Recovery periods can be short (30-90 seconds), or of an equal time or distance to the reps. Running at harder than race pace for short periods not only improves speed, but also allows you to work on your running form. When you're pushing hard, it's important to concentrate on things such as arm and hand motion, posture and stride length. If you can keep these together during a hard session of reps, it will be easier to do so during a race. Don't attempt reps until you've tried other types of speedwork for a couple of months.

● TEMPO INTERVALS These are longer than ordinary intervals in that they take between 90 seconds and 10 minutes (or between 400m and two miles) and are run a little slower than your 5K pace. These work a bit like threshold runs – they raise the point at which lactic acid builds up in the muscles.

● FARTLEK Fartlek is Swedish for "speed play" and is the fun side of speedwork. Best done on grass or trails, you simply mix surges of hard running with periods of easy running with no set structure. Run fast bursts between phone boxes, lampposts or trees when you feel like it, and as hard you like. Great for newcomers to speedwork.

● HILLS Simple: find a hill that takes between 30 seconds and five minutes to climb at 85-90 per cent effort, and run up it. Jog back down to recover. A great alternative to track intervals.

20 SESSIONS TO BUILD SPEED

These routines will keep your training fresh and make you faster, especially when you want to kick for home at the end of a race

BEGINNERS

If you haven't tried speedwork before, here are some (relatively) gentle introductory sessions.

1 KEEP IT SHORT
You could start with a session of brisk efforts. Six minutes brisk, one-minute walk, six minutes brisk, one-minute walk, six minutes brisk and so on.

2 ADD SOME FARTLEK TRAINING
To begin, add some quick bursts into your shorter runs. Each burst can be as little as 20 seconds or as much as a few minutes.

3 DO AN INTERVAL SESSION
6 x 1 minute, with three-minute jog/walk recoveries, or 5 x 2 minutes with five-minute jogs.

4 GO FOR SHORT REPS
After two months or so of speedwork, try your first session of short repetitions: 5 x 300m, with four-minute recoveries; 5 x 200m, with 3-minute rests; or try 10 x 200m with 3-minute recoveries.

5 GLIDE DOWNHILL
On down slopes during long runs, go with the hill and allow it to pick up your pace to around 80-85 per cent of flat-out, allowing gravity to power you downhill. Don't go any further than 150m. The idea is to speed up without using any extra energy.

INTERMEDIATES

Once you've tried a few sessions, you may want to build up your efforts with some of these...

6 DO A PYRAMID SESSION
So called because you start with a short distance, gradually increase, and then come back down again. For example, start at 120m, add 20m to each rep until you reach 200m, then come back down to 120m. Run these at 400m pace, with a walk-back recovery.

7 TRY FAST REPS
For 200m or 300m: run 6-10 x 200m, with three-minute recoveries, or 5-8 x 300m, with five-minute recoveries. Start both at 800m pace, eventually running the last reps flat out. You can also combine the two, for example 3 x 200m, 2 x 300m, 3 x 200m.

8 DO A SIMULATION SESSION
This should replicate an 800m race. Run two sets of either 500m + 300m, or 600m + 200m, at your target 800m pace, with 60 seconds or less to recover.

9 BUILD YOURSELF UP
Find a large, open area such as a sports ground. Mark out a circuit of roughly 800-1,000m. Once you've warmed up, run a circuit at your 5K pace, jog for five minutes, then run a second circuit about three seconds faster than the last. Continue speeding up by three seconds until you've completed five circuits.

MAKE STRIDES
These training tips will get
you from A to B faster

10 KEEP GOING

Now try 5 x 800m at a pace 10 seconds faster per 800m than your usual 5K pace. Recover between intervals for the same amount of time it takes you to run them. As you get fitter, increase the reps.

11 PILE ON THE MILES

Begin with a three-mile warm-up, then 4 x 1 mile at a pace faster than your 10K pace, with a three-minute jog between each. Jog to warm down.

12 BUILD YOUR PYRAMIDS

They work for long distances too. Try 1,000m, 2,000m, 3,000m, 2,000m, 1,000m at your half-marathon race pace, with a four-minute recovery between each.

13 OR DO A HALF PYRAMID

If you're short on time, try 400m, 800m, 1,200m, 1,600m, 2,000m, each run faster than your 10K pace but not flat out. Jog 400m between each.

14 CARVE UP A 2K SPEED SESSION

Divide 2,000m into: 400m at 5K race pace, with a 400m jog; 300m at race pace, with a 300m jog; 200m slightly quicker than race pace, with a 200m jog; 100m slightly quicker, but still not flat out, with a 100m jog.

15 GO LONGER

Run five miles, alternating three-minute bursts at 10K pace with 90-second recoveries between each.

16 GO OFF-ROAD...

Find a flat stretch of trail or grass and jog for 10 minutes, then run at your mile pace for 1:40; slow down to a jog (don't walk), and recover for three minutes, then repeat another 100-second burst. Try four of these sessions to begin with, and gradually work up to 10. These 100s work on speed without the need for a track.

17 ...OR USE A TRACK

At a track, warm up, then run eight laps, alternating fast and slow 200s. The fast 200s should be hard, but not a full sprint – you'll soon learn just how fast you need to go. Add an extra lap as you get fitter.

18 BUILD UP TO 5K

5 x 1,000m. Run the first 800m at your 10K race pace, then accelerate to 3K pace for the last 200m, with three-minute recoveries.

19 BREAK UP THE LONGER RUNS

Run at marathon pace for five minutes, then increase your speed to 10K pace for one minute. Continue this sequence until 30 minutes have elapsed.

20 DIVIDE YOUR TIME

Here's a great session for 10K+ distances, particularly the marathon. If you want to complete a marathon in three hours 27 minutes, run 800m reps in three minutes and 27 seconds. If you aren't planning a marathon, run them at 10-mile race pace.

HEIGHTS OF PASSION

It's worth learning to love them – with the right approach, hills can help you become a much better runner

Hills are hard. That is why many of us run round them rather than over them in training. It's not just training, either, it's possible to avoid hills at races if you always choose flat courses. But while running hills might be exhausting and demoralising if you're not used to them, with the right training and attitude, hills will make you not only faster but a stronger, tougher runner too, both physically and mentally.

"Hills are a challenge but bring huge rewards for those who regularly include them in their training mix," says Nick Anderson, British cross-country coach and runner. He ensures that all his athletes' training schedules include hills, even when they're racing on the flat. "Hills make you tough and give you confidence," he says. "If you can work for 10 minutes uphill, then working for 10 minutes on the flat will seem easier." And easier running means faster running.

Hills won't just make you faster and harder – they'll make you stronger too, which is good news if you're a runner who focuses on weekly mileage at the expense of improving muscular strength. "Running hills will make you physically stronger and improve both speed endurance and mechanical efficiency," says Anderson. In other words, if you skip circuit training or weights at the gym, hills will give your body the strength to run faster for longer without breaking down.

GOOD HEALTH

The strength you build when training on hills will also help you to run injury-free. Hills, especially when run off-road, provide a great total-body workout that will protect against stresses and strains. "I pick up fewer injuries when I train on hills," says Angela Mudge, who became the Buff Skyrunner World Champion in 2006 after completing a world-wide series of trail races at altitude. "The ever-changing terrain means that each foot placement is subtly different, so you don't tend to develop the repetitive injuries experienced on roads." The ascents will make you a more powerful runner but the descents are just as helpful: the balance and need to constantly change stride length when you're coming downhill will make you more agile.

Try this Train off-road as often as possible. The forgiving terrain protects against injury, while uneven surfaces improve your balance and core strength.

SKILL SET

"Off-road hill running suits athletes who can easily change their rhythm," says Mudge. Unlike the track or road, the terrain changes quickly and you need to be able to adapt – from walking up a steep incline to breaking into a run as soon as the gradient levels out. You also need to be good at descending: there's no point becoming powerful enough to hammer up the climbs if you hold back on the descents.

Try this Work on your mental toughness. What might seem like an easy climb at the start of a race will be harder towards the end, but if you're determined, running inclines instead of walking them will make a real difference to your overall race time.

CHECK YOUR PACE

If you find that you start every ascent full of energy and enthusiasm only to fade alarmingly before you're even halfway up, you're setting off too fast. And that, as you will find out to your cost, can spell disaster further into the run. "If your oxygen and energy consumption

are too high early on, you'll pay back your oxygen debt later by slowing down and running out of glycogen," says Anderson. You're also likely to experience that burning in your legs (from lactic acid) much sooner.

Forget speed when you start running hills: it's effort that you should focus on. "Aim to keep your effort constant," says Anderson. Try to keep your heart rate at a constant level to preserve energy. You can use a heart-rate monitor to keep track of this. If you're having to put more effort in, it's okay to slow down. You can even walk but make sure your effort level remains constant.

Try this Hold back a little on the climb. "You'll be able to descend much more quickly because your body will be fresh enough to react to the terrain," says Mudge. There is one exception to the "even effort" rule: "It's okay to hammer the descents in shorter races," says Mudge, "as long as you take them easier if you know there are several ups and downs in longer events."

ON THE UP

You'll develop your own strategies for conquering hills, but borrowing tips from elite runners can help. As well as organising the Montrail Ultra-running Championships (runfurther.com) – a series of 12 mountain and trail races of over 30 miles – Mark Hartell is a former winner of the elite class of the Lowe

Alpine Mountain Marathon, and the record-holder for the most Lake District peaks climbed during the 24-hour Bob Graham Round. He always prepares himself for an upcoming hill. "If you know there is a big ascent coming up, slow down a little, try to relax and prepare yourself mentally to 'float' up the hill," he says. "Running hills is about getting your breathing right too. It should be quite a meditative process. Try to breathe in time with your footsteps."

Try this Hartell suggests running three strides as you breathe in – making sure you pull air right into your lungs – and three strides as you exhale, forcing the used air out a little more quickly.

OVER THE TOP

When you're near the top of a hill, work your arms hard to maintain rhythm. "Always push for a point just beyond the summit," says Hartell, "and keep your faster breathing pace going for longer to help to expel built-up lactic acid." The oxygen you take in will speed up this process.

Try this Aim to maintain the same strong effort for at least one more minute when you've reached the summit, even if you feel like easing off a little.

ROUTE MAP

Becoming fitter will help you to run more quickly on both the ascents and descents, but there are other ways to save time when tackling hills. "Learn to navigate," says Mudge. "You can save time if you follow the best route rather than the runner in front." Start with shorter races where you can practice navigating in a safe environment.

Try this Think about investing in a pair of off-road shoes. These specialised models feature studs on the outsole for extra grip and a lower-slung sole so you're less likely to turn an ankle. Inov-8 and Walsh shoes are popular with fell runners.

THE PERFECT HILL

"The perfect hill to train on is the one nearest to you," says Hartell, "because what matters is that you get out there and do it." Different gradients do suit different types of training though. Do short repetitions on steep slopes and longer repetitions on gradual gradients. If you only have a short hill to train on, you'll just have to run up and down it more times. In terms of the surface you choose to run on, grass and forest trails are easiest on the body, but the only hills that aren't suitable to train on at all are ones where you can't get a good grip.

THE SCIENCE OF HILLS

To really understand how hills work to improve running capacity, you need first to understand that the movement of the human body during running is similar to the bouncing of a ball. When a ball hits the ground, its shape changes and it decelerates until the energy is released and it springs back into shape as it bounces off the ground. Like the human body, the ball flies upwards and forwards to its next impact with the ground. Athletes can improve their running efficiency by letting the stretch and recoil of muscles do even more of the work needed to "bounce" them forward.

The energy that returns after each footfall is greater when a runner trains on an incline. Studies have shown that, on hills, calf muscles contract more quickly when the foot is on the ground. The calf muscles become more powerful by working at a higher rate.

THIS WAY UP

Proper form helps you power up any incline

➲ HEAD
"Keep your head upright and your neck relaxed," says running coach Richard Holt (momentumsports.co.uk). This will help you maintain a steady breathing pattern. "There's no need to jut it forwards to lean into the hill," he says.

➲ EYES
"Keep your eyes focused about six metres directly ahead of you," says ex-British fell-running champion Keith Anderson (fullpotential.co.uk). "This will help keep your head straight – and keep your eyes away from the task ahead."

➲ HANDS
"Keep your hands loose," advises Paula Coates, author of *Running Repairs: A Runner's Guide to Keeping Injury Free* (A&C Black). Loose hands help your whole body stay relaxed.

➲ LEGS
"Push your legs off and up, rather than into, the hill," says US Olympian Adam Goucher. This helps you feel as if you're "springing" up the hill.

➲ GOING UP
"If the gradient is constant, keep your pace constant," says Anderson. Otherwise, create a strategy to manage it. "If necessary, adopt a fell-runner's walk," advises Anderson. "Place your hands on your legs above the kneecap and below the

quadriceps, and use them to push off."

➲ BRAIN
"You need a bring-it-on attitude," says Anderson. "You'll need to drive to reach the top. Remember that your training is evidence that you can beat the hill, so go for it."

➲ TORSO
"Lean into the hill slightly," says Coates. "This will keep your pelvis in position to drive through the legs and maintain momentum."

➲ ARMS
You need to drive those arms to get to the top, but don't overdo it. "Keep the motion of your arms proportionate to the effort the hill requires," says Anderson Keep your elbows at 90 degrees. "Focus on driving the elbow behind you – it will come forward all on its own," says Holt.

➲ FEET
You need to stay on your toes – literally. "Push yourself off from your forefoot using your calves and your quads," says Holt. "The braking action of a heel strike would be even more exaggerated than it is on the flat, slowing you down significantly."

➲ GOING DOWN
Downhill running is "an art form in itself", says Anderson. Your feet should land beneath you, and a shortened arm swing helps shorten the strides.

Try this Find a hill with a gradient of about 10 per cent. "That means not too steep and not too shallow," says Anderson. The important thing is that you can maintain good form on the ascent.

TRICKS OF THE TRADE

No matter how hard you train, some hills will always present a mental as well as physical challenge. It can help to break a hilly training run or race into manageable chunks. "If I know a race has seven hills, I never worry about each one until I'm climbing it," says Ian Holmes, four-time British fell-running champion.

You might also be able to push yourself harder if you try to stay with the runner in front. "If I'm struggling, I try to hang on to the group I am with until I get over my bad patch or they leave me for dead," says Mudge. "I think about the next part of the race where I will be able to use my strengths, and try to get there fast."

You can even stop thinking about the hill entirely: "Looking at the left-right, left-right of my feet helps to increase the metronomic effect," says Hartell. Imagining a beat in your head will also help you to maintain a steady rhythm.

Try this If you're struggling up a hill, stop thinking about it and focus instead on how much fun you'll have when you reach the top and begin to descend.

NEED FOR SPEED

Some runners use hills as a substitute for speedwork but Anderson advises against this. True speedwork on the flat is conducted over distances of less than 50 metres, but hill running can be a good alternative to longer intervals on the flat. "If you spend time in an endurance phase of training, running lots of miles, putting in threshold runs and hill sessions, you will probably be able to run faster for sustained periods in longer intervals on the flat," says Anderson.

Try this Hills shouldn't replace short repetitions on the flat, but add them to your schedule if you're currently just focusing on longer interval sessions.

HAVE MORE FUN

If the burning sensation in your lungs and legs leads you to avoid hills, there are ways to make them more tolerable. "I found that running hills became fun when I started passing other people in races. It was that simple," says Hartell. If you're training, run with other people and reward yourself after your effort.

Try this "Pick an area with gorgeous views and enjoy them on the way up," says Mudge.

HILL STARTS

Whether you're training for a 5K or marathon, these hill sessions created by Nick Anderson will toughen you up

➔ THRESHOLD HILLS

Hills run at threshold pace (the speed you can sustain with good form for around 40 minutes) with a downhill recovery run at a similar effort will build endurance and strength. Find a gradual gradient that you can run up for between 45 seconds and five minutes at 80-85 per cent of maximum heart rate. **Try this** Run one minute uphill followed immediately by one minute downhill. Repeat 12 to 20 times. If you're new to hills, break the session into segments and build up to one continuous block of effort. **Best for** The muscular endurance benefits are massive. They really benefit marathon runners who fatigue in the later stages of a race.

➔ SPEED ENDURANCE HILLS

These hills increase power, strength, speed endurance and mechanical efficiency. They are run at speed (85-90 per cent of maximum heart rate) with the arms driving and pumping hard and with a long, bounding stride and high knees. These hills are tough and run above threshold, creating high lactate levels. **Try this** Complete a session of eight to 12 times 30 to 45-second hills on a good gradient, with a walk or jog back to the start to recover. **Best for** Try these if you're a cross-country, 5K, 10K or middle-distance track runner.

➔ OFF-THE-TOP HILLS

You wouldn't run hard up a hill in a race only to start walking when you reach the top, so train by running hard up the hill and to continue at a hard pace once you've reached the summit. **Try this** Find a route that has hills that take 30 to 90 seconds to climb and run these hard each time you hit them. Then run for the same time at the same effort after you reach the top. **Best for** Giving you confidence to put some time into your rivals at the top of hills during races.

It's all in the training...

Whatever the event you choose to participate in, please do it for Guide Dogs and make your place count.

Guide Dogs receives no government funding and depends entirely on public donations to continue its work.

0845 600 6787

events@guidedogs.org.uk

www.guidedogs.org.uk/events

Guide Dogs

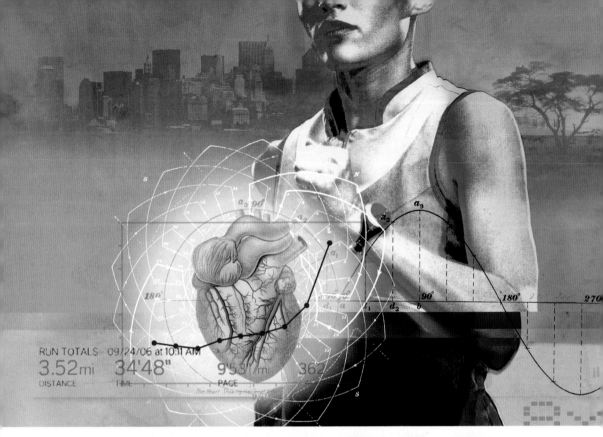

RUN TOTALS 09/24/06 at 10:11 AM
3.52 mi   34'48"   9'53"/mi   362
DISTANCE   TIME   PACE

PERFECT TEMPO

The 'comfortably hard' run is the key to clocking your fastest time, at any distance. Here's how to make it work for you

Pssst! Want to run like a world-beater? Okay, you might not make it to the very top, but your training regime can help you achieve new PBs, simply by incorporating the same method that helped propel the likes of Ethopian world-record holder, Haile Gebrselassie, and his Kenyan predecessor, Paul Tergat, to greatness.

The secret? The tempo run – that faster-paced session also known as a lactate-threshold, LT or threshold run. One US-based coach championing this method is Toby

Tanser. In 1995, when Tanser was an elite young track runner from Sweden, he trained with the Kenya "A" team for seven months. They ran classic tempos – a slow 15-minute warm-up, followed by at least 20 minutes at a challenging but manageable pace, then a 15-minute cool-down – as often as twice a week. "The foundation of Kenyan running is based almost exclusively on tempo training," says Tanser. "It changed my view on training."

Today, Tanser and many running experts believe that tempo runs are the single most important session you can do to improve your speed for any race distance. "There's no beating the long run for pure endurance," says Tanser. "But tempo running is crucial to racing success because it trains your body to sustain speed over distance." So crucial, in fact, that it trumps track sessions in the longer distances. "Tempo training is more important than speedwork for the half and full marathon," says Gale Bernhardt, author of *Training Plans for Multisport Athletes*. "Everyone who does tempo runs diligently will improve." However, you also have to be diligent about doing them correctly.

WHY THE TEMPO WORKS

Tempo running improves a crucial physiological variable for running success: metabolic fitness. Most runners train their cardio system to deliver oxygen to the muscles, but not how to use it once it arrives. Tempo runs teach the body to use the oxygen for metabolism more efficiently.

How? By increasing your lactate threshold (LT), or the point at which the body fatigues at a certain pace. "During tempo runs, lactate and hydrogen ions – by-products of metabolism – are released into the muscles," says Dr Carwyn Sharp, an exercise scientist who works with NASA. The ions make the muscles acidic, eventually leading to fatigue. The better trained you become, the higher you push your threshold, meaning your muscles become better at using these by-products. The result is less acidic muscles – in other words, muscles that haven't reached their new threshold, so they keep on contracting, letting you run further and faster.

DOING IT PROPERLY

But to garner this training effect, you've got to put in enough time at the right intensity – it's easy to get it wrong with runs that are too short and too slow. "You need to get the hydrogen ions in the muscles for a sufficient length of time for the muscles to become adept at using them," says Sharp. Typically, 20 minutes is sufficient, or two to three miles if your goal is general fitness or a 5K. Runners tackling longer distances should do longer tempo runs during their peak training weeks: four to six miles for the 10K, six to eight for the half-marathon and eight to 10 for 26.2.

How should tempo pace feel? It should feel what we call "comfortably hard". You know you're working, but you're not racing. At the same time, you'd be happy if you could slow down. You'll be even happier if you make tempo running a part of your weekly training schedule, and get results that make you feel like a champion – even if you're not quite as fast.

UP TEMPO

A classic tempo or lactate-threshold run is a sustained, hard effort for two to four miles, with a decent warm-up before and cool-down afterwards. The sessions below are geared towards experience levels and race goals

➔ GOAL: GET STARTED

Coach Gale Bernhardt uses this four-week progression for tempo newbies. Do a 10- to 15-minute warm-up and cool-down.

Week 1: 5 x 3 minutes at tempo pace, 60-second easy jog after each one (if you find that you have to walk during the recovery, you're going too hard).

Week 2: 5 x 4 minutes at tempo pace, 60-second easy jog recovery.

Week 3: 4 x 5 minutes at tempo pace, 90-second easy jog recovery.

Week 4: 20 minutes steady tempo pace.

➔ GOAL: 5K TO 10K

Run three easy miles, followed by two repeats of two miles at 10K pace or one mile at 5K pace. Recover with one mile easy between repeats. Do a two-mile easy cool-down for a total of eight or 10 miles.

➔ GOAL: HALF TO FULL MARATHON

Do this challenging long run once or twice during your training.

After a warm-up, run three (half-marathoners) or six (marathoners) miles at the easier end of your tempo pace range. Jog for five minutes, and then do another three or six miles. "Maintaining that comfortably hard pace for so many miles will whip you into shape for long distances," says coach Toby Tanser.

➔ THE RIGHT RHYTHM

To ensure you're running at the right pace, use one of these four methods to gauge your intensity.

RECENT RACE Add 30 to 40 seconds per kilometre to your current 5K pace or 15 to 20 seconds to your 10K pace.

HEART RATE Run at 85 to 90 per cent of your maximum heart rate (use a heart-rate monitor).

PERCEIVED EXERTION An eight on a one to 10 scale (a comfortable effort would be five; racing close to a 10).

TALK TEST A few words should be possible, but not conversation.

FLIGHT TO THE FINISH

Leave the competition behind with our five steps to a killer kick

Go on, admit it: you've dreamed about breaking the tape at a race. At the sharp end of a race, prizes and pride hang on how you run the last few metres, but learning to burst over the line is just as useful for everyone else. Finishing strong puts on a great show and is a superb confidence booster, but most importantly, a sprint finish is the difference between hitting and missing your targets.

Some people are naturally good at putting in a last spurt. "Most good sprint finishers are born, not made," says Steve Smythe, a coach and distance runner. "A runner with lots of natural fast-twitch muscle fibres will usually beat the one-paced endurance runner, but there are things you can do to redress the balance."

If you've taken up running in adulthood, it can take time to work out which camp you fall in to, because nearly all recreational runners are slow enough to have something left for a final push. As you become faster and race more often, you'll soon learn when and where to push the pace, but even if you're lucky enough to be a naturally strong finisher, you can work on your overall race for a better time and placing.

1 BUILD THE FOUNDATIONS

A strong finish is the icing on your running cake, but you need to bake the cake first. Yes, that means building up mileage slowly and introducing new training elements gradually – especially intense speed sessions. "There's a lot to be said for running 200m or 400m intervals with short recovery periods in the build-up to a race," says Nick Anderson, British cross-country team coach. "But you need to put in the basic training first."

For a fast finish, your base shouldn't just include mileage, though. Include core training – working on your abdominal and back muscles – to develop good sprinting form, and strength training, which helps to develop the fast-twitch muscle fibres needed to go up a gear. One or two sessions per week should do the trick – try gym classes if you're not sure where to start. When you do start sprint sessions in training, think about your form from the outset: relax your face and neck and pull up tall. Pump your arms back and forth (not out to the sides), your leading knee should drive up high and your foot should be planted firmly in front of you.

2 BECOME FIT TO BURST

The strong finish is all about a sudden fast burst, especially at the front of a race where intimidating your rivals is almost as important as the speed itself. To learn this, you need some short, fast intervals. Smythe recommends a session of 100m sprints: warm up, then try five to eight reps of 100m (or 15 to 20 seconds very fast) with walk-break recoveries. Time your efforts and try to run quicker each time.

3 RUN ON EMPTY

Running short sprints in training can be fun. At the end of a race, though, you'll be sprinting off the back of your very last reserves of strength. This isn't fun, but thanks to the good old rule of specificity (training as you want to race), you'll need to practise fast running when you're tired just as much as the sprinting. The best way to do this is to make your hard sessions slightly harder. "I always try to finish a speed session with a hard final effort, so my body does it automatically in a race," says Smythe.

Change your approach to your long runs: promise yourself you'll never trot down to your front door at the end, and pick a point – perhaps

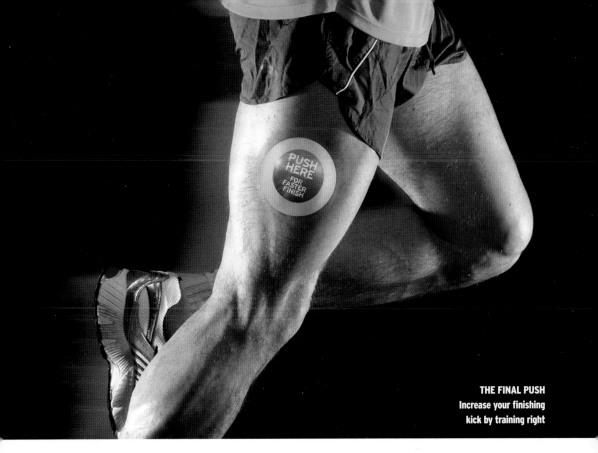

THE FINAL PUSH
Increase your finishing
kick by training right

at the end of your street, or when you see a familiar landmark – to race home from.

4 PLAN FOR THE END

To finish a race really well, you need to know what's coming. "To make sure you judge your effort at the right place, familiarise yourself with the end of the course before the race," says Smythe. If there's a nasty hill, narrow path or difficult ground in your way, factor that in to your final approach.

If you're in contention for a top-three place, try to suss out your competition. If you don't know who you'll be up against, it could be worth checking previous years' results – are there any regular winners? Is the finish usually close, or is the winner usually minutes ahead? Race standards change from year to year, but often particular events will have a reputation for being particularly fast or not, and this could help you to plan your tactics.

In the race itself, don't focus so much on the finish that you forget about your pace the rest of the time – your sprint can buy you seconds, but your overall pacing puts you in pole position for that sprint. Over long distances, it can be tempting to distract yourself from the passing miles, but research has shown that concentrating on your body and your performance has a better outcome, so make sure you're switched on from at least one-third in to the race.

5 THE FINAL PUSH

By the time you reach the end of the race, you'll know where your strengths lie and who you're racing for a place. For middle-of-the-pack runners, your task is simple and satisfying: speed up gradually to pick off runners as you approach the finish. Further up the field, you'll need to be more precise with your timing of the final big push. "If you don't have a killer kick and want to beat a rival, make your effort 400m to 800m from the finish to draw the speed out of your opponent," says Smythe.

For most of us, the sight of the finish line is enough to spur us on – but when you reach that point, remember that however unpleasant you feel physically, it won't last long. So give it everything you've got.

RULES OF ACTION

Discover the perfect training strategy for you by listening to the needs of your body – and following these five universal rules

R unning isn't rocket science. But figuring out a training strategy can seem just as tricky. How many miles should you run? At what speed? What is VO2 max again? And lactate threshold? Is that related to glycogen stores?

The fact that every runner is unique further complicates matters. So it's crucial to learn the quirks and requirements of our own bodies and play by its rules.

Luckily, there are some principles that, regardless of individual mileage and pace, apply to almost every runner – whether you're slow or fast, training for a marathon or for life. Conceived by coaches and employed by elites, these time-tested rules will help you stay motivated, avoid injuries and run strong year after year.

1 MINIMAL TRAINING FOR OPTIMAL RESULTS

If you've improved by running 25 miles a week, you could be so much better by running 50, right? Not exactly. Training isn't a matter of cramming in as many miles as you can. It's about finding the balance of miles, days per week, and types of workouts that get you to your goals without injury or exhaustion. Tim Noakes, in his book *Lore of Running*, describes this concept as the "individual training threshold". And that threshold is uniquely yours. One runner may excel on 55 miles a week over six days with extra tempo running, while another runner may do well on 25 miles a week over four days, with a focus on short, fast repeats.

Action Experiment with different mileage levels. If you've been logging megamiles (50+ per week), back off for a while and see if you can still hit your goal times in workouts. If you've been doing the bare minimum (three days per week), try adding a day or two. Keep a detailed log, noting how your body and your race times respond.

2 BALANCE HARD EFFORTS WITH REST

Imagine running as hard as you can one day, then again the next day, and the next. Sooner or later, you'd barely be able to run at all. That's the scenario that exercise physiologist Jack Daniels uses to illustrate the necessity of the work-rest cycle. "The benefits of stressing the body come during recovery," he says. On easy or off days, your body is busy repairing muscle fibres, increasing your ability to process nutrients and oxygen, building new blood cells and eliminating waste. If you don't give your body time to recover, sooner or later you will tear it down.

Action As a rule of thumb, put in one easy day between hard workouts (more if you're feeling fatigued) and take at least one full day off a week. During training, reduce your mileage by 15 to 20 per cent every fourth week, and if you find that a certain week is particularly difficult, keep training at that week's level until it becomes comfortable.

3 EXPECT PEAKS AND PLATEAUS

You drop three minutes off your 10K time. The six-mile loop that used to feel impossible now feels easy. At some point, though, the improvements will slow, or stop. That's not necessarily a bad thing. It means you've adapted to your training and you've climbed to a higher plateau. But now is the time to change your workload.

Most of us see the greatest improvements early in our running careers. Once you reach a certain level (predetermined by genes and influenced by age), you'll

ILLUSTRATION: CELIA JOHNSON

have to work harder, and perhaps rest more, to gain seconds off a race.

Action Adding hills, increasing the time of your tempo run, or trying longer or faster repeats are a few ways to intensify your training and advance to a new level. However, if you're already training at a high level – 50 or more miles a week with a mix of intervals, tempo miles, hills and long runs – a plateau may be a sign you need rest.

4 BE CONSISTENT

Ask a coach what the single most important factor is in training, and most will answer "consistency". You won't improve if you run only once a week, or if you repeatedly run hard for a week, then take the next week off. Better running comes from regular running. Consistency, however, doesn't mean you need to train all-out year-round. Periods of structured training, paired with months of fewer miles, help you avoid physical and mental burnout.

Action Maintain a minimum, even if that's 30 minutes, two or three days a week, and run in the morning so you're sure to get it done. Plan your 'down' months

for times you know it'll be harder to run – winter weather, big projects, life changes, and so on.

5 PRACTISE PATIENCE

Piling on the miles or pushing the intensity too soon won't get you in shape faster (your body needs time to adapt), but it might get you injured. So whether you're a new runner or returning after a break, increase quantity and quality gradually.

Action When we say to step up gradually, this translates into an increase in mileage or time by only 10 per cent a week. It's conservative, but that's the point. The increase should be applied to more than one run. So say you put in 20 miles a week, including one long run and one speed session. You could add a mile to your long run and a half-mile to an easy run, while increasing your speed session by one 800m rep for a total of two additional miles across the whole week. Avoid increasing intensity and distance simultaneously (for example, don't pick up the pace of your 800m in the same week that you add another one). New runners should focus on going further before going faster.

RUNNING ROADMAPS

If you want to get the most out of your running, make a plan

Running goals can be tricky things. Set them too high, and they're bound to frustrate you. Set them too low, and they won't challenge you. Set them just right, and they'll be a powerful source of motivation, driving you to achievement. To set the perfect running goals, follow the five-step plan below. Don't forget, the paths you take to reach your running goals are just as important – and just as rewarding – as achieving the goals themselves.

1 MAKE A LIST

In order of importance, write down two to four running goals you'd like to achieve in the next six months. They can be as general as to run injury-free; to feel good on almost every run; or to balance your running with your family life and career, or they can be more specific, such as completing a particular race or achieving a certain time. You'll need to review this list every so often to make adjustments as needed. For example, as the date of a 5K goal race gets close, it will move higher on your list than when it was months away.

2 PENCIL IT IN

With your list of goals in hand, you can begin to sort out how you'll achieve each one by plotting the key sessions you'll need in a training log, notebook or on a calendar. If one of your goals is to enjoy your runs more, you'll need to schedule social runs, runs in scenic locations or runs with your favourite four-legged friend. Time-specific goals mean you'll need to chart a series of speedwork sessions, and if you're looking to complete a marathon or half-marathon, you'll need to map out your long-run

strategy. Use a pencil to schedule these runs, just in case changes need to be made later.

3 MAKE IT STICK WITH INK

After you've pencilled in all the sessions, you need to make sure you have time to achieve those goals – so take an overall look at your calendar to assess things. Do you have the time and the resources to follow through with your plan as scheduled? Are you able to make the sacrifices necessary to achieve your specific race and time goals? If so, take out a pen and make your schedule permanent. If not, scale down your goals, and set up a new programme based on your time and energy constraints. Then put it in ink.

4 BREAK IT DOWN

Big goals are achieved much more easily if you divide them into smaller goals you can use as stepping-stones to reach the final goal. For example, instead of trying to make the "good-for-age" qualifying times for the London Marathon before you've even run a half-marathon, aim to finish a 10K in the next two months. As this goal approaches, plan your second goal of finishing a half-marathon in the next three months. Finishing your first marathon might follow in the months leading up to the end of the year. Write down each intermediate goal in your training log, and fill in the long run and speed sessions needed to prepare for them. If any of these smaller goals become too stressful, add another stepping stone.

5 TAKE A REALITY CHECK

How do you know your time goals are achievable? By running a 5K, you can predict your

JULY

RUNNER'S

MONDAY	TUESDAY	WEDNESDAY	THURSDAY	FRIDAY	SATURDAY	SUNDAY
			1 Tempo run	**2**	**3**	**4** RACE
5	**6** Lunch-time run	**7**	**8** Tempo run	**9**	**10**	**11** RACE
12	**13** Lunch-time run	**14**	**15** Tempo run	**16**	**17**	**18** Long run
19 Taper	**20**	**21**	**22**	**23**	**24**	**25** → RACE
26	**27**	**28** Recovery run	**29**	**30**	**31**	

potential finishing time in a 10K, half-marathon or marathon. There are a number of prediction charts around, such as those at www.runnersworld.com/calculators that will calculate your predicted race time at a given race distance based on your actual time at another race distance. If your goals are more qualitative (eg to enjoy running more), look over the notes in your log every few weeks to see if you're on the right track. If not, make the training adjustments necessary to give you a realistic shot of reaching your goal.

6 PLANNING A RACE SEASON

Once you are used to running, you might want to plan the events you enter so you can make the most of your training, and maintain your interest as the months pass. Each year there are well over 5,000 running races in Britain, ranging from a mile to 100Ks and more, with options over trail, countryside,

fell, track and road. Some people may manage 100 races in a year, including 30 marathons, but it isn't advisable if you want to maximise your performance and keep injury and boredom at bay. Variety and recovery should be your keywords. It's also valuable to decide what, for you, are going to be the three or four most important races of the year. This not only helps focus your training, but also affects the way you approach the other races in your year.

April, of course, is when the London Marathon takes place, so if you're running it, the first months of the year will be largely about training. As the weather heats up during the summer it's a good time to enter a 5K or 10K race, especially if you're recovering from the rigours of London. But there are some great events throughout the year, even in winter when it's an ideal time to go cross-country. Go to runnersworld.co.uk/events for details on races.

RISE OF THE MACHINE

Looking to broaden your running experience? Perhaps it's time you spent some quality time with "it indoors" – the treadmill

I n 1980 Benji Durden had a secret. The soon-to-be US Olympic marathoner was sneaking over to the local univerity physiology lab to work out on (gasp!) a treadmill. "I didn't tell other runners I was using a treadmill," he recalls, reflecting the derisory attitude toward treadmills of the time. "They would have thought I was strange. Even the lab staff thought I was mad." They soon revised their thinking when Durden clocked 2:09 and won many marathons in the following years.

Still, it took many years for the idea of treadmills to take hold. At the time, they were considered tinny, cheap, noisy contraptions that cluttered the spare room and did little else (except deliver pangs of regret to their owners). It seemed, like the hula hoop, Rubik's cube and mullet hairstyle, they were doomed to be nothing more than a fad. Few serious runners owned one and those that did kept it quiet. The distance-running ethic was an outdoors one – no matter the conditions. To run indoors on a rattly machine was... well, a sellout really. Treacherous. Weak.

Fortunately that attitude has changed – as have treadmills, which are vastly superior machines today. Just as cross-training doesn't diminish you as a runner, neither does engaging in a treadmill session. Once you've decided to try treadmill running, you just need to work out how to incorporate it into your schedule to maximise its potential (and yours). The advantages of treadmills are numerous: from convenience to workout precision to injury prevention.

BEAT THE COLD

It's February and freezing outside, so you step on your treadmill for a six-mile run that beats scampering about on icy footpaths hands down. This is the most obvious reason to use a treadmill. Severe winter weather can be tough to train in – as well as potentially dangerous. You may know people who prided themselves on running every winter day, no matter how miserable the weather was – that is, until they

INJURY PREVENTION

Dr Ken Sparks, an exercise physiologist at Cleveland State University in the USA, recommends treadmill training to come back from injuries – or avoid them altogether

➔ "First of all, there's less pounding of the joints on a treadmill than on the roads," says Dr Sparks. "The treadmill belt gives when you land on it, unlike concrete and asphalt."
➔ "Second, there's no camber on a treadmill as there is on roads. That slope forces you to overpronate (your feet rotate too far inwards on impact) and can lead to shinsplints, Achilles tendinitis and knee problems."
➔ "And third, on a treadmill, there's no lateral pressure on your knees and ankles as there would be if you were running around a track, and this kind of pressure can lead to injuries."

NO SLIP-UPS
Treadmills avoid the
risk of falling on ice

hit an ice patch and ended up in a cast for two months and out of running for four. "I don't mind the cold too much," says Bob Kempainen, a 1992 Olympic marathon runner. "But if it's icy, I'll do my 10-mile run on a treadmill. Why risk it?"

BEAT THE HEAT

Severe heat is another reason to head to the health club or wherever there's a treadmill. On a really hot day, an air-conditioned gym may be more attractive than a sticky road surface and punishing sun.

WORK VS WORKOUTS

Sometimes a quick 30-minute run on the company treadmill at lunch is the only way to fit in a workout between job commitments. Durden, who coaches several runners by fax and phone, remembers a particularly busy month when he and his treadmill became very close. "I did 23 days in a row on a treadmill," he says. "I was afraid that if I went out on a long run I'd miss a lot of calls. It was either that or take a mobile phone with me. Mobile phones were pretty big back then so it wasn't really practical."

PRECISION TRAINING

"Treadmills give you a much more evenly paced workout than running on a track," says world-class masters miler Dr Ken Sparks. "For instance, if you're doing 400-metre repeats on a track in 90 seconds, you might run the first 200 in 43 seconds and the second in 47. On a treadmill, you can't do that. Each 200 will be exactly 45 seconds."

PERFECT HILLS

Hill workouts are a special feature of treadmill running that win many over – even those, like Durden, who live in hilly areas. "You can duplicate your hill sessions from week to week almost perfectly," says Durden. "If you want to do a two per cent gradient and a one per cent recovery, you just punch some buttons. It's very precise and very easy to do."

RACE-COURSE WORKOUTS

Computerised treadmills come with built-in programmes that can take you up and down or increase and decrease the pace during your run. They also let you programme your own courses. Extreme marathoner Matt Carpenter is a regular treadmill trainer. Carpenter programmes in the exact ascent gradients in upcoming races and sets the pace at

slightly faster than the course record. One year, Carpenter won a race but missed the record by 33 seconds on a day when rain made the footing slippery. "You can't put mud on a treadmill," he quips.

ESCAPE THE LONELY ROAD

Finally, treadmills come in handy for those who don't appreciate the loneliness of the long-distance runner, or those concerned with the safety of solo jogging.

GETTING YOUR TREADMILL LEGS

Once adjusted to treadmill running you can begin to explore the myriad ways to employ it, from speed training to hill sessions to recovery runs. Like a new pair of running shoes, a treadmill needs to be broken in – or, rather, you need to be broken in to the treadmill if you are to derive maximum benefits. "The first few times on a treadmill, start off slower than you think you should," says Benji Durden. "You need to become accustomed to it so you don't feel awkward or as though you're going to fall off."

Take Carol McLatchie and her husband, Jim, for example. They are both keen runners, although Jim has had some treadmill "issues". "Jim has been periodically banned from the McLatchie treadmill," says Carol with a laugh. "He just can't get the hang of it. He keeps falling off it. Once he fell off and was lying half-stunned, pressed against the wall, while the belt was whipping around and thumping on his leg. Finally, he reached over and unplugged it."

Jim is a rare case, however. Most people have no problem on a machine once they adjust to the initial strangeness of a moving surface – it's like learning to ride a bike. Once you get the hang of it, it's easy.

"When I'm on the treadmill, I always have this feeling I'm going faster than on the roads," says Carol McLatchie. "Without visual cues, like scenery going by, I get thrown a bit and my equilibrium can be slightly off when I step off. It's as if I was out at sea, and now I'm on land again. I have sea legs for a few minutes. But you get used to it pretty quickly."

THE TRICK IS NOT MINDING

The monotony of treadmill training is a big complaint, and even dedicated treadmill trainers won't argue with you on that point. Instead, they'll tell you how they get around it. World-class marathon runner Ken Martin blasts music while on his treadmill. Durden watches

BEAT BOREDOM
Programme hills, intervals and race courses for variety

THE GREAT OUTDOORS, INDOORS

With few exceptions, anything you can do outside, you can do inside. Prior to his 2:09:38 second-place finish at the 1989 New York City Marathon, Ken Martin logged all his long runs on a treadmill. "I'd just get into a nice rhythm and stay controlled," he says. "I also thought it was good because I had my drinks right there beside me, so I didn't have to stop to drink, and I could practise drinking on the run."

But Martin's may be a special case. Many runners can't tolerate a two-hour easy run going nowhere, even if audio-visual enterntainment is on hand to ease the pain and/or boredom. Other workouts, such as tempo runs, hills, speedwork and specially designed race-course sessions, are more suited to the treadmill because the session is broken up into more easily digestible segments.

MAKING SPEEDWORK COUNT

Dr Sparks has been running intensive speed sessions on a treadmill since the late 1960s, when he was a graduate student for Dr David L. Costill, director of the Human Performance Laboratory at Ball State University in Indianapolis. "I didn't have much time back then, and some of my workouts would actually be jumping on a treadmill and running a four-minute mile, then jumping off," he says.

Nowadays, on his homemade treadmill, Dr Sparks clicks off 63-second 400m intervals with a one-minute jog in between. But don't try this at home – or at the health club. Most treadmills won't go faster than a 75-second 400m pace. Therefore, you might want to limit your speed sessions on a treadmill to longer repeats of say, 800m or miles.

Olympics re-runs. McLatchie's treadmill is next to a window that looks out on her garden.

Another option is to schedule your treadmill sessions for peak hours at the health club, so you can socialise, or at least have something to look at. (But be aware that most health clubs have a time limit on treadmills, usually 20 to 30 minutes.) Avoid clock-watching. "If I look at my watch, time crawls by unbearably slowly on a treadmill," says Carpenter.

There's one perfect way of avoiding monotony on a treadmill. You simply take your cue from Peter O'Toole in Lawrence of Arabia, who, after extinguishing a match between his fingers, explained "the trick is not minding". And how do you not mind a treadmill workout? Throw in a little pain.

"I never get bored on my treadmill," says Dr Sparks, who treadmill trains alongside garden hoses, rakes and spades in his garage. "I know when I step on my treadmill, I'm going to do an intense speed workout." A positive attitude, as ever, is of crucial importance.

TOP TIPS

→ Treadmill running is precise, convenient, safe and can reduce injuries.
→ Take the time to accustomise yourself to treadmill running to avoid accident and injury.
→ Treadmills are blissfully immune to extreme weather.

→ If your employer has a treadmill, employ it for extra lunchtime runs.
→ Make the most of your treadmill's interval and hill settings.
→ Input a race's exact gradient changes and distance to gain an edge.

RUN STRONG

Work out your running muscles to improve performance and injury-proof your body

HOW TO DO THIS CIRCUIT

Check with a healthcare professional if you're new to exercising. Start with a 10-minute warm-up of gentle jogging or cycling. Perform the exercises in order, taking the minimum possible rest between each one. Rest for three minutes before repeating the circuit. Do this session two to three times a week for up to six weeks.

➡ THE PENDULUM

① Stand on one leg with your shoulder blades drawn back and core braced.
② Lift one leg straight up behind you while reaching to your toes with the opposite arm. Keep your hips level.
REPS 10 (each leg)
WHY This move works the muscles at the side of your backside to prevent lateral hip movement.

➡ REVERSE LUNGE INTO STEP-UP

① Step back into a lunge with your right leg until your left thigh is level with the floor.
② Drive forwards lifting your right leg up onto a step and stepping up. Drive your left leg up and forwards before stepping back with it.
REPS 10 (alternate legs)
WHY It trains your leg muscles to be strong, as they lengthen as well as contract.

➡ PLANK TO ONE-ARM ROW

① In the plank position, hold your body in a straight line from ankle to neck.
② Take one hand off the floor, and without tilting your torso or moving your core, lift the hand until the elbow goes past your ribs. Hold for two seconds.
REPS 10 (each arm)
WHY Your core will work hard to stabilise your body.

➡ SQUAT TOUCH-DOWN

① Contract your abdominals and take one foot off the floor.
② Squat by bending at the hip, knee and ankle, lowering your right hand to the outside of your left foot.
REPS 10 (each side)
WHY Improving neuromuscular stability across your body and overall leg strength will make you a stronger runner.

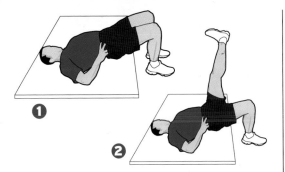

→ SINGLE-LEG BRIDGE

1 Lie with your knees bent. Lift your hips to form a line from shoulder to knee, resting your hands on your hips.

2 Lift one foot off the floor, making sure that your hips don't tilt or buckle. Straighten the leg if you can.

REPS 10 (each side)

WHY Poor weight transfer through your pelvis after each footfall can lead to injury.

→ TOE RAISE

1 Stand with hands on hips and shoulders drawn back.

2 Raise your right toes off the floor while keeping your heel on the ground and hold for five seconds.

REPS 10 (each side)

WHY Despite the small movement, this exercise is vital for overpronators, and will prevent shin splints. It will also give you lower-leg strength and stability.

STRETCH IT OUT Follow every workout with a good stretching routine

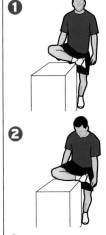

→ KNEELING STRETCH

1 Place your right knee on the floor and bend your left leg. Raise your arms.

2 Lean forwards to feel the stretch in your hips and side abs. Hold for 30 seconds.

REPS 3 x 30 seconds (each side)

WHY Stretches your hip flexors and core to ease the tension that running causes.

→ INVERTED V

1 Get onto hands and knees.

2 Take your knees off the floor and press your heels into the floor with your bottom in the air.

REPS 3 x 30 seconds

WHY This stretch was used by female winner in the Cuba Trail Marathon 2007, Kyrin Hall, to loosen up hamstrings, calves and lower back.

→ QUADS STRETCH

1 Lie supporting your weight on your left arm, and place a foam roller under your left thigh.

2 Brace your core and glutes and roll forwards and backwards slowly.

REPS 30-90 seconds (each side)

WHY Stretches the quads without tensing ligaments.

→ STANDING PIGEON

1 Rest your right leg on a table so it is at 90 degrees to your body.

2 Step back slightly with the supporting leg and relax your upper body over the leg on the table.

REPS 3 x 30 seconds (each side)

WHY Targets the glutes, lower back and calf.

BE A PART OF IT
Joining a club means
lots of new friends

JOIN THE CLUB?

Thinking about signing up with a running club? Here's all you need to know before committing – or not

The days when running clubs were the sole preserve of ultra-competitive elite racers hell-bent on crushing the opposition at all costs and putting in more hours than Haile Gebrselassie or Paula Radcliffe are thankfully long gone. With hundreds of clubs catering for runners up and down the country, there's literally something for everyone, from beginner fun-runners to serious pace-setters. Indeed, it's possible to join a running club without ever racing, without being able to make it round the athletics track in under 90 seconds and without finding it fascinating to discuss the relative merits of control versus stability shoes.

Not everyone feels the need to be coached as part of a group – after all, getting away from the crowds has always been one of the main pulls of our pastime. But with the help of the country's finest club coaches and input from regular runners, we've come up with the ultimate guide to help you decide whether joining a club could help you reach your goals, or realise that you're better off flying solo.

HOW TO CHOOSE A CLUB
SUIT YOURSELF

If you're simply keen to get out there and meet other recreational runners, you need to know you're not joining a club packed with elite racers. "While everyone will change their goals over time as a runner, you need to make sure there's a group, at least at the start, that's on the same wavelength as you," says Fraser Smart from Kirkintilloch Olympians (kirkintillocholympians. co.uk). All clubs will claim to be "friendly", but that depends on your outlook. "Prioritise what it is you're aiming to get from your club, and email or call one of their coaches to see if it tallies with their approach – it's better to be upfront from the start than leave after a couple of months with a bitter taste in your mouth."

GO LOCAL

If the club's not convenient, you'll find your reasons not to go. "There'll be times when the last thing you want to do is go for a run, so it has to be easy to get to and from," says Clare Naden from Clapham Chasers (claphamchasers.co.uk). "If it takes you an hour to get home, it'll impinge too much on your stress levels, which defeats the point – it's supposed to be enjoyable, not a strain." Add in the problem of commuting time and you're also less likely to make any post-run socials that are an integral part of any club's cohesion. "Mine's on my way home from work, so it's virtually impossible for me to justify not going – and I can enjoy a relaxing drink afterwards knowing I've got an easy 10-minute jog home." Find clubs by postcode and proximity at goodrunguide.co.uk.

FRINGE BENEFITS

As well as potentially reduced race costs, there are other extras you might want to ask about. "The £20 a year I pay is more than offset with discounts at local running shops, not to mention the contacts you make in terms of physios when you get injured, and massage therapists," says Lucy Colquhoun from City of Edinburgh AC (edinburghac.org.uk). "Any good club should at least be aware of local physios and other running-specific professionals who can help you out, either with discounts or just priority treatment."

CLUB TOGETHER
Sharing a ride to races is part of the fun

And once you enter the circle of trust, you won't be simply relying on the first ad you see on yell.com to iron out any issues.

MAKE THE RIGHT FRIENDS

While being sociable is no doubt top of every runner's list, that probably stops short of drinking yards of warm lager out of dirty training shoes as part of Frat-party-worthy initiation rites. "The post-run environment is absolutely essential for you to make friends, determine running partners and discuss issues with coaches," says Rory McDonnell from Clapham Chasers. "I've known clubs that have really frowned

> ### 'The post-run environment is absolutely essential to make friends, determine running partners and discuss issues'

on any post-run drinking, which I find as off-putting as compulsory drinking – you just have to know what you want first," he says. "You'll also be sharing cars to races, and helping each other through problems, so you have to know you're vaguely on the same song sheet as your club mates." See if you can meet up for a couple of post-run sessions to get to know the runners.

MAKE CONTACT

While running is probably the oldest sport known to man, most clubs have moved with the times, with websites that provide information and contact details. "If there are lots of pictures of runners at a recent race or meet, you've got an idea that the club is run efficiently and for the runners," says Guy Regis from Serpentine Running Club (serpentine.org.uk). "Too many clubs stagnate under bureaucratic committees who've lost touch with what they're trying to achieve." But don't always judge a book by its cover. "There should at least be an email address for someone on the site – if they don't get back to you in a couple of days, I'd give it a wide berth, as you could be left similarly stranded once you join."

READ THE SMALL PRINT

While yearly subs of up to £20 might seem reasonable, once you're in the club you might well get stung for some extra hidden costs. "Often you have to buy their club-branded running bibs and shorts, at prices that seem far from reasonable," explains Lesley Foster from Sunderland Strollers (sunderlandstrollers.co.uk). "Also ask if there are any monthly admin charges, or what you have to pay for each session throughout the year. "If money's an issue, say it is and see what reaction the club gives. "If they don't suggest they'll waive or cut costs if you're hard-up or unemployed, it gives a pretty good indication of the people running it."

GIVE IT A TRY

As well as asking questions of the coaches, see if you can trial a few sessions before signing up. "It often takes more than one session to get to really know a club, so don't base all your judgements on one evening," says Michael Morris from Morpeth Harriers (morpethharriers.co.uk). And don't try three Monday evenings in a row. "Different sessions and evenings often have different focuses and people, so dip your toe in several spots before making up your mind."

THINK THE WORST

While no runner goes out looking for injuries, they inevitably hit us all from time to time. "Ask the coaches their views on over-training and limiting sessions to see if they're generally aware of your long-term safety," says Rob Pullen from the Owls running club in Leicester (owlsac.org.uk). Ask what contingencies they have for injuries during runs, whether they have insurance, and ask if they have a group for runners who are coming back to fitness from injury. "It's all well and good catering for the flag-waving front runners, but you need even more attention if you're coming back to fitness, and one day that will be you."

PAY BACK

Clubs aren't just about running. "There's a whole load of other activities, from organising socials to marshalling races to helping out at water stations, which some clubs expect you to take part in," says Ken Rushton from Trentham Club in Stoke-on-Trent (trenthamrunningclub.co.uk). "With our club it's voluntary – I seem to have a right arm that shoots into the air every time someone mentions cross-country – but a lot of clubs have a strict rota that you might not want to get involved in, so always check first." Likewise, if you don't want to be part of a club where runners don't want to get involved in the dirty work, the same rule applies.

MAKE FRIENDS
Social gatherings are
a good way to get advice

'I THANK MY CLUB'

**BEN MILLAR
32, Clapham Chasers**
I'd been running for years, but thought that a club could help take my running up a gear. I decided to go for one that I could get to easily. They got back to me straight away and were really welcoming, which clinched it.

We have fully qualified coaches on hand to discuss our issues with. It's not just their qualifications, but their willingness and approachability that make the difference to me.

I've found good local sports therapists through the club, something I'd never have considered as a lone runner. I've also discovered good local routes for long runs.

Principally, I've found that training with other runners has pushed me to my limits – and not beyond them, so I avoid injury. We do a variety of training sessions, which I probably would never have had the courage to try on my own.

Racing's another key draw for me – we have regular race fixtures that most of us attend. It makes a huge difference to the amount and type of races we do, often leading up to a big event like a marathon.

For me, the numbers speak for themselves: my marathon PB was 3:48, and after just four months with the club it went down to 2:56. I can't overstate how much I enjoy my running now, thanks to everyone there.

10 GOLDEN RULES FOR GOING IT ALONE

You may prefer not to sign up. That's fine – but these tips from top clubs' coaches can still help you on your way

1 PLAN AHEAD

"Always make sure you know in advance what your training schedule's going to be for that week (at least) and what each session is supposed to achieve. Write a list of your motives and goals and how it all works in the bigger picture, from fartleks to longer endurance runs. On a purely practical level, this means that you can get the right kit together at the start of the week, so when work and other things start interfering with life, it's all laid out and ready – if you're going off-road or travelling to get to a run, your training should be something that falls into place without impacting on those around you."

Neil Aitken, Clapham Chasers
(claphamchasers.co.uk)

2 ASK FOR ADVICE

"Always look for early signs of overtraining, from a tighter running gait all the way through to nausea – and don't be afraid to talk things through with your coach, medical professionals or even other runners on online forums. Any uncertainty or fear will eat into your enthusiasm and hold you back."

John Gannon, Striders of Croydon
(stridersofcroydon.co.uk)

3 SET A ROUTINE

"Your running has to become a routine reflex action – like brushing your teeth – that you don't question. If you train hard for six or 12 weeks and then go on holiday and do no training, you'll lose all the benefits. If you're finding it too hard, you're on the wrong programme. Becoming the best runner you can be takes years, not weeks, of hard work."

Jim McLoone, Kirkintilloch Olympians
(kirkintillocholympians.co.uk)

TEAM STRATEGY
Clapham Chasers plan ahead each week

4 DON'T FORCE IT

"Try not to blame yourself if you don't always get the results you want, when you want them – and in particular you should make sure you get checked by your GP if you suddenly have low energy, which could be a condition that you can't help. Understand that there are some things that are simply out of your control, and don't try to catch up on missed sessions by overdoing it – it's far better to enjoy your running than to seriously injure yourself."

Simon Nurse, Les Croupiers Club
(lescroupiersrunningclub.org.uk)

5 MIX AND MISMATCH

"Don't pigeon-hole yourself by running with the same people every session. Whatever your levels of ability and fitness, running with beginners can be as advantageous as running with elite runners – you pick up tips and cement your knowledge whoever you run with. The trick is communication, exposing your weaknesses and strengths, and supporting each other. Running with people who aren't as fit or as fast as you are can really boost your motivation (but don't rub it in – that's not nice) at the same time as giving you an easier run when your body needs a break. And

the process of giving advice and support actually makes you analyse your own running more too.
Paula Coates, Clapham Runners
(claphamrunners.com)

6 PUSH YOURSELF

"Focus on your weaknesses as much as your strengths – it sounds obvious, but ask yourself how often you choose to do the runs or gym sessions you find hardest. By facing your Achilles' heel head-on, you'll see your times improve, and also feel a stronger runner mentally. Don't see your weaknesses as 'problems', but areas that can take you up a level."
Rupert Pepper, Poole Runners
(poolerunners.com)

7 GET TOGETHER

"Socialise with other runners away from running – this provides invaluable time for you to communicate concerns away from the fear of judgement from your peers, and become a 'real' person. Don't be afraid to hand out your email address or mobile number so you can discuss concerns on non-training days – but make sure it's not a work email address! Instead, set up a different one with a webmail accessible address, like gmail.com, to pick up messages in the evenings and reply when possible."
John Wood, City of Sheffield AC
(sheffieldathletics.co.uk)

8 BE PATIENT

"Increase frequency, duration and intensity gradually. One good week doesn't mean you're ready to move on immediately, so consolidate gains before pushing yourself too hard. The bravest thing a runner can do is make the choice not to run."
Alex McEwen, City of Edinburgh AC
(edinburghac.org.uk)

9 CROSS-TRAIN

"If you want to avoid injury, complement your running with other activities such as swimming, resistance work in the gym and cycling – if nothing else, it stops you going insane and gives you something to do to maintain fitness when injury does strike."
Karen Hancock, Serpentine Running Club
(serpentine.org.uk)

10 EAT RIGHT

"Understand the importance of nutrition and hydration to get the most from your sessions, and most importantly, to aid recovery after sessions – you'll enjoy your running more and your times will come on leaps and bounds. You could even suggest a peer-review of food diaries – the process in itself makes you more self-aware of your diet and provides the motivation you need to put the right fuel in the tank."
James Hayden, Notts AC
(nottsac.co.uk)

'I LIKE TO TRAIN ON MY OWN TERMS'

TIM HOLSGROVE
26, former club runner
from Bath
After entering a few full marathons, two years ago I decided to have a crack at ultras, and have been doing them since. From my days as a club member before university, I knew that environment wouldn't suit my training needs now – there was always so much messing around before and after; a quick session simply took too long.

Essentially, I think I'd become much more self-aware and had the confidence to train myself, and with such different goals from most other club runners, I didn't feel there was much to learn from others. And when coaches had told me what to do, I didn't always understand why I was doing it. Now I'm doing what works for me.

I only do two races on average each year, so all my training hours build towards those. Often it feels like a completely different sport to regular distance running. But I feel I've learnt more on my own about the training zones that are specific to my distance needs than I ever could with a general running-club coach.

I still appreciate the need to glean knowledge, and I do train with other runners. If you feel like you could benefit from the support of a running club, then I'd definitely suggest giving it a go. Personally, I prefer to mix it up and enjoy training on my own terms – that's just my personality. Whether I run well or badly is up to me and I love that pressure to come from within.

Whatever race you're running, make a real difference.

By joining Team Macmillan we'll ensure you have an unforgettable experience with the highest level of support. But more importantly, you'll help us change the lives of people affected by cancer now and far into the future.

Be part of the action. For more information or to join the team, visit **macmillan.org.uk/running** or email **running@macmillan.org.uk**

WE ARE MACMILLAN. CANCER SUPPORT

BE PART OF SOMETHING BIGGER

PERFECT FORM

Give your gait a makeover to run stronger, longer and injury-free

There is actually no such thing as "perfect" form. There, we said it. Runners – like everyone else – come in far too many shapes and sizes to take a one-form-fits-all approach to our sport. However, there are certain elements of form that, if you get them right, can make your technique more efficient. Take these eight examples, and then perform the drills to help you be a better runner.

❶ UP YOUR UPPER BODY
Core strength is essential for good posture. An upright posture with a slight forward lean ensures efficient forward acceleration and reduces stress on the body.
DRILL Stand on the balls of your feet, just less than shoulder-width apart, and use your abdominal muscles to control your posture for 60 seconds while keeping your balance.

❷ KNEE-SY DOES IT
Increase your knees' range of motion during the swing phase. With your knee more bent, you can move faster with less effort.
DRILL Stand in your push-off position, with your left foot forward and your right foot back. Lift your right heel like you're toeing off. From here perform a high knee lift. Replicate this in your runs for 10-15 seconds on each side.

❸ DON'T CROSS THE LINE
Beware the crossover gait. If you imagine a line between your legs as you run, you need each foot to land either side of that line. If they cross it, you'll be landing more on the outside of your foot, adding stress to your muscles and tendons.
DRILL Find a line on a track or football pitch, and run eight 100m reps, keeping your feet either side of the line.

❹ POWER UP YOUR QUADS
The forces experienced as your foot hits the ground can be up to three times your bodyweight. Strong quads control the flexion and minimise the shock.
DRILL Squats. Keeping your arms at your sides, bend at the hips and knees to lower your body until your thighs are parallel to the floor, hold, then press back up. Perform three sets of 10 reps.

IMAGES: LEVON BISS

⑤ HAPPY LANDINGS

For optimum efficiency, avoid excessive flexion through your joints as you land. Pronounced flexion of the ankle, knee and hip reduces the impact shock but decreases your rebound. Minimising it can keep you on the go, faster.

DRILL Cadence counts. During a run, count the number of right footstrikes achieved in 20 seconds. Aim for 30.

⑥ GET IN THE SWING

If your arms swing across your chest, this can translate to your legs and upset your form. An equal arm swing will help keep your legs straight.

DRILL Stick two labels on your running top, on the side of your ribcage two inches below your chest. Perform 50m warm-up sprints, drawing your shoulders back and swinging your upper arms forward and back to touch the labels.

⑦ GO FORWARDS

Focus on pushing forwards through your hips with each step. This will utilise your gluteal and hamstring muscles in the push-off and keep your centre of gravity consistently rolling forward.

DRILL Tyre sprints. Tie a tyre behind you, and using the resistance, lean forwards and perform six 60m sprints, fully extending your legs, with walk-back recoveries.

⑧ UP AND AWAY

Get the most from your push-off – from the point where your foot is flat on the ground to where your hip, knee and ankle are fully extended. Improving this will help you achieve a faster flight phase.

DRILL High hops. Perform six 50m reps high-hopping on alternate legs with a walk-back recovery. Ensure your leg is fully extended on take-off every time.

RAVE RUN
Scout Moor, Lancashire

3 Nutrition

FUEL'S PARADISE

As with most forms of production, low quality input equals low quality output. So if you want to produce good running, be good to yourself and consume foods that favour your best running efforts

Runners are not average citizens. We are different to the sedentary folk for whom dietary recommendations were created. We need more calories and protein. More carbohydrates. We need more nutrients in general. And runners covet foods that never figure in government recommendations – like carbohydrate and protein drinks and energy gels.

That's why we've designed this food plan, aimed specifically at runners, that, as well as being tasty, will help keep you on the move.

GET YOUR TIMINGS RIGHT

Many runners know exactly what they should eat and when they should eat it. It's the practical application of this theory that messes them up. You are either ravenous when you don't want to be (during training) or not hungry when you should be (immediately after training). The problem is when you are planning your run around a busy work schedule, your brain, leg muscles and stomach aren't always in sync.

An early morning run, for example, can leave you feeling fatigued during your working day. A midday training session may become no more than an afterthought if hunger overrides your motivation. And an after-work jaunt may press your dinnertime perilously close to bedtime.

If you are looking for ways to get back into sync, read on. The following advice will help coordinate your meals with your training schedule, based on the time of day you run.

DAWN PATROLLING

To eat or not to eat? That is the eternal question of those who like to run as the sun is coming up. The answer is, if you can, you should fuel up before your morning run. This performs two functions. First, your muscles receive an energy supply to help you power through the run. Second, your entire body, especially your brain, receives the fuel and nutrients it needs for optimal functioning.

It shouldn't be a surprise that studies support this and that eating before a run boosts endurance compared with fasting for 12 hours. People who eat before working out rate the exercise as being better yet less rigorous compared with non-eaters.

That said, not everyone can eat before a morning run. If you're the type of person who sleeps until the minute before you head out the door, you might not be able to fit in a meal. Also, eating too close to your run may spoil it by causing nausea or cramps. On the other hand, if you're a true early bird, you may eat breakfast, read the paper and wash up before you head out.

SMOOTH OPERATOR
Snack on fruit – or blend
it with protein powder
for extra benefit

EGGING YOU ON
Eggs on toast can help you
recover from a hard run

Here are a few refuelling strategies for both types
of morning exercisers:

EARLY RISERS

Choose high-carb foods that are low in fat and
moderate in protein. Aim for about 400-800 calories,
which will fuel your training without making you feel
sluggish. Drink about half a pint of water two hours
before your run to offset sweat loss.
Try these 400- to 800-calorie pre-run breakfasts:

- Two slices of toast, a yoghurt and a piece of fruit.
- Cereal with skimmed or semi-skimmed milk
and fresh fruit.
- A toasted bagel topped with low-fat cheese
and tomato slices.

LATE SLEEPERS

Most runners fall into this category and don't have
time to eat and digest a full meal before they head
out the door. If you fall into this camp, experiment
to see what you can stomach before you train. But you
could start off by trying:

- Half a pint of a carbohydrate drink.
- An energy gel washed down with water.

EVENING MEAL SPECIALISTS

If none of these sits well with you just before a run,
then fuel up the night before with a large dinner. As
long as you don't plan a long or intense run in the
morning, a high-carbohydrate evening meal should
power you through your pre-breakfast session.

ON THE RECOVERY

Whether you're an early or late riser, your body needs calories from carbohydrate, protein and other nutrients after you have finished running. A recovery meal will help fuel your morning at work, preventing post-run fatigue. Eat within an hour of your training and be sure to include both carbs and protein. Some options include:

➜ A fruit smoothie made with a tablespoon of protein powder.

➜ Eggs on whole-wheat toast, juice or fresh fruit.

➜ Leftovers from dinner – pasta, soup, chilli or even vegetarian pizza are proven winners.

THE LUNCHTIME CROWD

People who run during lunch hours sometimes find hunger gets the better of them. That's because if you ate breakfast at 6am, you've gone six hours without food. By noon, your fuel from breakfast is long gone and your blood sugar may start to dip. Rather than increasing the size of your breakfast (which may just leave you feeling sluggish), you should bring a light, pre-run snack to work.

Eat one to four hours before your run to allow enough time for food to leave your stomach, and consume 100-400 calories, depending upon your body size and how much you had for breakfast. Select foods that are rich in carbohydrate, low in fat and moderately high in nutrients. Try these mid-morning snacks:

➜ A breakfast or energy bar with five grams of fat or less.

➜ One slice of wholewheat toast topped with fruit spread.

➜ A 75g serving of dried fruit with a glass of vegetable juice.

➜ One packet of instant oatmeal made with skimmed or semi-skimmed milk.

POST-RUN LUNCH

The obvious problem with lunch-hour exercise is that you don't have time for lunch. But you need fluid and food to recover and fuel your brain for the rest of the working day. Packing your own lunch becomes a must – unless you have a work cafeteria where you can grab food for desktop dining. A well-rounded packed lunch can be put together in less time than you might think. Try these tips:

➜ Opt for convenience and shop for items that save time, such as yoghurts, raisins, nuts and health bars.

SERVING SENSE

When we recommend 8-15 daily servings of high-carbohydrate food, you may think you'll have to gorge yourself day after day to get the necessary nutrients. But a serving in each of the food groups isn't as hefty as most people think (or hope). Here are a few examples:

➜ **CARBOHYDRATE** 100g of cooked pasta, beans, couscous or other grains (about the size of a computer mouse); one slice of bread; 25g of cereal.

➜ **VEGETABLES** 200g of raw leafy vegetables (about the size of a cricket ball).

➜ **FRUIT** One medium piece of fruit (about the size of a tennis ball); 250ml of juice; 100g of chopped fruit.

➜ **CALCIUM** One pint of milk; 200g of yoghurt; two slices of cheese.

➜ **PROTEIN** 200g of soybeans; 50-75g of fish or lean meat (about the size of a deck of cards); two eggs.

➜ **HEALTHY FOODS** 25g of nuts (about 20 almonds); an eighth of an avocado; two teaspoons of olive oil.

➜ Always add fruit. Toss one or two pieces of fruit in your lunch bag for a reliable source of nutrient-packed carbohydrate.

➜ Make the most of leftovers. Choose any food from the previous night's dinner that you've already packed in a sealed container ready for transport, reheating and eating. Of course.

EVENING EXERTIONS

After a stressful day at the office, there's nothing like a run to burn off tension. The problem is you don't always feel like heading out the door if you're hungry or just exhausted. If you do manage to run, sometimes you return home so ravenous you'll gorge yourself on anything in sight as you make your evening meal. Then you might eat dinner as late as 9pm and end up going to bed with a full stomach. Not so good.

Subscribe to RUNNER'S WORLD

ONLY £3
for the first 3 issues*!!

SAVE £9.60 ON YOUR FIRST 3 ISSUES

PLUS all our subscribers have access to our exclusive content on www.runnersworld.co.uk

No matter what your health and fitness goals are, running works. It's the simplest, most accessible and beneficial activity you can do.

Whether you're young or old, male or female, fast or slow, everyone can benefit. RUNNER'S WORLD magazine shows you the best ways to do this.

Subscribe securely online at
www.qualitymagazines.co.uk/rw/SB26
Or call today and quote offer code SB26
0844 848 1601†

Order lines open 8am-9.30pm (Mon-Fri), 8am-4pm (Sat)

†BT landline calls to 0844 numbers will cost no more than 5p per minute; calls made from mobiles and other networks usually cost more.

Terms and Conditions: This offer is available for UK subscriptions only, when paying by Direct Debit only. All orders will be acknowledged and you will be advised of commencement issue within 14 days. This offer cannot be used in conjunction with any other Natmag-Rodale Ltd subscription promotion and closes 31 January 2011. The minimum subscription term is 12 months. The normal cost of 12 issues is £50.40 based on a basic cover price of £4.20. *All savings are based on the basic cover price of £4.20. After the first 3 issues your subscription will continue at the low rate of £16 every 6 months. For subscription enquiries, please call 0844 848 5203; if calling from outside the UK call +44 1858 438838. This subscription may not include promotional items packed with the magazine.

WHAT TO DO?

It's very simple – if you can stick to the following
two principles:

➜ Eat healthily during the day to avoid any intestinal
upset that might thwart your training plans. Also eat
often and enough that you're adequately fuelled for
your session to avoid the "I'm too hungry" excuse.

➜ Eat lightly after exercise to recover well without
causing digestion to interfere with your sleep.

BETTER LATE THAN NEVER

Evening exercisers may also want to keep the following
in mind:

➜ Never skip breakfast. Try to eat at least 500 calories
for your morning meal. For example, throw together a
fruit smoothie made with yoghurt, fruit and juice while
you are preparing your toast. Or try cereal topped with
nuts, skimmed milk and a piece of fruit.

➜ Make lunch your main meal of the day. Focus on
high-quality protein, such as fish, tofu, lean beef or
lamb, chicken or bread with cooked grain, along with
fresh fruit. A smoothie, juice or natural yoghurt drink
are also great, healthy lunch foods.

➜ Always eat a mid-afternoon snack. Around three
hours before your run, have some fruit or an energy
bar together with half a pint of water.

➜ Drink more fluids. Grab a drink as soon as you
step back through the door after your run. And keep
drinking as you prepare your meal. This helps replace
sweat loss and may prevent you trying to eat the
contents of your kitchen cupboards in one go.

➜ Eat moderately at dinner. Some people worry
about eating too close to bedtime because they fear the
calories will go straight to their fat cells. That's simply
not true. Your body will use those calories to stockpile
fuel in your muscles. On the other hand, if you eat more
calories than your body needs – no matter what time of
day or night – your body will store the excess as fat.

HEALTHY SNACKS

If your runs last longer than an hour, you can use
energy bars, gels or carbohydrate drinks and other
performance foods to boost your energy levels.
Because these foods contain easily digestible carbs,
they make great pre- and post-run snacks as well.
Consume about 30-60g of carbs during each hour
of running (most bars contain 30g or more of carbs;
most gels contain about 25g). Foods such as jelly
babies, fig rolls, dried fruit and honey also supply
fast, digestible carbohydrate.

BERRY GOOD
Fruit smoothies
are a quick and
easy breakfast

TOP TIPS

➜ If you run in the morning, try to eat at least
an hour before you begin. If you don't have
time to prepare and eat food, experiment with
carb drinks and energy gels. Or eat a large
meal the night before.

➜ If you run at lunch, have a mid-morning
snack and pack your own lunch to eat
afterwards at your desk. Always eat fruit.

➜ If you run in the evening, eat well during
the day to prevent post-work slothing. Make
lunch the main meal of your day and eat
healthy morning and afternoon snacks.

➜ Eating junk food occasionally is not the end
of the world. If it's not out of control, don't
beat yourself up. Enjoy the treat.

40 TASTY TIPS

You don't need a magic potion if you want to shift some weight, fight colds, boost your endurance, protect yourself against major illnesses or run faster and better – all you need is good food

We've put together some of the best nuggets of nutritional know-how – some weird, some wonderful – that will help make you healthier, fitter and even happier. Incorporate some of these ideas into your daily eating plan, and you'll be eating smarter and running faster.

1 USE HEALTHY GARNISHES

One secret of weight-loss is making bland foods taste great. Smear mustard on a low-fat turkey sandwich and it becomes delicious. Use Worcestershire sauce to spruce up broccoli and other healthy foods. Lightly brush barbecue sauce on grilled veg, and you'll find yourself craving that aubergine.

2 DRINK GINGER ALE INSTEAD OF COLA

Besides packing too many empty calories, colas (including the diet kind) are high in phosphorous, a mineral that can prevent the absorption of calcium. Ginger ale is a better carbonated drink. It has no phosphorous and as many as 30 fewer calories per glass than regular cola.

3 CHEW GUM, NOT SECONDS

When sanity dictates you stop shoving food into your face at the buffet or dinner table, pop mint-flavoured gum into your mouth. It changes the flavour of everything, and makes that extra helping of lasagne almost impossible to swallow.

4 MAKE YOURS A PINT

Drinking one beer a day has been associated with a 40 per cent lower risk of developing kidney stones. One explanation is that the hops in beer help prevent calcium leaching out of bones and taking up residence in your kidneys.

5 FREEZE YOUR VEG

One easy way to improve your diet is to stock your freezer with bags of frozen vegetables. Not only do they provide a variety of nutrients, they're also convenient. Throw a handful in soups, stews, stir-frys and instant rice dishes. The veg is usually frozen within a few hours of harvest, so their nutritional value can actually be greater than their fresh cousins.

6 BLOT YOUR PIZZA

By blotting the grease with a kitchen towel you'll lose at least a teaspoon (4.5g) of fat per slice.

7 FORK OUT ON CHINESE

Eating Chinese takeaway with chopsticks isn't just a way of showing off – it's much healthier than shovelling your chow mein down with a spoon. Scoop your takeaway out of the carton or bowl with chopsticks – or a fork – and you'll be more likely to leave behind the fatty, artery-clogging sauce.

DON'T FORK UP
Eating with chopsticks
reduces the amount of
fatty sauce you gobble

STAB FAB
Prick the skin to reduce
the fat in chicken

8 POKE THE CHICKEN

Barbecued or grilled chicken is tasty, but there's a catch-22: leave the skin on and the bird will be as fatty as beef; peel the skin off, and it'll be drier than the Gobi Desert. A quick solution: poke a few dozen holes in the skin with a fork before cooking. This will let the fat drip out, but will keep the meat moist.

9 FREEZE SOME MELON BALLS

Substitute frozen melon balls for ice cubes in fruit drinks; 110g of honeydew melon has 230mg of potassium and 20g of vitamin C.

10 HAVE A BABY BOOM

Jelly babies are one of the best secret weapons a runner can pack. A handful of low-fat sweets will help keep your blood glucose stable during long runs and races. (Low blood glucose causes the dips we see in performance as the body switches from burning the carbs in your system to burning your fat stores.)

11 HAVE A HEALTHIER MARINADE

When grilling chicken, try this oil-free marinade: combine three small glasses of apple juice and two cloves of crushed garlic with a cup of reduced-salt soya sauce.

12 DRINK LEFTOVER MILK

Your favourite breakfast cereal may be fortified with a veritable alphabet of vitamins, but that doesn't mean you're getting all the nutrients listed on the side of the box. Up to 40 per cent of the vitamins in the cereal can quickly dissolve into the milk. To make sure you obtain the most vitamins from fortified breakfast cereals, pick up the bowl and slurp all the milk down.

13 MARK THE ALMONDS

All nuts are good for you, but almonds are among the best. A 30g serving gives 160 calories, with about two-thirds coming from heart-healthy fats. Almonds have been shown to lower heart-disease risk thanks to their healthy fats and phytochemicals.

They're also a great source of vitamin E, an antioxidant that's hard to find in food sources. Almonds are great on their own but also add flavour to cereals, yoghurts, salads and even stir-frys.

14 MAKE A BETTER FISH FINGER

Fish fingers are the seafood version of hotdogs – delicious, easy, but not the healthiest of options. Here's a healthier, DIY version: cut a salmon or tuna steak into finger-size portions. Dip the sticks into an egg-white batter and roll them in a bowl of breadcrumbs. Stick a few in the freezer, and when you're feeling peckish simply bake.

15 OBSERVE THE THREE QUARTER RULE

Three-quarters of your dish should contain fresh produce and grains, with the last quarter saved for fish, meat or chicken. This combination will supply longer-lasting energy and fuel for many hours.

16 CHANGE YOUR DIPS

Instead of buying fatty sour cream-based dips to drag your nibbles through, think black-bean dip or go Middle Eastern and buy some hummus. It's made from chickpeas, which are high in fibre, and it's great with raw vegetables like celery and carrots.

17 BE A BREADWINNER

Shopping in the bread aisle, you naturally grab a loaf of something brown – it must be higher in fibre than the white stuff, right? Well, no – that dark complexion may be courtesy of molasses or food dyes. Likewise, a loaf with seeds or oatmeal flakes gracing its top isn't necessarily high-fibre either; they could just be decoration. To be sure you're a breadwinner every time, look for the phrase "100 per cent wholewheat or whole grain" on the package.

18 SHAKE IT, DON'T BAKE IT

To cut back on salt, don't add it to food during cooking. Instead shake it on when the plate reaches the table. Research shows people given totally unsalted food – but a free hand with the shaker – put in one fifth of the amount originally called for in the recipe.

19 FEEL THE BURN

Spicy food makes you eat slowly, fills you up more quickly and increases your metabolism so you burn more calories – three reasons to put some cayenne on your chicken.

20 MAKE COURGETTE CHIPS

Fancy chips? Try the courgette variety. Slice two courgettes, sauté in half a teaspoon of oil in a large pan over medium-high heat until lightly browned. Sprinkle with basil.

21 BUY THE BEST BERRIES

Before you buy strawberries or raspberries, turn the carton over. You're looking for nature's expiry date: juice stains. Dripping fruit is one step away from rotten fruit. If you've already bought berries that are going soft, place a single layer of them on a baking sheet and freeze for 20 minutes before you scoff them.

22 KICK OUT THE JAM

Fruit is good for you, so the best yoghurt must be the kind with fruit in it, right? Not necessarily. For the most nutritious yoghurt, skip the "fruit on the bottom" varieties. The fruit will be mostly jam, which packs the equivalent of eight or nine teaspoons of sugar per pot – nearly as much as a can of fizzy drink. Instead, choose plain low-fat yoghurt and add your own berries. Fresh berries also provide a healthy dose of fibre.

23 MAKE IT AN ORANGE

Any fruit is good, but oranges are the king. They offer a massive dose of immune-system boosting vitamin C – over 130 per cent of the RDA. They also contain a good helping of potassium, folic acid and pectin, a fibre that helps balance blood sugar levels and keep hunger at bay. If that's not enough, there's a big bunch of cancer- and heart-disease-risk-reducing flavanoids, too.

GET LEAN
Rinse and strain the fat off mince for a healthier dinner

24 HALVE YOUR BEEF AND EAT IT

Here's a way to make meaty chilli, bolognese or meatballs with a good deal less fat: start with extra-lean minced beef. Crumble your meat and brown it in a frying pan. Next, dump the browned beef on to a dish covered with a double thickness of kitchen paper. Place another paper towel over the meat and blot up the grease. To remove even more fat, put the beef into a strainer and rinse it with hot water. Squeeze out the water and add the meat to your sauce. Blotting and rinsing can cut 50 per cent of the fat from your beef. And you won't taste the difference.

25 TAKE POT LUCK

A pot of low-fat yoghurt provides half the recommended daily allowance of calcium, and as studies have shown the dietary calcium intakes of athletes with bone injuries such as stress fractures are abnormally low, you should eat more yoghurt. You don't have to just spoon it from the pot, though. Why not add it to your favourite low-sugar cereal; or use plain yoghurt instead of sour cream on top of baked potatoes.

26 DRINK BRAIN JUICE

A slug of orange juice first thing in the morning will kick start your day. That's because fruit juice is the best source of energy for the brain. Overnight the brain's fuel – blood glucose and liver glycogen – drops so we feel sluggish by morning. Fruit juice is packed with fructose, the sugar that restocks liver glycogen supplies, and as it's liquid, it's absorbed quickly.

27 GET THE MISSING ZINC

Another way to keep your bones healthy is to load up with zinc. This mineral helps manufacture healthy bone and cartilage cells. We need about 15mg a day and the easiest places to get it are from red meat and zinc supplements. Or you could be really fancy and start necking oysters. As well as – allegedly – doing wonders for your love life, these little shellfish are mega zinc-givers – down five and you'll consume 41mg of the mineral.

28 GO BETA BY MILES

It's long been known that the beta-carotene found in carrots protects against diseases such as cancer and can protect against muscle damage and soreness, but this antioxidant can also make you faster. In one US study, 5K runners were given the equivalent of five carrots' worth of beta-carotene a day. At the end of the 30 days, the runners ran on average 30 seconds quicker than before. If you don't fancy becoming Bugs Bunny, other good sources of beta-carotene include peaches, apricots, and red and yellow peppers.

29 SAY HI TO HONEY

You'd think something that tasted as good as honey would have to be bad for you. Nope. Honey is a mixture of glucose and fructose, so it's great for a quick energy boost. Pure honey also contains a huge range of vitamins such as B6, thiamine, riboflavin and patothenic acid, as well as calcium, copper, manganese, phosphorous potassium, sodium and zinc. Added to that, it also contains several different amino acids and antioxidants. So go on, smear it on your toast.

30 DO SOME PORRIDGE

A true wonder brekkie, not only is porridge a great source of carbohydrates – it's also a great weapon in the battle of the bulge. It contains a high

IMAGES: GETTY, SIÂN IRVINE, SAM STOWELL, JON WHITAKER

amount of water-soluble fibre so it keeps you full for longer – hence the saying "it sticks to your ribs". Oats also lower blood cholesterol.

31 RAISIN THE BAR

Sprinkle raisins into yoghurt, on your cereal or just snack on them throughout the day, as they are a fantastic energy snack. Four tablespoons of raisins contain 79g of carbohydrates, 302 calories, as well as potassium, iron and phytochemicals. And they're virtually fat-free, too.

32 MELLOW YELLOW

Bananas are chock full of vitamin B6, which helps boost your body's production of the feel-good chemical serotonin. This helps elevate mood, giving you a calm, positive feeling. Slice a banana over cereal or eat one as a mid-morning snack.

33 TAKE YOUR TIME

After a run, it's easy to stuff food down without it touching the sides. By not rushing your meals, though, you'll actually lose weight. US researchers found people who extended their meal times by four minutes, simply by chewing more slowly and enjoying their food, burnt more body fat than greedy guzzlers.

34 PUT A LID ON IT

You can reduce the amount of oil needed to pan-fry foods simply by keeping the lid on the wok. The lid catches and returns moisture that would usually escape, thus preventing the need for more oil.

35 ENJOY THE BROWN STUFF

Obviously, scoffing 10 Mars Bars every day might lead to weight (and pimple) gain, but every now and then a chunk of chocolate is quite a healthy treat. Chocolate, especially the darkest varieties, contains the same phytochemicals found in red wine that have been shown to fight heart disease. In fact, some studies have found chocolate contains more phytochemicals than other powerhouses such as tea and strawberries.

36 CRUNCH BUNCH

Between meals snack on crunchy foods to wake up your mouth and your mind. Fresh vegetables such as radishes, broccoli and cauliflower dunked in a spicy dip – such as chilli, lime and low-fat yoghurt – will stop you flagging at your desk mid-morning.

37 CHEERS FOR TEARS

Onions might make you cry, but they'll also stop your nose weeping. Along with other vegetables from the allium family (such as garlic or leeks), onions contain quercetin, an antioxidant that smothers invading bacteria. So if you want to avoid the sniffles, add onions to everything.

38 PACK TWO LUNCHES

Not an excuse to gorge yourself on two Big Mac meals a day, instead a rather clever nutritional trick. We tend to feel hungry every four hours, but most of us don't eat to that timetable. Instead, we scrimp on breakfast and lunch before stuffing our faces in the evening. Instead, eat two 600-calorie "lunches" a day. Have one at 12pm and the next at 4pm and you'll boost your energy and "ruin" your appetite so that you don't stuff yourself in the evening.

39 GUZZLE GRAPE JUICE

The best health drink for people with heart trouble is a glass of purple grape juice after a daily aspirin. The aspirin protects your heart by preventing bloodclots, but this effect can be blocked by the adrenalin that exercise and stress produce. Flavonoids in grape juice may stymie that response.

40 TEA'S UP

A brew doesn't just provide you with vital fluids, it also helps protect against a number of age-related ailments. Tea, especially the black and green varieties, contains catechins and flavanols, phytochemicals that fight the free radicals that lead to illnesses such as cancer, Parkinson's and osteoporosis.

TO YOUR HEALTH

We all know staying well hydrated is important, but few of us are aware we can have too much of this particular good thing

As he passed his family on Tower Bridge during the 2007 London Marathon, 22-year-old David Rogers did a star jump. "He saw us and waved, and then leapt in the air," said his father, Chris. "He was doing what he wanted to do."

Tragically, just hours after completing the race, David died in a London hospital, having collapsed once he'd crossed the finish line. The cause? Hyponatraemia, following kidney failure due to sodium deficiency, which is caused by excess fluid consumption.

We live in a water-obsessed society. Water bottles have replaced orange segments as the half-time refreshment at football and rugby matches; water coolers are as pervasive as tea bags in office kitchens, and schools increasingly encourage you to send your child to school with their own drink bottle. Why? At least in part because every fitness article in every newspaper and magazine insists you absolutely, positively must drink eight big glasses, or two litres, of water a day.

But where's the proof? Amazingly, there isn't any. Even in marathons, the available evidence indicates overhydrating is as potentially dangerous as underhydrating, with David Rogers' story serving as an unfortunate exclamation mark. Yes, we runners need to drink generously – no one questions that – but we need to drink with a fuller understanding of the facts, the medical science and the potential risks.

WATER, WATER EVERYWHERE

Water is by far the largest constituent of the human body, making up about 60 per cent of total bodyweight. This large pool of water performs many crucial functions, including nourishing the cells, carrying food throughout the body, eliminating waste, regulating body temperature, cushioning and lubricating the joints, and maintaining blood volume and blood pressure. Inadequate levels of fluid consumption have been associated with kidney stones and higher rates of urinary tract infections, bladder and colorectal cancers, and even heart disease.

Given this information, all experts agree that an adequate water supply is crucial to the body's optimal functioning. But how much is "adequate"?

THE TWO-LITRE MYTH

Most adults – at least those who read the health pages of newspapers or magazines – have come to believe that they should drink two litres of water a day, but there's little to no evidence supporting this rule.

Heinz Valtin, the Professor Emeritus of Physiology at Dartmouth Medical School, USA, committed himself to searching out medical-scientific verification for this theory. He couldn't locate any. "I have found no scientific proof that we must drink two litres of water a day," concluded Valtin. "The published data strongly suggest that we probably are drinking enough, and possibly even more than enough."

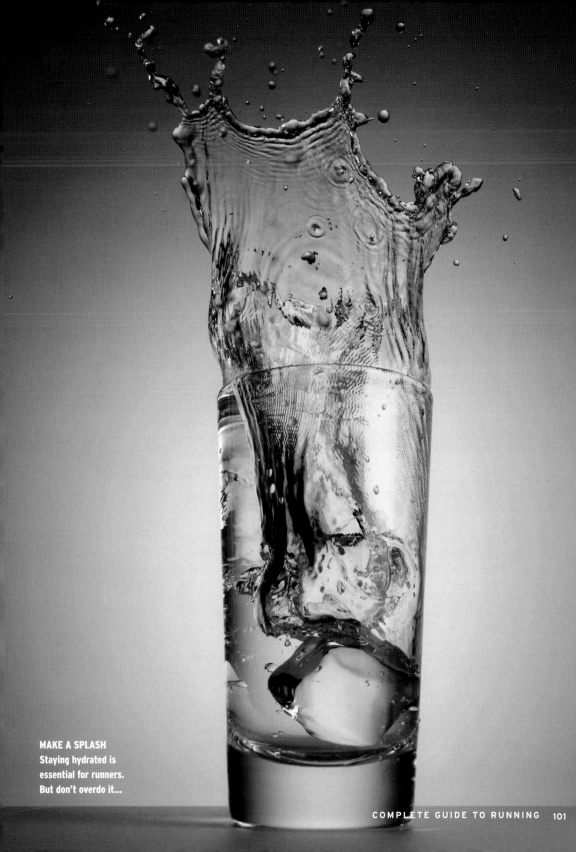

MAKE A SPLASH
Staying hydrated is
essential for runners.
But don't overdo it...

Ron Maughan, Visiting External Professor of Loughborough University and the foremost researcher on hydration in the UK, agrees. "You hear this advice from magazines, but where is it actually coming from? Not the Department of Health."

Tim Lawson, director of Science In Sport, a UK-based sports nutrition company, believes the two-litre rule might only apply if "you were eating dehydrated food". He says the figure is misquoted because it fails to take into account the moisture content from food (especially fruit and vegetables) and the fluid intake from other drinks.

Of course, Valtin was researching the hydration habits of non-exercising people. Runners sweat heavily and need to drink more than non-exercisers, and the heavier and more muscular you are, the hotter the weather and the faster you run, the more you sweat.

THE TRUTH ABOUT CAFFEINE

Meanwhile, a survey of 2,818 adults by the American-based International Bottled Water Association (IBWA) revealed an average adult drinks 4.5 litres of fluid a day. The IBWA argues that 1.5 litres of this amount is alcohol and caffeine drinks (both considered diuretics, meaning they increase urine production), and should be subtracted from the total.

However, subsequent research has reversed the age-old wisdom that caffeinated beverages are diuretics. Actually, to be more precise, the research confirmed that caffeinated beverages are diuretics but only to the same degree as plain water. If you drink a lot of water, you need to go to the toilet. It's the same with caffeinated beverages – no more, no less.

"The research indicates caffeine stimulates a mild diuresis similar to water," says heat and hydration expert Larry Armstrong. Maughan also reviewed the literature to find a diuretic effect occurred only when high caffeine doses of over 300mg were given to research subjects whose caffeine intake had been restricted for a few days prior to the test. He also noted the same myths surround alcohol – especially beer – which isn't, he claims, that much of a diuretic.

BEATING A PATH TO THE BATHROOM

If anything, truth be told, we're overhydrated. This isn't necessarily a bad thing. It's probably just adding to your daily mileage and calorie burn, with all those trips to the bathroom, but there's little evidence for dehydration ills – fatigue, headache, dry skin, lack of concentration and so on – put forth by some.

GET IT WHILE IT'S COLD
Even 2% dehydration can affect race performance

"Without any convincing data, I remain sceptical of all these so-called dehydration problems," says researcher Barbara Rolls, author of *Thirst*, and a leading expert on hydration. "It's a myth that's being perpetuated. The thirst mechanism is exquisitely tuned to keep us in fluid balance."

Maughan confirms the view that thirst is a useful mechanism, maintaining that it is simply a learned behaviour. Unlike children, who demand a drink as soon as they feel like it, but then only have a sip and are unable to finish the drink, adults learn to restrain the immediate impulse to drink.

A MATTER OF SEX

When it comes to sweat rates and fluid-replacement needs, men and women come from different planets. Because men are, on average, significantly heavier than women and have more muscle mass, they sweat more than women and need to drink more.

efficiency, increases heart rate and raises body temperature, but a modest dehydration is a normal and temporary condition for many marathoners, and doesn't lead to any serious medical conditions. Extreme fluid consumption, on the other hand, can be deadly.

THE LONG AND SWEATY ROAD

The first dehydration studies with marathoners were done at the Boston Marathon in the USA in the 1960s, an era when runners were advised to avoid water-drinking because it caused stomach cramps. At any rate, race organisers provided no fluids en route. The result was that the runners lost five to six per cent of their bodyweight through sweating, but apparently suffered no particular ill-effects.

A FULL TANK

Since then, research has shown that anything more than a two per cent dehydration will worsen performance, and experts agree that it makes sense to limit dehydration as you run. Some runners can even train themselves to drink more. Studies have also shown that the more fluid there is in your stomach, the more will reach your blood, where you want it. Hence the good advice to run with a comfortably full stomach and to "top up your tank" frequently.

Women, meanwhile, have a smaller blood plasma "tank" than men, which is easier to overfill. Many women who are new to marathons are happy to finish in five hours or more. They reach the 20-mile mark exhausted, and think, "If I can force myself to drink more I'll feel better," even though this is not necessarily the best course of action.

For these reasons, a woman's hydration need can be up to 30 per cent less than a man's. This essential fact has been largely overlooked and is particularly important for female runners, because most of the marathoners who suffer from hyponatraemia, including a number who have died from marathon-related hyponatraemia, have been women.

HYDRATION, PERFORMANCE AND RISK

Dehydration diminishes performance, because it thickens the blood, decreases the heart's

OUT OF THE LAB, ONTO TO THE ROAD

Nonetheless, in the real world, most runners who finish a marathon in three to four hours will sweat about twice as much per hour as they can drink. This can easily lead to greater than two per cent dehydration. Why this scenario? Because the body doesn't like to run hard and drink hard at the same time. At about four-hour pace, it seems, runners are going slow enough, perhaps with walking breaks, to drink sufficiently to avoid most dehydration.

With regards to the often-quoted warnings to avoid greater than two per cent deydration, Maughan emphasises that, "there is no sudden cut off point – dehydration depends on performance and the individual." He does however acknowledge that even one per cent dehydration is enough to have a negative effect on performance.

THE SWEAT-RATE PARADOX

As we get fitter, we sweat more. This means we dehydrate faster – a cruel blow, it would seem. In any given marathon, in fact, the winners are probably the most dehydrated runners on the course. At pace, they produce tremendous amounts of heat and sweat, and have no time for drinking. Of course, the body is clever. It knows it can cope with modest dehydration.

Heatstroke is the serious danger. So the body increases your sweat rate as you get fitter, because sweat promotes cooling, which helps keep heatstroke at bay. Dehydration can certainly contribute to heatstroke (which is one of the prime reasons why all athletes are admonished to drink regularly), but it doesn't cause it.

RISE OF HYPONATRAEMIA

As marathon running has boomed, and particularly as it has attracted more women and recreational runners, hyponatraemia has intruded on our sport. It means "low blood sodium", but it's caused by excessive fluid consumption, which lowers the concentration of sodium in the blood. As we've seen, in extreme cases, hyponatraemia can lead to brain seizures and death. Maughan describes the condition as "a significant danger for a small number of people".

In 2002, America's Boston and Marine Corps Marathons had their first-ever fatalities attributed to hyponatraemia. Hyponatraemia is also beginning to appear in other endurance athletes, including ultramarathoners, Ironman triathletes and long-distance walkers.

WATER IN, WATER OUT

Your daily water supply comes from three sources, and you lose water in four ways. The percentages shown here are averages for non-exercisers. Runners sweat more, and need to drink more, than non-exercisers. Actual percentages will vary considerably depending on the weather, your diet, the amount you exercise and other factors.

WATER INTAKE	PER CENT	WATER LOSS	PER CENT
Fluids	60%	Urine	50%
Food	30%	Sweat	35%
Metabolism	10%	Respiration	10%
		Faeces	5%

Approximately 10 per cent of your daily water supply comes from metabolic water – fluid that's "liberated" within the body when you burn fats and carbohydrates.

WATER RATES

The hyponatraemia issue has forced sports and medical groups to take a new look at their hydration guidelines, and several have already adjusted their recommendations. Recently, the International Marathon Medical Directors Association (IMMDA) issued the first fluid-consumption guidelines from a medical organisation that was completely focused on and tailored towards runners.

IMMDA, which represents some 150 major marathons on all seven continents, suggests marathoners should consume 385-800ml of fluid per hour (you'll need more the hotter it is, the harder you run or the heavier you are), with an absolute ceiling at 800ml. See www.aims-association.org/immda.htm.

That's just over half the fluid requirement proposed since 1996 by the widely-quoted "Exercise and Fluid Replacement" stance of the American College of Sports Medicine, which calls for 590-1,180ml per hour. Clearly the scientific jury is still out when it comes to appropriate water consumption.

The Boston Marathon now provides all 20,000 runners with a fold-out pamphlet from the American Running Association and the American Medical Athletic Association. It advises runners to stay hydrated but not to over-drink, to maintain a salty diet, to favour sports drinks and to recognise warning signs.

The Gatorade Sports Science Institute (www.gssiweb.com) has recently published one of the most comprehensive advisories on hyponatraemia, *Hyponatraemia in Athletes*. It reinforces the idea that hydration is important, and that each of us sweats at a different rate, produces varying amounts of sodium in our sweat and reacts differently to heat stress.

WATER FORESIGHT

We also believe it's a good time to review your hydration practices. Runners need to pay more attention to their daily fluid consumption than most people, but we don't need to be obsessive. Given half a chance, the body will self-regulate to a normal, healthy state of fluid balance.

If you drink a lot of water and get a little overhydrated during the day, that's okay. Your body will simply send you to the toilet. Conversely, if you can't drink quite enough during a marathon, that's also okay. Sit down with a sandwich and carbohydrate drink after the race, and your body will soon soak up the water it needs. Don't rush and don't over-drink. After a race, you've got plenty of time to rehydrate.

HYDRO THERAPY

Keep the following in mind and water consumption should never become an issue for you:

Drink generously, but appropriately Know yourself and your needs, and make adjustments for the weather. A runner training while away on holiday in Greece may well need to drink more during and after a slow 10-mile run in August than during or after an all-out marathon effort on a cool spring morning. Listen to your body.

Use carbohydrate drinks Before, during and after training and races, drink carbohydrate drinks made with electrolytes. These contain the water you need, appropriate amounts of carbohydrates and small amounts of sodium, all of which are essential.

Pay particular attention to post-exercise rehydration You're likely to become dehydrated during a long, hard run, so make sure you drink enough afterwards. The same goes for food. Take your fluids, take your carbohydrates, take a little sodium, take a little protein.

Weigh yourself daily during periods of intense training If you're losing weight, make sure it's from fat loss, not chronic dehydration. Maughan's recommendation is to restrict actual weight loss to one

DON'T OVERDO IT
All runners need water, but women need 30% less than men

per cent of body mass. You can also check your urine colour. It should be clear or light yellow (unless you have recently taken some B vitamins, which can turn the urine bright yellow).

When running long and slow – three or four hours or more – monitor your fluid consumption Be sure you're not drinking more than you need. Also, consider running with a salty snack that you consume at the 20-mile mark. If you're a woman, pay particular attention to these recommendations.

Drink when you're thirsty While it's true that your thirst doesn't kick in until you're one- to two-per cent dehydrated, there's nothing wrong with that. Remember that your body has an "exquisitely tuned" water-balance mechanism. Use it.

RUNNER'S WORLD

REAL GOOD EATS

★ ★ ★ ★ ★

A HEALTHY, WHOLE-FOODS EATING PLAN IN SIX COURSES

1 Colourful fruits and vegetables

2 Meat and Poultry

3 Cold-water Seafood

4 Foods with Skins

5 Seeds, nuts and grains

6 Dairy Foods

Put down, for a moment, your energy bars, nutrient-enhanced drinks and other fortified foods. When it comes to fuel, 'real' foods, such as fruits, vegetables, whole grains and lean meats, are a far better option. Within the body, vitamins, minerals and other essential nutrients work together with thousands of other compounds, such as colour pigments in fruits and vegetables, special starches and fibres in whole grains, and unique fats in seeds, nuts and dairy.

And it's the whole package, working together, that promotes good health and peak athletic performance. Getting the 50-plus nutrients every runner needs daily, from real food, is easy. Follow these six rules every day, and your body will get everything it needs for better health and better running.

RULE 1 | EAT FIVE DIFFERENT-COLOURED FRUITS AND VEGETABLES DAILY

A plethora of pigments lights up the fruit and veg aisle, each offering health benefits. The red in tomatoes comes from lycopene, while orange in sweet potatoes comes from beta-carotene. These, and other pigments, lower risk of cancer and heart disease. And since most pigments act as antioxidants, they can help reduce inflammation caused by heavy exercise. For maximum benefit, these pigments need to interact with different colour compounds in other fruit or veg.
PLATE IT Aim for nine daily servings of colourful fruit and veg. Of these, try to eat five colours. A serving equals a medium-sized fruit such as an apple; 60g of dried fruit; 160g of raw veg; 90g of cooked veg; or a bowl of green salad.

COLOURFUL FRUITS AND VEGETABLES

BASQUE GRILLED VEGETABLE SKEWERS WITH LIME CHIMICHURRI SAUCE

An energising lunch that will power you through an afternoon workout

YOU WILL NEED...
(Makes 8 skewers, serves 4)
- 3 peppers (green, yellow, red), sliced
- 2 Portobello mushrooms, quartered
- 2 courgettes, sliced and halved
- 1 red onion, cut into 3cm chunks

FOR THE VEGETABLE RUB...
- Salt and freshly ground black pepper
- 1/2 tbsp chilli powder
- 1 tbsp dried orange rind

FOR THE BASQUE-STYLE GREEN SAUCE...
- 6 garlic cloves, chopped
- 3 dried bay leaves
- 3 limes
- 1 green chilli, 1 red chilli
- 20g fresh flat-leaf parsley, chopped
- 15g fresh oregano, chopped
- 30g fresh basil, chopped
- 80ml olive oil

HOW TO MAKE IT...
➔ Cover the veg with the rub and let them rest. Preheat grill. Make the green sauce with a pestle and mortar or in a blender until a smooth paste. Transfer to a bowl. Add herbs and juice the limes. Whisk in oil in and set aside. Skewer veg and grill. Serve on steamed brown rice and drizzle sauce over.
Per serving: Calories: 220; Fat: 11g; Carbs: 29g; Protein: 7g

RULE 2 EAT MEAT, POULTRY OR EGGS FROM FREE-RANGE OR GRASS-FED ANIMALS

By eating lean meats, poultry and eggs, along with dairy products, runners can easily meet their increased protein needs and take in minerals that can be hard to get elsewhere. Meats are a great source of iron and zinc, which support healthy red blood cells and a strong immune system. Studies suggest that diets balanced with fruit, veg, whole grains and lean meat, including beef and skinless poultry, help to lower blood-cholesterol levels, blood pressure and the risk of heart disease.

PLATE IT Aim for around 140-200g of lean meat, or the equivalent (one egg equals 30g of meat, protein-wise) a day. Having 85g of meat supplies 20-25g of protein (25 to 30 per cent of your daily needs). Trim away fat, and grill or bake rather than fry.

MEAT AND POULTRY

KOTA KAPAMA
A post-long-run cinnamon chicken dinner to refuel and repair working muscles

YOU WILL NEED...
(Serves 4)
- 1 chicken (around 1.35kg) cut into 8
- 1 tsp ground cinnamon
- 2 tsp salt
- 1 tsp freshly ground black pepper
- 5 peeled garlic cloves, crushed
- 1¹/₂ tbsp extra-virgin olive oil
- 2 peeled, chopped medium yellow onions
- 120ml (half a glass) dry white wine
- 235ml water
- 235ml chicken stock
- 140g tin of tomato purée
- 1 tbsp fresh oregano, chopped

HOW TO MAKE IT...
➡ Boil water with some salt and set aside. Mix the cinnamon, salt and pepper in a small bowl. Rub over the chicken.
➡ Heat oil in a large, deep pan over a high heat. Add the chicken and brown for 4-5 mins on each side. Remove from heat.
➡ Fry onions and three garlic cloves over a medium-high heat. Cook until the onions are a golden brown. Add wine. When that has evaporated, add water, chicken stock, purée, oregano and remaining garlic. Add chicken.
➡ Cover and simmer over low heat for an hour or until chicken is tender. Serve over a bed of quinoa or cous cous.
Per serving: Calories: 360; Fat: 11g; Carbs: 18g; Protein: 40g

RULE 3 — EAT FOODS THAT COME FROM COLD WATER

Fish and other seafood provide a unique combination of nutrients important to runners. Seafood is an excellent source of protein (runners need about 50 per cent more protein than non-runners) and also contains zinc, copper and chromium – minerals that are often low in a runner's diet. But the omega-3 fats are what really count, as they lower the risk of heart attack, vascular disease and stroke. The fats in fish have anti-inflammatory capabilities, so can counter muscle soreness.

PLATE IT Eat one or two seafood dishes a week. Fish from colder waters, such as Scotland, have the greatest amount of omega-3 fats. Swordfish, shark and king mackerel are the most contaminated fish, so go for salmon, prawns and scallops.

COLD-WATER SEAFOOD

SALMON LETTUCE PARCELS

A protein-packed recovery meal that's light on the stomach

YOU WILL NEED...

(Serves 4)

- 4 110g salmon fillets
- 2 tbsp olive oil, plus more to brush fish
- Juice of two limes
- 1 level tbsp chilli powder
- 1 tbsp cumin
- 1 tsp cayenne pepper
- 1 head butter lettuce
- 1 head radicchio
- 1 tomato, diced
- 1 onion, diced
- 125g prepared tzatziki
- 25g chopped spring onions

HOW TO MAKE IT...

➡ Preheat grill to the high setting. In a baking dish, combine oil, lime juice and spices. Add fillets and turn them so every side is coated. Marinate for 10 mins.

➡ Form the parcels by gently separating the heads of butter lettuce and radicchio. Line a whole leaf of round lettuce with radicchio for each serving.

➡ Brush fillets with oil. Grill until they begin to turn opaque on top. Fish should be firm to the touch, flaking easily.

➡ Flake fish into each parcel. Top with tomato and onion. Drizzle with tzatziki, then garnish with spring onions.

Per serving: Calories: 350; Fat: 22g; Carbs: 9g; Protein: 31g

RULE 4 EAT PLANT FOODS WITH THEIR SKINS INTACT

Lose the peeler. The outer skins of plants protect them from UV light, parasites and other invaders. As a result, those skins are bursting with a wide range of phytochemicals that also protect your health. Grape skins, for example, are high in resveratrol, and onion skins contain quercetin, both of which can help lower your risk of heart disease and colon and prostate cancer, and boost your immunity. Skins are also rich in resistant starches and various types of fibre, which promote the growth of healthy bacteria in the intestines and help keep body fat low.

PLATE IT The less you fuss with fruits and veg, the better. Wash them, but leave the peels and skins on. When using high heat, wrap veg in foil to protect their skins.

FOODS WITH SKINS

CURRIED LENTILS WITH BUTTERNUT SQUASH

A satisfying night-before-the-race dinner that won't slow you down

YOU WILL NEED...

(Serves 2 as a main dish, 4 as a side dish)
- 190g dry lentils
- 1 butternut squash
- 1 tbsp olive oil
- 1 tbsp curry powder
- 1 tsp ground ginger
- 1 tsp chilli powder

HOW TO MAKE IT...

➤ Spray a baking dish with cooking spray and set aside. Pour lentils into a deep pot and cover with cold water. Bring water to boil, reduce heat, and add raw chunks of the squash (leave the skin on, remember). Simmer for one hour (or until squash is soft).

➤ After an hour, remove from heat, drain and set aside. With tongs, pull out the chunks of squash and mash them roughly.

➤ Preheat the oven to 200°C. In a large bowl, mix the lentils and mashed squash with the olive oil and the spices (including salt and pepper to taste). Spoon the mixture into the baking dish.

➤ Bake for around 20 mins until piping hot. Serve warm with spinach or cabbage.

Per serving: Calories: 530; Fat: 8g; Carbs: 94g; Protein: 32g

RULE 5 · EAT SEEDS, OR FOODS MADE FROM SEEDS

Seeds, many beans and even tree nuts (such as cashews, almonds, pecans and walnuts), contain the mix of nutrients necessary to grow a new plant, which means they are packed with health-boosting compounds. In addition to protein and essential fats, seeds contain bioactive compounds, which act as antioxidants. Eating a diet rich in seeds can improve health and help maintain healthy body weight. They also lower the risk of Type 2 diabetes and certain cancers.

PLATE IT Eat four to five servings of whole grains daily (equal to 100g of brown rice or one slice of 100 per cent whole-grain bread), a 130g serving of beans most days of the week, and a 30g serving of nuts or seeds five days a week.

SEEDS, NUTS AND GRAINS

WALNUT AND BLUEBERRY BRAN PANCAKES

A pre-run breakfast to top up your fuel tank

YOU WILL NEED...

(Makes 8 pancakes, serves 4)
- 350ml whole milk
- 80g instant oats
- 95g sifted all-purpose flour (or a blend of white and whole-wheat flours)
- 25g oat flour or oat bran
- 110g blueberries
- 60g chopped walnuts
- 1 tbsp baking powder
- 2 tbsp honey
- 2 eggs, beaten

HOW TO MAKE IT...

➡ Sift together the flour, baking powder and salt. Then pour milk over the oats and lightly stir in the eggs.

➡ Add the mixture of dry ingredients, and the honey, to the oats mixture, stirring until combined. When the batter is thoroughly mixed, stir in the blueberries and walnuts. Ladle batches of the batter onto a preheated greased or non-stick frying pan and cook until tops are bubbly and edges look cooked. Turn over and finish cooking the other side.

Per serving: Calories: 400; Fat: 16g; Carbs: 52g; Protein: 15g

RULE 6 — DRINK MILK AND EAT MILK PRODUCTS THAT COME FROM ANIMALS

Mammal milk (as opposed to soya milk) and other dairy products, such as cheese and yoghurt, should be a part of every runner's diet. Milk supplies calcium for strong bones, and animal milk provides whey protein to speed recovery and boost the immune system, as well as lower your blood pressure and your risk of heart disease. Studies have also shown that dieters who include dairy lose more fat than those who simply cut calories. Fermented dairy products, such as yoghurt and cream cheese, contain live bacteria, which also bolster immune health.

PLATE IT Include two or three servings of low-fat dairy each day, with one being fermented (240ml of milk, a yoghurt or 40g of cheese).

DAIRY FOODS

SEASONAL FRUIT SMOOTHIE

An anytime snack that boosts energy and recovery

YOU WILL NEED...
- 70g seasonal fruit (such as peaches, berries, mangoes)

- 180g low-fat yoghurt
- 240ml milk
- 6 almonds
- 1 tbsp honey (optional)

(Makes 2 servings)

HOW TO MAKE IT...
→ Peel the fruit, if appropriate, and cut into small pieces. Put all the ingredients into a blender and purée until smooth. Pour into a chilled glass and serve with a straw. You may want to add ice or use frozen fruit if you want to serve it really cold.

Per serving; Calories: 170; Fat: 6g; Carbs: 19g; Protein: 12g

GET REAL — A three-day whole-foods eating plan

Day 1

→ **BREAKFAST**
Small bowl (50g dry oats) porridge, 30g almonds 250g plain yoghurt with kiwi and strawberries

→ **LUNCH**
Burrito with 240g black beans, 30g grated cheese, 120g chopped tomatoes, 2 tbsp chopped olives, lettuce, and salsa, on a whole-grain tortilla 75g raisins

→ **SNACK**
1 pear, 215ml low-fat milk

→ **DINNER**
115g baked salmon topped with fresh herbs 4 or 5 small red potatoes, steamed

Large bowl of mixed green salad with 2 tbsp olive-oil vinaigrette 245g mashed butternut squash

Day 2

→ **BREAKFAST**
2 eggs, scrambled 1 whole-grain English muffin spread with 2 tbsp soft goats cheese 1 banana and 85g melon

→ **LUNCH**
225g low-fat cottage cheese topped with 75g cherry tomatoes, 60g diced cucumber and 30g toasted wheat germ 4 whole-grain rye crackers

1 oatmeal cookie 1 green apple

→ **SNACK**
245g plain low-fat yoghurt blended with 150g frozen mixed berries and 2 tbsp honey

→ **DINNER**
Stir-fry with 115g lean top sirloin beef steak cut in thin strips, 1 tbsp peanut oil, 275g frozen stir-fry veg, and 2 tbsp cashews with 280g brown rice

Day 3

→ **BREAKFAST**
2 tbsp peanut butter on 2 slices of whole-grain oatmeal bread or toast 245g yoghurt topped

with 1 chopped apple and 4 dried apricot halves

→ **LUNCH**
360g lentil soup 2 slices of a whole-grain toast, drizzled with 2 tbsp honey Big handful of raw snap peas and carrot sticks 215ml low-fat milk

→ **SNACK**
50g nut and raisin mix 235ml pomegranate juice

→ **DINNER**
1 chicken leg and thigh baked with 2 tbsp pesto 180g cooked bulgur pilaf (with onions, garlic and parsley) 125g steamed cauliflower 1 plum, handful of dates

→ **DAILY NUTRIENT TOTALS:** 2,300 calories; 110g protein; 330g carbohydrates; 40g fibre; 70g fat

BETTER TOGETHER

Mix and match different foods to get more nutrients from every bite

Runners know that fruits, vegetables and whole grains are good for us because they contain nutrients that fuel our runs and repair our muscles. But many of us might not realise that while each of these foods is individually nutritious, when they're paired with a complementary counterpart, they can provide more bang with every bite.

"Nature put nutrients in foods to act in synergy with each other," says nutritionist Lisa Blair. "When certain foods are eaten at the same time, their nutrients can work together in a way that provides unexpected health benefits." The following duos are perfect examples of how two can most definitely be better than one.

BAKED POTATO + SPINACH

WHAT IT DOES Boosts iron absorption.
FOOD SCIENCE Iron is responsible for transporting oxygen in the blood. Low iron levels can lead to anaemia, resulting in fatigue, weakness and dizziness. The body absorbs as little as two per cent of iron from plant foods, compared with up to 25 per cent from meat sources. However, says Blair, if we know how to put them together, in the right combinations, we can enhance the overall nutrient value.
PUT IT TOGETHER Have a baked potato and baby spinach salad with dinner. Or stir-fry red and green peppers (a handful provides double your vitamin C RDA) with tofu, edamame and kale – all good sources of iron.

RED PEPPER + FETA CHEESE

WHAT IT DOES Cuts heart-disease risk.
FOOD SCIENCE Colourful vegetables (red peppers, tomatoes, carrots) are rich in carotenoids, pigments that reduce risk of heart disease. Add some fat, and your veggies get even better, says Dr Steven Schwartz, professor of food science at Ohio State University in the USA. "Fat helps carotenoids become more soluble so they can be better absorbed in the intestine and into the bloodstream," he says. Schwartz found that people who ate a salad with avocado absorbed five times more carotenoids than eating it with non-fat dressing.
PUT IT TOGETHER Top your salad with feta cheese, avocado or dressing. Or sauté vegetables in olive oil or butter.

ROSEMARY + BEEF

WHAT IT DOES Reduces compounds in grilled meat that may cause cancer.
FOOD SCIENCE Researchers at Kansas State University, USA, found that the antioxidants in rosemary inhibit the formation of carcinogenic compounds called heterocyclic amines (HCAs) that form when meat, fish or poultry are cooked at high temperatures. The herb can reduce the level HCAs by more than half.
PUT IT TOGETHER Add some finely chopped rosemary to dry rubs or marinades. Basil, oregano, sage and mint can also protect against HCAs.

BROCCOLI + FISH + TOMATO

WHAT IT DOES Slows cancer-cell growth.
FOOD SCIENCE Fish contains lots of selenium, a mineral that raises levels of a cancer-fighting enzyme; broccoli has sulforaphane, a chemical that boosts the same enzyme. When scientists combined the two nutrients, they discovered the pairing was 13 times more effective at slowing cancer-cell growth than when

PERFECT PAIR
Match foods and eat
together to draw even
more nutrients out

each was consumed individually. Add tomatoes and the news gets better: studies show that prostate tumours grow less in males who eat broccoli andtomatoes in tandem rather than separately.

PUT IT TOGETHER Enjoy your grilled halibut, salmon or tuna topped with a tomato salsa and a side of steamed broccoli. Or choose another cruciferous vegetable, such as cabbage or cauliflower.

OATMEAL + STRAWBERRIES

WHAT IT DOES Lowers the likelihood of a stroke or heart attack.

FOOD SCIENCE Oats are rich in antioxidants called phenols, which keep free radicals from damaging LDL ('bad' cholesterol). That's good news because the more stable LDL is, the less likely it is to stick to artery walls and cause a heart attack or stroke. Researchers at Tufts University, USA, found that these phenols work even harder in the presence of vitamin C (250g strawberries provides more than your RDA), making LDL twice as secure as when the oat phenols are consumed alone.

PUT IT TOGETHER Have a bowl of high-fibre oatmeal topped with strawberries. Or drink a glass of orange juice to get the same benefits.

TURMERIC + BLACK PEPPER

WHAT IT DOES Reduces muscle inflammation and pain.

FOOD SCIENCE The active compound curcumin, contained in the yellow Indian spice turmeric, reduces the inflammation from exercise-induced muscle damage, according to a 2007 study in the *American Journal of Physiology*. Mixing the spice with black pepper – which contains the active component piperine – significantly increases the absorption of curcumin, upping its anti-inflammatory effects.

PUT IT TOGETHER Why not use as a dry rub for grilled chicken – which contains protein for muscle repair – for the perfect post-run recovery dinner.

PEANUT BUTTER + BREAD

WHAT IT DOES Promotes muscle growth.

FOOD SCIENCE On top of zinc to up your immunity, and heart-healthy fats, peanuts contain amino acids – the building blocks of protein. When added to those present in bread, they form a 'complete' protein, providing a foundation for muscle growth and repair – making this the perfect snack before or after training.

PUT IT TOGETHER Wash your sandwich down with a glass of milk. It's rich in conjugated linoleic acid

(CLA), a fatty acid compound that has been shown to help increase muscle mass and decrease body fat.

SALMON + SESAME SEEDS + KALE

WHAT IT DOES Builds bone strength.

FOOD SCIENCE Sesame seeds and kale are good sources of calcium, as are all dark-green leafy vegetables – essential to maintaining good bone health. The vitamin-D hit found in the salmon – and other fish with natural oils – stimulates the intestinal absorption of this mineral, promoting bone growth. Sesame seeds are also rich in zinc, needed for the enzyme that controls the development of the bone structure.

PUT IT TOGETHER For a bone-building boost, serve sesame-seed-crusted salmon fillets with a portion of lightly steamed kale. If kale is hard to find, broccoli or spinach are decent replacements.

RED APPLES + GRAPES

WHAT IT DOES Prevents arteries from clogging.

FOOD SCIENCE Red apples – particularly their skin – contain high levels of the flavonol quercetin, while grapes' seeds and skins are a good source of catechins. A study reported in the *American Journal of Clinical Nutrition* demonstrated that pairing these two antioxidant compounds together may help improve cardiovascular health by making blood platelets less sticky, reducing the chance of them clumping together and clogging the arteries. Grapes also protect LDL cholesterol from the free radical damage that initiates LDL's artery-damaging actions.

PUT IT TOGETHER Serve in yoghurt for breakfast – or pack in a fruit salad with other heart-healthy fruits, such as oranges, grapefruit and other citrus fruits.

MARJORAM + SALAD

WHAT IT DOES Speeds post-training recovery.

FOOD SCIENCE According to a 2005 study in the *British Journal of Nutrition*, adding just a small amount of the aromatic herb marjoram to a salad of lettuce, tomato, onion, carrot and cucumber boosted its antioxidant value by 200 per cent, producing a combination that can help reduce free-radical damage caused by training. Dressing salad with olive oils and wine or apple vinegars also increases the antioxidant capacity.

PUT IT TOGETHER Top your salad with artichoke, beetroot and broccoli, which in the same study were found to have the highest antioxidant values of the vegetables tested.

WHAT YOU STAND FOR

MAKES YOU STAND OUT

When you run for team**GO** you will be helping end cruelty to children across the UK. We're at every major running event in the calendar, from the **London Marathon** to the **Great North Run**. So join us and make a stand for vulnerable children.

For more information visit nspcc.org.uk/teamgo **email** gorunning@nspcc.org.uk **or call** 020 7825 2621

teamGO

NSPCC ●
Cruelty to children must stop. FULL STOP.

EAT FOR BRITAIN

With the help of top nutritionists, we've tweaked some of the nation's teatime favourites to make them more runner-friendly

VENISON HOTPOT

1 Venison contains a meaty hit of carnitine, an amino acid that helps the body use fat as an energy source to power the heart and muscles, according to nutritionist Kim Pearson.

2 Shitake mushrooms are one of the few vegan sources of bone-boosting vitamin D. "The compound lentinan will power up your immune system," says Pearson.

3 "Antioxidants in rosemary help to protect the body's cells from damage by free radicals created during exercise," says Pearson. "It's also a rich source of vitamin E, another powerful antioxidant."

4 In studies, mice that were fed resveratrol, a powerful antioxidant found in red wine, had increased endurance when tested on a mini-treadmill.

YOU WILL NEED...
(Serves 4)
- 700g venison
- 150g shitake mushrooms
- 30g flour
- Sea salt and pepper to taste
- 1/2 tsp paprika
- Olive oil
- 1 onion
- 2 carrots
- 3 large cloves of garlic
- 1/2 bottle dry red wine
- 240ml water
- 2 sprigs of fresh rosemary
- 2 sprigs of fresh thyme
- 450g potatoes

HOW TO MAKE IT...
➔ Cut the venison into chunks. Mix flour, salt, pepper and paprika and coat the meat. Brown off in a pan over a medium heat with 1 tbsp of oil. Place in a pot.

➔ Finely chop onions, carrots and garlic, then fry over a medium heat with 1 tbsp of olive oil for 5 mins, stirring occasionally. Add to the pot. Chop mushrooms, and add to the pot with the water, wine, rosemary and thyme.

➔ Bring to the boil, cover, then cook in at 160˚C/Gas Mark 3 for one and a half hours. Add chopped potatoes and cook for 30 mins.

IMAGES: RGB DIGITAL

TOFU AND LENTIL CURRY

1 Antioxidants in ginger – gingerols – can help banish muscle pain and inflammation. The spice also contains vitamin B6. "This is used in the formation of red blood cells and in the breakdown of glucose for energy production," says nutritionist Lisa Blair.

2 Lentils are rich in iron, which helps deliver oxygen around the body and is also used in enzymatic reactions involved in energy production. "Without enough iron your aerobic capacity is hampered and fatigue sets in," says Blair.

3 The vitamin C in apples is vital for the formation of collagen. "This helps keep connective tissue, such as ligaments and tendons, healthy," says Blair. There's also a hit of quercetin, a powerful anti-inflammatory.

4 Low-fat and protein-dense, tofu also delivers a dose of vitamin B1. "This is essential for energy production as it plays a key role in the enzyme used to turn both glucose and fats into energy," says Blair.

YOU WILL NEED...
(Serves 2)
- 250g tofu
- 100g pre-soaked red lentils
- 1 small apple, peeled and chopped
- Vegetable oil
- 470ml coconut milk
- 1 chopped onion
- 1 crushed clove garlic
- 1/2-inch piece of fresh ginger, finely chopped
- 1 peeled, chopped carrot
- 240ml water
- 1/2 chopped green pepper
- 1 tbsp curry powder
- Olive oil
- 1/2 tsp cumin seeds
- 1/2 tsp garam masala

HOW TO MAKE IT...
➜ Heat 1 tbsp of oil in a pan. Cook onion and garlic until onion softens. Add curry powder, ginger, carrot, green pepper and apple and cook for 2 mins. Add lentils, water and coconut milk and bring to the boil. Simmer for 20 mins.

➜ Heat 2 tbsp of olive oil. Add cumin and cook for 1 min, stirring. Add sliced tofu and stir fry. Add the garam masala and cook for 2 mins.

➜ Transfer to the lentil mixture. Cook for 5 mins. Serve with rice and coriander.

SESAME AND OAT-CRUSTED COD, CHUNKY CHIPS AND MINTED MUSHY PEAS

1 "A complete protein, cod is perfect for post-training muscle repair," says Blair. The white stuff is also high in anti-inflammatory Omega-3 fats and selenium, an antioxidant that prevents tissue damage caused by exercise.

2 Peas are a good source of bioflavonoids, health-boosting antioxidants, and contain high levels of bone-building vitamin K – and the olive oil will enable the fat-soluble vitamin to be better absorbed.

3 The phytosterols in the sesame seeds and beta-glucan in the oats give this coating a healthy hit of heart protection, says Blair. "Both help lower cholesterol." Manganese and calcium in the sesame seeds promote healthy bones.

4 Put the peeler away: most of the nutrients found in a potato are in its skin. "And they're a rich source of vitamin B6, required to break down glycogen – a key process in the production of energy for endurance," says Blair.

YOU WILL NEED...

(Serves 2)
- 2 x 180g skinless cod fillets
- 100g fine cut oats
- 1 tbsp toasted sesame seeds
- 1 egg
- 1/2 tsp dried thyme
- 2 large potatoes
- Olive oil
- 1 small bunch spring onions
- 1 handful of mint leaves
- 250g frozen peas
- Knob of butter
- Salt and black pepper

HOW TO MAKE IT...

Leaving the skins on, cut potatoes into large chips and place onto a baking sheet. Brush lightly with olive oil and season. Bake at 200°C/Gas Mark 6 for 30 mins, turning a couple of times.

Toss the oats, sesame seeds, thyme and pepper. Beat the egg. Dip the cod into the egg, then dip into oat mixture until coated. Heat 1 tbsp of oil in a pan over a moderately high heat, then fry cod for 2 mins each side (depending on the thickness).

Chop onions. Heat 1 tbsp of oil in a pan and add the onions, mint and peas. Cover and steam for a few minutes. Mash, then add the butter.

THE ULTIMATE RUNNER'S ROAST

1 With a third more immune-boosting zinc than chicken, turkey is not just for Christmas, says nutritionist Kate Cook. "Lean protein helps repair the muscles, while the phosphorus boosts bones."

2 Delicious roasted, beetroot packs plenty of potassium, helping to keep your blood pressure in check. It's also high in antioxidants that protect your body's cells from the ravages of oxidation damage caused by workouts.

3 Not only are Jerusalem artichokes a good source of energy, they're also very rich in inulin, a carbohydrate linked with good intestinal health due to its prebiotic properties. "Leave those skins on for maximum nutritional benefit," advises Cook.

4 An excellent source of slow-release carbs, sweet potatoes are great for energy (84 calories per 100g), as well as being packed with beta carotene, which is transformed into vitamin A to strengthen the immune system.

YOU WILL NEED...

(Serves 4)
- 1 small turkey
- 6 unpeeled beetroots
- 500g Jerusalem artichokes
- 500g sweet potatoes
- 1 onion
- 1 lemon
- 1 bunch of sage, thyme and rosemary
- Olive oil
- Salt and black pepper

HOW TO MAKE IT...

Juice the lemon. Halve the onion and place inside the turkey with lemon and herbs. Smear turkey with oil and season. Place breast-side down on a lightly oiled roasting tin, and cook at 180°C/Gas Mark 4. To cook, allow 20 minutes per 450g of weight, plus an extra 20 mins. Turn it 40 mins from the end, then let it rest for 20 mins.

Drizzle beetroots with oil and roast for one and a half hours, or until tender.

Preheat 2 tbsp of oil in a roasting tray. Peel and cut potatoes, then par-boil for 8 mins. Scratch with a fork and roast for one hour.

Slice artichokes, toss in oil and season. Roast for 50 mins, or until tender.

FUELLING YOUR FIRE

Run out of gas during a long run and you will crash to the Tarmac. The perfect nutrition strategy of personal mobile pit stops will have you clocking faster times and feeling stronger

You've been running for months. You've spent more early mornings in trainers than you have tucked up in bed; you've done short runs, long runs, quick ones and slow ones, all of them at paces ranging from "race" to "rather not actually, thanks". You've burnt through three pairs of shoes and set new personal bests along the way. You may be planning to enter a race, or simply to run faster for your own entertainment.

But despite all the hours of hard work, you won't reach that finish line or see the time you were hoping for on your watch if you're not prepared to provide your body with the fuel it needs along the way. A good nutrition strategy is as important to your success as registering for a race on time or doing up your laces. The time to start forming your mid-run habits is a long time before you're limbering up on the start line. It should start a few weeks into your schedule of marathon preparation – and should become a habit for all long runs.

WALL TO FALL

Regardless of whether it's a gel, a drink, a bar or even just sweets that you're knocking back on the move, you're doing it for one very visceral reason – the wall. The wall is what distance runners hit, traditionally somewhere after 18 miles. They feel light-headed and utterly without energy. In short, they would much prefer to just potter off home for a lie down than carry on going.

Is this you? And, if so, what happened? How could collapsing into a sofa or a bath become a viable alternative to strong running? When your body senses that your easily accessible reserves of carbohydrate energy have fallen to 40 or 50 per cent, it starts to use its fat as a source of fuel. It simply cannot let your blood sugar reserves empty completely, because your brain relies on them.

The trouble is that fat can't be turned into energy nearly as fast as blood sugar can, so your body becomes forced to either slow down or increase

its effort dramatically to maintain the same speed. In both cases, you'll find yourself breathing more heavily, because fat conversion requires more oxygen.

"When running you burn through your main source of stored energy – glycogen – very quickly, and the faster you go the more quickly you burn it," says coach Nick Anderson. "With shorter distances, 5-10km say, you need to remain hydrated for optimal performance, but you haven't got to worry about completely depleting your carbohydrate stores.

"However, once you're out there for longer than 90 minutes you can expect to see a depletion of those glycogen stores. You will slow down dramatically and hit the wall."

So, very simply put, if your body runs out of glycogen, it has no fuel left and to keep running it has

to resort to its only other fuel source – stored fats. Processing stored fats requires a lot more oxygen, so you slow down to a jog or even a walk so that less of the oxygen you breathe in goes to your muscles and more is available to break down the energy. From the wall onwards it's a mental battle to the end of your run.

You don't want to hit the wall. It's not a clever name – walls hurt and this one will, too. Fortunately, with the right nutrition you don't have to experience the full horror of the face-brick interface. In fact, by maintaining your glycogen levels your face need never come near anything vaguely brick-like whatsoever.

"It's a mix of people running too hard and not using the right nutrition," says Anderson. "Someone who has a good nutrition strategy will run even splits throughout a long run."

GLOW AHEAD
The right food and drink
will fire up your long runs

EAT UP THE ROAD

Keeping yourself topped up during a race is great, but you've got to start with a full tank of gas. Nutritionist Anita Bean tells you how to fill up the right way

➡ THE DAY BEFORE

Your goals for the day before your race are to top up your glycogen stores, stay hydrated and avoid any pitfalls.

GRAZE Eat little and often throughout the day. Choose high carbohydrate, low-fat, moderate-protein meals to avoid overburdening your digestive system.

AVOID FEASTING It's not a good idea to gorge the night before a race as this can play havoc with your digestive system and keep you awake at night. You may feel sluggish.

STICK WITH FAMILIAR FOODS Eat only foods that you know agree with you and eat them in normal-sized amounts. Don't try anything new.

AVOID ALCOHOL Sounds obvious but beyond the hangover alchohol is a diuretic and, if you have even a bit too much, you will definitely feel well below par the next day.

BEWARE OF THE GAS Avoid gas-forming foods such as baked beans and other pulses, cruciferous vegetables (broccoli, Brussels sprouts, cauliflower), bran cereals and spicy foods the night before the race.

TAKE TO THE BOTTLE Keep a water bottle handy so you remember to drink regularly throughout the day. This is especially important if you are travelling to the race venue on this day, as it's easy to forget to drink.

➡ RACE DAY

By now, your muscle glycogen stores should be fully stocked and you should feel ready to go. All that remains to be done before the race is to top up your liver glycogen stores at breakfast time as liver glycogen is normally depleted overnight.

EAT 2-4 HOURS BEFORE A carbohydrate-rich pre-event meal means that you will start exercise fully fuelled.

AVOID FRY-UPS Dodge anything high in fat, such as sausages, bacon, croissants and pastries. These take longer to digest and will sit heavy.

LIQUID MEAL If you can't eat because of nerves, have a meal replacement shake, smoothie or yoghurt drink.

DRINK ENOUGH Have at least 500ml of water, a sports drink or diluted fruit juice during the two hours before the race, then another 125-250ml just before the race.

Fundamentally, your nutrition strategy for any long run is to take on board carbohydrates every 40-45 minutes that you're on the road. Remember that and stick to it. Whatever distance you're running, if you're going to be running for longer than an hour you should be putting in some fuel. So for a marathon you may need 4-5g, for a half-marathon perhaps just 2g and on a 10K most people will have finished before your body needs anything. The products are very rapidly absorbed as your body is, understandably, extremely keen to grab what it needs. Just don't wait for a telegram telling you quite how desperately it needs it.

"The classic mistake is to feel woozy and then reach for a drink or a gel," explains Anderson. "They are both packed with sugars as well as complex carbs, both of which work as efficiently as each other. But if you wait

FUEL ON THE MOVE
Okay, you don't have to wear them, but easily digestible snacks boost energy

until halfway through a marathon to take something on, it's far too late for you to gain the full benefits."

PRODUCTS OF YOUR TIME

What you take on is more than a matter of mere taste. A Holland & Barrett-sized myriad of sport-specific products exists, each one vying for that place in your race-day kit bag. But all products are not created equal. Oh no. You can choose from carbohydrate gels to isotonic drinks; energy bars to the famous Jelly Babies; every one offering different combinations of nutritional benefit to your body while it's busy setting your personal best for you.

DRINKS The original performance enhancer is still as good as they always have been. They are easy to take on and quickly absorbed thanks to their liquid format, and they replace the minerals you lose through sweat when you're putting in the hard yards. "Isotonics are a closer match to your body's fluids, so get to work immediately," says track and field coach Chris Husbands. "Intersperse with water, though, as some can be too dense for comfortable digestion."

GELS If the race organisers are only offering water on the day then you should tuck some gels into your pockets to ensure you have access to the energy, electrolytes and vitamins you'll need along the way. Again, just watch your hydration levels. "The efficiency and convenience of gels have resulted in many competitors drinking less during races, causing dehydration and, ironically decreased performance," says Nick Mitchell, head coach and founder of Ultimate Performance (upfitness.co.uk).

SWEETS The gel or liquid format has taken over from tablets or chews, being more efficient and easier to digest. That's not to say that something sweet doesn't have its nutritional merits. "Eating Jelly Babies or Haribo towards the end of a run will do everything a gel does a little slower but taste a lot better," says Anderson. "After all, if you're out there for 3-4 hours or longer then you're entitled to a treat."

➔ **BARS** In theory, the absolute best, packing in the most carbohydrate and therefore providing the most energy. But – and this is a worthy of note – they can be difficult to eat on the run. "Cyclists use them all the time because their upper body is static," says Anderson. "And ultra-runners can slow down for the time it takes to eat and digest one." Running puts the stomach walls under constant stress, so giving them something solid to deal with can have less than favourable results if you're not used to them.

PREPARE TO SUCCEED

On a pragmatic level, if your body is not well acquainted with the product you choose then it will be unable to extract the optimal amount of energy at exactly the time when it needs it. So, regardless of which carbohydrate source you choose, it's vital to practise on-the-move refuelling during training, and especially before a race. Different events have different sponsors, meaning differently branded cups are going to be out at the hydration points.

"You've got to make a decision based on the event are you training for and what is available on the day," says Anderson. "London has Lucozade; the Great North Run Powerade. If you're not an elite athlete, you can't put your own drinks out, so you need to practise with what the specific sponsors will be providing around the course."

That done, take a firm hold of the things you can control – the gels, bars or sweets you intend to carry with you. Practise taking on board your carbohydrates during the long runs of your weekly training but, if you are planning on being at a start line any time soon, do it at race pace. Your body needs to adapt to digesting your nutritional weapon of choice at speed, as that's exactly what it will have to do three-quarters of an hour after the start on the big day. Which, it's fair to say, is not a time to give your stomach any surprises.

Finally, on the morning of any race, do yourself and your nutrition strategy a favour – look up. The weather influences more than what top you wear. On a hot day you burn through your glycogen more quickly, which means adapting the timings of your fuelling to come five to 10 minutes more often, every 30 minutes in extreme cases. But it's not just the scorchers you have

to worry about. "On a very cold day people don't take on very much at all," says Anderson. "They don't think they're sweating but it's just that the moisture is being absorbed by technical clothing. On a very cold day you still need a good hydration and nutrition strategy."

Pick your product, practise with it in training, and stick to your strategy. The rules of mid-race nutrition are that simple and based upon even more straight-forward biological principles. Your body uses energy to power you onwards, if that energy runs out you will have nothing to go on with besides grim determination. After all, grim determination, though sometimes enough, is nowhere near as tasty...

SPECIAL EXTRAS

Energy drinks or gels will contain glucose, maltodextrin and perhaps fructose to deliver fast energy. Sodium and potassium are often also present to replace lost electrolytes and speed rehydration. However, many products on the market now include these extra ingredients designed to enhance performance:

➔ **Caffeine** As evidence stacks up that caffeine can boost athletic performance, so more manufacturers include it in their energy products. Don't worry – it won't dehydrate you, and may genuinely help you to run faster.

➔ **Guarana** This stimulant is a Brazilian plant. It contains caffeine and acts in a similar way.

➔ **B-vitamins** (Including niacin, thiamin and pantothenic acid). This group of vitamins helps your body to release energy from food and drink, so is used during races.

➔ **Minerals** (Often magnesium, calcium). These help with muscle contractions and nerve function.

➔ **Antioxidants** Vitamins A (including carotenes), C and E are antioxidant vitamins that may be included in your energy products. They'll also help to protect your immunity.

➔ **Protein** Though carbs are the best energy source for runners, protein can also be used to fuel your muscles, and helps to protect them from damage caused by long sessions.

➔ **Amino acids** These are the building blocks of protein, and are used for energy. Some products contain Branched Chain Amino Acids (BCAAs) which may prevent mental fatigue towards the end of a long run.

RAVE RUN
Broughty Ferry, Dundee

IMAGE: TATIANA OKORIE

4 Health & Injury

10 WAYS TO AVOID INJURY

Even if you train right, injury can strike. But if you obey these commandments you can stack the odds against it in your favour

Most runners know about injuries. They're almost part of the game. Run long enough or hard enough, and you'll probably come down with an ache that will temporarily sideline you.

Fortunately, most running injuries are short-term. After a few days or weeks of rest, you can return to your regular routine. Still, there is a better way: don't get injured in the first place. If you adopt the principles outlined on these pages, you'll have a reasonable chance of running in good health indefinitely. Ignore them, and... well, you know. You reap what you sow.

1 WARM UP, COOL DOWN

When you first get up in the morning, your muscles and soft tissue are tight. In fact, at that time, your muscles are generally about 10 per cent shorter than their normal resting lengths. As you move around, they stretch out. Then when you start to exercise, your muscles stretch even more, to about 10 per cent longer than their resting lengths. This means you have a 20 per cent change in muscle length from the time you get out of bed until your muscles are well warmed up.

According to the basic laws of physics, muscles work more efficiently when they are longer; they can exert more force with less effort. This means, too, that longer muscles are much less prone to injury.

Make it a habit to warm up before a run or race. Pedal for a few minutes indoors on a stationary bike, or skip with a rope for a few turns before you head down the road. If you'd rather warm up on the run, begin with a walk or a slow jog and gradually speed up.

Cooling down can also help you avoid injury. An easy jog after a hard session or race has been shown to speed recovery by helping to remove any lactic acid that may have accumulated. It also gently brings your muscles back to a resting state.

A good warm-up and cool-down are especially important before and after a hard run in which you push your muscles to their limits. The extra time you spend warming up your muscles before a training run or race and cooling down afterwards is worth the effort in improved efficiency and decreased risk of injury.

2 STRETCH OUT

Without flexibility, you are an injury waiting to happen. Tight muscles cannot go through their full range of motion. Lack of flexibility is probably the biggest cause of Achilles tendinitis and is a major factor in plantar fasciitis and shin splints. Although your hamstrings tend to be the workhorses, don't forget to stretch those in the fronts of your legs as well.

Stretching is not the same as warming up. Trying to stretch "short" muscles may cause injury. The best time to stretch is after a run, when your muscles are warm and elongated. Make stretching part of your routine every day.

3 CHILL OUT

Let your training schedule be your guide – but never your jailer. One of the surest ways to become injured is to train hard on a day when you're tired or feeling soreness or the pain of an injury about to happen. If you feel fatigued or overly sluggish, or if you notice twinges of muscular pain, ease up. You will not lose fitness over a few days of rest. Remember that any schedule is built on the assumption that you aren't experiencing pain. Listen to your body.

IMAGES: STEVE BOYLE, GETTY

4 KNOW YOUR GROUND

To stay injury-free, mix your training surfaces to match your type of run

❶ TARMAC ROADS

Firmer training surfaces absorb less energy, meaning more power and speed from every push off the ground. Good for PB-chasers, but hard roads are also hard on the shins and knees.
STEP TO IT Avoid pounding the pavement for long runs and do fartlek sessions, using lampposts as markers to speed up or slow down.

❷ SYNTHETIC TRACK

Perfect for precision speedwork, and more cushioned than Tarmac. But the curves can tighten calf muscles and irritate your iliotibial bands (ITBs).
STEP TO IT Run at 90 per cent of maximum effort on the straight sections, slowing to a recovery jog on the curve before repeating for four or five laps.

❸ LOOSE EARTH

A medium-soft surface, rural dirt roads lower the risk of overuse injuries such as ITB syndrome. Gravel is also worth a try. More resistant than grass, and softer than Tarmac, it's another great mid-way surface.
STEP TO IT Take to the trails for your weekly long runs, running at a minute or two slower than target marathon pace.

❹ GRASS

The softest option is far less strenuous on the joints and bones, because it absorbs most of the energy from your footfall. The uneven surface also makes stabiliser muscles work – just tread carefully.
STEP TO IT Play the field for your long run, and/or two to three maintenance runs a week of about three to seven miles at conversational pace.

❺ SAND

Use sand for strength training. Italian researchers found that athletes who did four weeks of sand-based plyometrics improved their sprint times as much as those who trained on grass, but with less soreness.
STEP TO IT Do 15 squat jumps to work your calves and quads: stand with feet shoulder-width apart, hands on your head. Squat deeply, then push up and jump as high as you can.

❻ TREADMILL

Treadmill running is about keeping stable. Your stride lengthens, foot turnover decreases and muscles don't work so hard. But increase the incline and you boost power output from quads, hamstrings and calves.
STEP TO IT After a two-minute jog at a 0.5 per cent incline, up the ante gradually every 20 seconds. Do six minutes before reducing the incline in 20-second increments.

PUT YOUR FEET UP
Proper rest can help
you in the long term

5 BACK OFF

If you train hard every day, you'll wear your body down rather than build it up. You need to recover after a tough training session or a race – give your muscles a chance to mend and stock up on glycogen for your next hard effort. This is why most experts recommend that you never schedule hard sessions two days in a row. Give yourself at least one day of easy running or rest between hard efforts. If you run fast one day, train slowly the next. If you run long one day, plan a short one for the following day. This is the hard/easy method of training.

Just as some people need more sleep than others, some people need more recovery. You may discover that your body performs best when you rest for two days after a hard training session. Or you may even need three easy days. Experiment with various combinations of hard and easy runs and compare the benefits of easy running versus rest or a different form of training. Which leads us to the next point...

6 BRANCH OUT

Runners once took a run-or-nothing approach to their sport, and many still do, believing that other sports cannot benefit their running and may in fact hurt it. The wiser runner explores other options, both to supplement running during periods of good health and as a substitute for running if they are injured.

Participating in another sport a couple of times a week gives your feet and legs respite from the constant pounding of running and strengthens muscles that running does not exercise. In both of these ways, cross-training can help to protect you from injury.

Replace an easy run or rest day with a cross-training workout. After all, it is often not total rest that your body needs but merely a break from the specialised action of running. The more muscles you can involve, the less likely you are to sustain an overuse injury. Additionally, by working more of your major muscle groups, you improve overall fitness.

If you do become injured through running and have been cross-training regularly, you will have an activity to turn to that will keep you fit while you recover. Overuse symptoms such as soreness or injuries caused by too much shock or jarring can be relieved through swimming or cycling. By using a stair-climber, rowing machine or cross-country ski machine, you can take the stress off an injured area and still benefit.

7 SPACE YOUR RACES

Racing pushes the limits of your speed and endurance, and too much racing can push you beyond your ability to avoid injury. Racing is hard, so give yourself plenty of time to recover after each event.

The general rule is to take one easy day or rest day for each mile you have raced, and certainly don't race again until that period has passed. For example, allow one easy week following a hard 10K and an easy month after completing a marathon. Top marathoners believe that they can run only two or three good marathons in a year – the gruelling event takes that great a toll.

8 WRITE IT DOWN

Keeping a training log of your daily runs may seem compulsive or boring, but charting your distance, pace and course, the weather and how you feel can give you perspective, and help you see if you've been training too little or too much.

Review your log weekly with a critical eye. Pretend it's someone else's training programme. You may be amazed at the training errors you find. Correct these errors, and you'll become a better runner – and one more likely to stay injury-free.

9 BUT IF YOU DO GET INJURED...

...come back slowly – much more slowly than you might think necessary.

After a layoff or an injury, your feet and legs, bones and joints are just not ready for any pounding. They have become somewhat soft and lazy, and it takes time to build them to the point at which they can take the forces of running without becoming reinjured.

Furthermore, it's possible that your injury hasn't healed completely, making you more susceptible to re-injury. If you stress your body too much too soon, the same symptoms are likely to reappear and you could end up with a more long-term problem.

Depending on how long your layoff is, you might need a walk/jog regime. Although you would rather eat asphalt than be caught walking, do it anyway. You'll gain fitness without the hard pounding of running.

If you try to take short-cuts or cheat your body's natural timetable, you're asking for trouble. You simply cannot rush your recovery. As you become stronger and start to run regularly, increase your weekly distance by no more than 10 per cent.

10 EAT WELL

During a layoff, many runners cut back on their diets to prevent weight gain. This isn't necessary. You need extra nutrients to help your body to mend the injured area and to fuel your training once you renew your running programme. If you do gain a few pounds during your recovery period, they'll just melt away when you begin running again. So eat, and train, wisely and you'll keep running year after year without injury.

THE MOST COMMON ROUTES TO INJURY

Sometimes avoiding injury is about what you *don't* do. These are some of the most common errors made by new and experienced runners alike

➔ **WEARING NEW SHOES ON RACE DAY** This is tempting, because new running shoes have a slipper-like feel. That might remain the case for a short while, but resist it. A plethora of foot and lower-limb problems are just a few miles away. **PREVENTION** Wear them in first.

➔ **WEARING OLD SHOES** It's easy to judge wear by the state of the outsole and the upper rather than (correctly) by the compression of the midsole. Joint or shin soreness is the most obvious result and are signs that they need replacing. **PREVENTION** Log the miles you've run in each pair of shoes, and change them every 500-600 miles.

➔ **WEARING THE WRONG SHOES** This could either be a model unsuited to your gait and foot, or a shoe inappropriate to the type of running you're doing. Either way, you have a problem. **PREVENTION** If you don't know what you're doing, shop at a specialist running retailer.

➔ **IGNORING PAIN** You have to learn to separate good pain, associated with increasing fitness, from bad pain, which tends to be unfamiliar, infrequent and localised in one area of the body. It is an early warning sign of injury. **PREVENTION** Ease off, and seek medical help where necessary.

➔ **COMMENCING TREATMENT WITHOUT DIAGNOSIS** Okay, so you have an injury, you know it's a bad one and you feel you know how to solve it. So you start treatment. The trouble is that you're a runner, not a medical expert. You may have misdiagnosed your problem and started the wrong treatment. **PREVENTION** See a professional.

➔ **NOT DRINKING ENOUGH** Dehydration affects your health and performance whenever you run. **PREVENTION** Drink fluid little and often throughout the day, every day.

Subscribe to RUNNER'S WORLD and receive a
FREE WATCH

PLUS all our subscribers have access to our exclusive content on www.runnersworld.co.uk

Runner's World is the best selling running magazine in the world, providing you with all the tips and expert advice you'll ever need to get into peak condition.

- 7 modes
- 4 alarms
- Lap Memory
- 3 count-down timers

Subscribe securely online at
www.qualitymagazines.co.uk/rw/SB27
Or call today and quote offer code SB27
0844 848 1601†

Order lines open 8am-9.30pm (Mon-Fri), 8am-4pm (Sat)
†BT landline calls to 0844 numbers will cost no more than 5p per minute; calls made from mobiles and other networks usually cost more.

SAVE 36%*
on the cover price plus receive a FREE watch!

Terms and Conditions: This offer is available for UK subscriptions only, when paying by Direct Debit only. All orders will be acknowledged and you will be advised of commencement issue within 14 days. This offer cannot be used in conjunction with any other Natmag-Rodale Ltd subscription promotion and closes 31 January 2011. The minimum subscription term is 12 months. The normal cost of 12 issues is £50.40 based on a basic cover price of £4.20. *All savings are based on the basic cover price of £4.20. Your subscription will start at the low rate of £16 every 6 months. For subscription enquiries, please call 0844 848 5203; if calling from outside the UK call +44 1858 438838.T his subscription may not include promotional items packed with the magazine. Gift is subjected to availability. Free gift is limited to the first 500 orders only.

INJURY CLINIC

If you suffer any of these five common running injuries, our doctors are in – and can fix you

1 ITB SYNDROME

2 RUNNER'S KNEE

3 SHIN SPLINTS

4 ACHILLES TENDONITIS

5 PLANTAR FASCIITIS

1 ILIOTIBIAL BAND SYNDROME

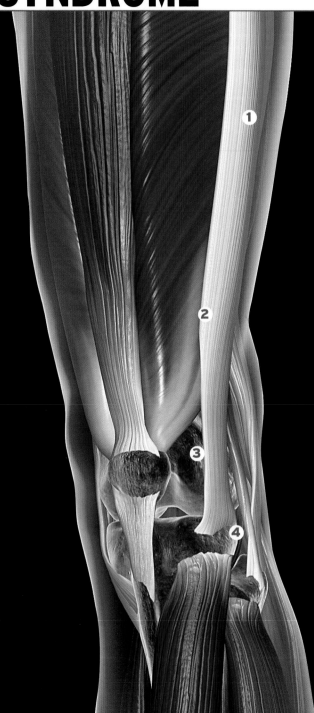

Leading sports performance specialist Dr Carlyle Jenkins explains why your knee feels like it's got a stake driven through it

❶ ILIOTIBIAL BAND
Your iliotibial band (ITB) is a ligament-like structure that starts at your pelvis and runs along the outside of your thigh to the outside of the top of your shinbone (tibia). When you run, your ITB rubs back and forth over a bony outcrop on your knee, which helps to stabilise it.

❷ BAND AID
If you have poor running mechanics, muscle imbalance, put on weight or start running hills, then your ITB can track out of line, slipping out of the groove created by the bony outcrop.

❸ SWELLING
As it tracks out of its natural alignment it rubs against other structures in your leg, creating friction on the band. This results in inflammation (but no swelling) and a click when you bend your knee.

❹ HOLD UP
The scarring thickens and tightens the ITB, and limits the blood flow to it. If you continue to run, you'll feel a stinging sensation. This can make you limp after a run.

HOW TO REHABILITATE IT

Decrease your training load by 50 per cent and apply the principles of R.I.C.E (rest, ice, compression and elevation), then use some of these rehabilitation tips from Jenkins

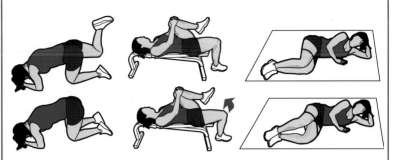

DONKEY KICKS

1 Get on all fours, resting your bodyweight on your knees and flattening your elbows on the floor into a position similar to that of The Sphinx.

2 Keep your right knee bent as you slowly lift your right leg up behind you so your foot rises towards the ceiling.

3 Hold that position for one second, then slowly return to the start. Perform four sets of 12 repetitions on each leg.

WHY This move strengthens your gluteus maximus and medius. Research in the journal *Physical Therapy in Sport* has found that these muscles are vital for keeping your ITB strong.

LYING ITB STRETCH

1 Sit on the edge of a bench or firm bed. Lay your torso back and pull the unaffected leg to your chest to flatten your lower back.

2 With your affected leg flat to the bench, maintain a 90-degree bend in its knee. Shift that knee as far inwards to the side (towards your other foot) as possible.

3 Hold this position for 30 seconds and repeat four times on each leg.

WHY "The ITB is difficult to elongate, as it doesn't have nerves that allow you to feel if you're actually stretching it. You might not feel this move in the ITB, but it does isolate the band," says Jenkins.

SIDE-LYING CLAMSHELL

1 Lie on your side bending knees and hips to 90 degrees. Wrap a resistance band around both thighs.

2 Lift your top knee up towards the ceiling, making sure that the insides of both feet stay together.

3 Perform 10 to 15 reps, or until you get a burn in the outside of your hip.

WHY "This move works your gluteus medius (on the outer surface of the pelvis). This muscle prevents your thigh from buckling inwards when you run, which is the root of ITB aches," says Richard Scrivener, a running and injury lecturer at Premier Training International.

HOW LONG UNTIL YOU'RE RECOVERED

According to Jenkins, these are the recovery rates of Achilles tendonitis depending on the severity of your injury

➔ **MILD INJURY**	100% after 2-4 weeks
➔ **AVERAGE INJURY**	100% after 7-8 weeks
➔ **SEVERE INJURY**	100% after 9-24 weeks

2 RUNNER'S KNEE

PAIN, EXPLAINED

Dr Ross Sherman, senior exercise physiologist and sports science consultant at Kingston University, London, explains what causes it

❶ QUADS

The thigh muscles above the knee hold your kneecap in place. When you run, your kneecap moves up and down your thighbone (femur) without touching it.

❷ KNEECAP

If your quads are weak or you have poor foot mechanics, your kneecap will move left and right, creating pressure, friction and irritation. As you clock up the miles and repeatedly stride out your misaligned steps, your kneecap rubs against the end of the thighbone.

❸ CARTILAGE

This wobbling and rubbing grinds down the cartilage underneath your kneecap so that it becomes rough, like sandpaper. This makes your kneecap unable to bend smoothly and efficiently.

❹ FRONT KNEE

When this happens, you'll experience a dull, aching pain under or around the front of your kneecap. The pinch will be the worst when running downhill, walking down stairs, squatting or sitting with a bent knee.

HOW TO REHABILITATE IT

After applying the rules of R.I.C.E (rest, ice, compression and elevation), take a rest from all sports for one to two weeks. Then do these moves from Sherman two to three times a week

LYING LEG LIFTS

❶ Lie flat on back. Bend your left knee at 90 degrees, keeping your foot flat on floor.
❷ Keep your right leg straight and lift it to the height of the left knee.
❸ Hold for five to 10 seconds and repeat five to 10 times on both legs.
WHY "When running, your body weight lands on a near-straightened knee," says Sherman. "This move strengthens your quads – the muscle that absorbs the blow – in the position they receive the impact. This stabilises the injured knee."

SWISS BALL HALF SQUATS

❶ Put a Swiss ball between your lower back and a wall.
❷ Bend your knees to lower yourself towards the floor. Stop when your knees are bent at 90 degrees.
❸ Straighten your legs to rise to the top without locking your knees.
WHY "Do four to five sets of 12 repetitions to strengthen your quads, lower back, glutes and core. These muscles work together to teach your knees to start bending through their natural range of movement," says Sherman.

FOOT TURNS

❶ Sit in a chair and stretch both legs out straight in front of you, feet pointed straight up towards the ceiling.
❷ Turn both feet out as far as possible. Hold for 12 seconds while tensing your quads.
❸ Turn them inwards for 12 seconds. That's one set; do six sets.
WHY "You'll strengthen your outer and inner quads, building the cartilage on either side of the knee cap, which stops it from tracking out of line in the future," says Sherman.

HOW LONG UNTIL YOU'RE RECOVERED

According to Dr Sherman, these are the recovery rates depending on the severity of your injury. If your injury is only mild you can be recovered in six weeks, as long as you take his advice to rest up for the first two weeks and do his rehabilitation exercises to help overcome the injury. If the injury is particularly severe, it could take up to six months to recover

➜ **MILD INJURY**
40-50% better after 1-2 weeks
60-75% better after a month
100% better after 6-8 weeks

➜ **SEVERE INJURY**
30-40% better after 2-3 weeks
50-60% better after 2 months
100% better after 4-6 months

3 SHIN SPLINTS

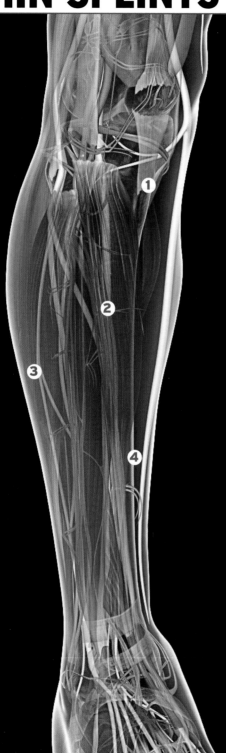

PAIN, EXPLAINED
Dr Carlyle Jenkins, a leading sports rehabilitation specialist, explains the reasons for that persistent ache in your shins

❶ TIBIALIS ANTERIOR
Shin splints are an overuse injury. The muscle most affected is the tibialis anterior, stretching from your knee to your ankle. A new or excessive running stress can irritate it.

❷ TIBIA
By resting and applying our rehab tips when you feel mild tenderness in your shin bone (tibia), you'll eliminate further damage. But if you soldier on with more miles, then you'll create micro-tears.

❸ OUTER SHIN
This is when you'll feel a razor sharp pain on the outer edges of the mid region of your lower leg, next to the shin bone. The aching area can measure 10 to 15 centimetres, and the pain often subsides after warming up and returns after the workout is finished.

❹ REST UP
Worst-case scenario is that the swelling in the muscle and sheath continues unabated, increasing the pressure in the sheath to intolerable levels. This can lead to 'Compartment Syndrome', a condition that can require surgery.

HOW TO REHABILITATE IT

Dramatically decrease your training load by 90 to 95 per cent and apply the principles of RICE (rest, ice, compression and elevation) then use some of these rehabilitation tips from Dr Carlyle Jenkins once a day

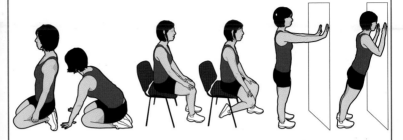

KNEELING STRETCH

1 Get into a kneeling position with your toes tucked under so that your weight is resting on the balls of your feet and you are sitting on the back of your ankles.

2 Lean forward and rest your fingers on the ground in front of you.

3 Gently sit back onto your heels so that your ankles almost flatten against the floor. Hold for 30 seconds and repeat as needed.

WHY "This move stretches the muscles and connective tissue in the front of your legs and will alleviate some of the pressure in the painful part of your shin," says Jenkins.

SEATED STRETCH

1 Sit on a chair with your feet hip-width apart on the floor and place your hands on your knees.

2 Bend your right leg behind you under the chair and rest the top part of your foot on the floor.

3 Push your foot into the floor and press down gently on your right knee with your right hand. Hold that position for 30 seconds, then switch legs and do the same again.

WHY "This move is very efficient at isolating and loosening your shin muscles and can be done at your desk at work several times during the day," says Jenkins.

STANDING STRETCH

1 Stand with your feet hip-width apart at arm's length from a wall.

2 Place your hands on the wall and keep your feet and knees straight.

3 Lean as far forward as possible while keeping your feet flat. Stop leaning when you feel an intense stretch and hold for 30 seconds.

WHY "If the muscles at the back of your calves become overly tight this can worsen and even cause shin splints," says Jenkins. This move gives these muscles a comprehensive stretch and resets the muscles of your lower leg into the correct position for healing to be done."

HOW LONG UNTIL YOU'RE RECOVERED

An online poll on the fitness website attackpoint.org found that these were the expected recovery rates for shin splints

➲ **MILD INJURY**   100% after 1-2 weeks

➲ **AVERAGE INJURY**   100% after 7-8 weeks

➲ **SEVERE INJURY**   100% after 9-24 weeks

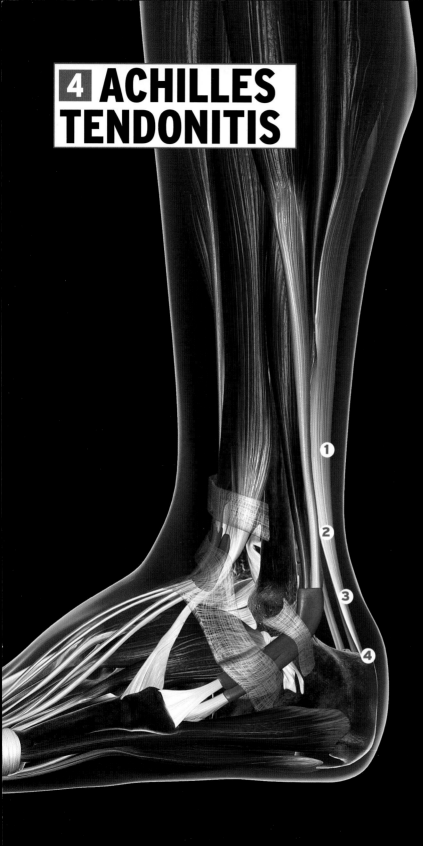

4 ACHILLES TENDONITIS

PAIN, EXPLAINED

Dr Carlyle Jenkins, a leading sports performance specialist, explains why your Achilles heel aches

❶ ACHILLES TENDON

This connects the calf muscles to the heel bone. It's the thick, springy tissue just above the heel and is used when you walk, run, jump or push up on your toes. Injury can occur if you up training frequency or intensity.

❷ FEEL THE BURN

Achilles tendonitis is a "chronic stress" injury where small stresses accumulate and damage the tendon. This strain is increased if you're inflexible or you overpronate.

❸ HEEL

The inflammation is often at the narrow point of the tendon just above the heel area. This is because that area has the smallest blood supply, which slows the healing time considerably. Rest to avoid further pain.

❹ ANKLE

You'll feel an ache at the back of your ankle and a burning or piercing pain. You'll experience redness on the tendon and/or severe pain when you take your first few steps in the morning or after sitting for a while. This will subside as you move around.

HOW TO REHABILITATE IT

Apply the principles of R.I.C.E (rest, ice, compression and elevation) and take a break from all weight-bearing sporting activities, such as running, for at least two weeks. Then do these scientifically backed stretching and strengthening moves once a day

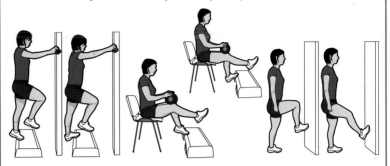

ECCENTRIC STRAIGHT-LEG CALF LOWERING

1 Stand with the balls of your feet on the edge of a step. Hold on to a support if necessary.

2 Rise up onto your toes then remove the unaffected leg from the step so you're holding the tiptoe position on only the sore leg.

3 Take five seconds to lower your affected heel as far down as is comfortable. Do three sets of 15 twice a day.

WHY A study at the University Hospital of Northern Sweden found that 12 weeks of this and the next exercise combined could eradicate Achilles pain.

ECCENTRIC BENT-LEG CALF LOWERING

1 Sit on the edge of a chair with your legs bent in front of you. Place a weight on top of your thighs and rest the balls of your feet on a ledge or step.

2 Rise up onto your toes then remove the unaffected leg from the step so you're on tiptoes on the sore leg.

3 Take five seconds to lower your affected heel as far downwards as is comfortable. Do three sets of 15 twice a day.

WHY The Swedish researchers noted that doing this exercise with a bent leg forces your deep calf muscle to work, which strengthens the major calf muscles needed to heal Achilles tendonitis.

WALL STRETCH

1 Stand with both feet parallel to each other, facing a wall at about arm's length away.

2 Put the affected foot on the wall at knee height and try to press its heel against the wall.

3 Do not lean towards the wall. Lift your chest until you are standing straight. Hold this position for three minutes on each leg, three times a day.

WHY A study in the journal Foot & Ankle International found that holding an Achilles tendon stretch for this exact period of time (three minutes on each leg) helped reduce pain.

HOW LONG UNTIL YOU'RE RECOVERED

According to Jenkins, these are the recovery rates of Achilles tendonitis depending on the severity of your injury

➜ **MILD INJURY**   100% after 2-10 days

➜ **AVERAGE INJURY**   100% after 7-8 weeks

➜ **SEVERE INJURY**   100% after 42-160 days

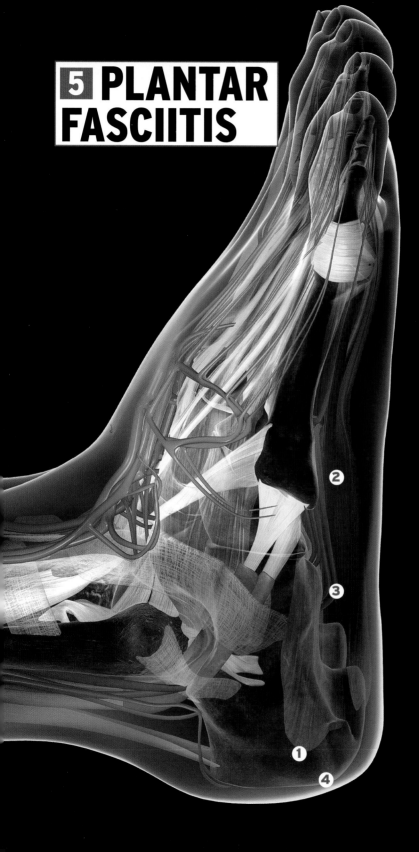

5 PLANTAR FASCIITIS

PAIN, EXPLAINED

Dr Ross Sherman, senior exercise physiologist and sports science consultant at Kingston University, London, explains why your heel aches

❶ FEELING PAIN?
This is an overuse injury so you won't remember one incident where you've damaged your heel. You'll sow the seeds if you've increased your training or started running hill sprints.

❷ PLANTAR FASCIA
It's a thick broad band of tissue that runs along the bottom of your foot. It supports your foot's arch and acts like a shock-absorbing bow-string. When an abnormally high load is forced on it you get a small split in this tissue.

❸ WAKE UP!
At the time, this rip will only create mild discomfort, which you probably won't even notice. But when you sleep, your body starts the repair process – making the plantar fascia stiff. Upon waking, it will be inflexible. When you take your first strides you'll stretch and tear it slightly.

❹ HEEL
The tear can lead to additional micro-tearing, which results in the stinging pain at the base of your heel pad, which can last all day if you're on your feet.

CAUSE & EFFECT

Why it happens and how to spot it

WHAT CAUSES IT?

The American Academy of Orthopaedic Surgeons cites these as the root of plantar fasciitis:

➜ A job that requires you to stand for long periods
➜ Poor foot mechanics, flat feet or high arches
➜ Being overweight – this places additional pressure on your plantar fascia
➜ Tight calves that limit the amount you can flex your ankles
➜ An aggressive increase in training load or exertion
➜ Arthritis can cause inflammation in the tendons at the bottom of your foot
➜ Diabetes increases your risk, as diabetics have less blood going to their feet
➜ Poor or worn-out shoes

SPOT IT!

Research at the Mayo Clinic, USA, found it's likely you have plantar fasciitis if you experience one or more of the following symptoms:

➜ A sharp pain in the inside of the bottom of your heel that may spread under the arch of your foot.
➜ Heel pain when you wake, stand or climb stairs.
➜ Heel pain after long periods of standing or after getting up.
➜ Heel pain after, but not usually during, exercise.
➜ Mild swelling in the heel.

HOW TO REHABILITATE IT

Rest from all weight-bearing sporting activities, such as running, for at least two to three weeks. Then do these stretching and strengthening moves from Sherman two to three times a week

FOOT ROLL

1 Sit at your desk or on a couch and place a tin of canned food (on its side) or tennis ball on the floor in front of you.

2 Rest the arch of your injured foot (without shoes on) on the can or tennis ball and press down slightly while rolling the can up and down your foot from your heel to your mid-arch.

3 Perform this for one minute, rest for 30 seconds then repeat twice more.

WHY "This tackles the problem at the source by lengthening and softening the offending plantar fasciitis in order to release the pressure that's magnifying the heel pain," says Sherman.

TOE FLEXES

1 Sit with your injured leg straight out in front of you. Loop a towel around your foot, holding the ends with both hands.

2 Position your foot so that the towel goes around the arch, and pull the towel tight towards you.

3 Keeping your injured knee straight, push your foot away from your body and apply resistance with the towel. Do three sets of 10 repetitions.

WHY "You'll strengthen your calf muscles and Achilles tendon while the force from the towel against your plantar fascia stretches it out, to provide a two-pronged approach to fast recovery," says Sherman.

PLANTAR STRETCH

1 Cross your legs and put your right ankle (assuming this is your affected foot) above your left knee so the underside of your foot is facing you.

2 Grab your toes and pull them back.

3 Hold this position for 10 seconds then release. Repeat 10 times. Do three to six times a day, starting when you get up.

WHY "This stretch isolates the plantar fascia, and after subjects did it for eight weeks there was a dramatic improvement over those who only stretched their Achilles," says orthopaedic surgeon Dr Ben DiGiovanni.

HOW LONG UNTIL YOU'RE RECOVERED

Studies in the *American Family Physician* journal state that these are the expected recovery rates

➜ **MILD INJURY**   100% after 2-6 months

➜ **AVERAGE INJURY**   100% after 9-12 months

➜ **SEVERE INJURY**   100% after 18 months

NEVER GET HURT

It's a very simple exercise plan. And it may just help you run injury-free for the rest of your life

At the gym, it's easy to spot the runners. They're the ones with skinny legs and 3D quads who are doing squats, hamstring curls and calf raises. There's only one problem: they're working the wrong muscles.

"Since the quads, hamstrings and calves propel you forwards, they're adequately strengthened through running," says Dr Robert Wilder, medical director of the University of Virginia Centre for Endurance Sport in the USA. "Other muscles, like your abs and glutes, aren't typically engaged when you run, but should be. They're the ones that need attention."

These underappreciated muscles provide the foundation for a strong pelvis. "Almost all common overuse injuries are related to a lack of pelvic stability," says Jay Dicharry, director of the University's Centre for Endurance Sport.

Here's why. Picture a weak, wobbly pelvis. As you stride, one side rotates forward as the other drops down, forcing your back to overarch and your striding foot to rotate inwards. Wilder says these events cause muscular imbalances and tightness, which can lead to iliotibial band syndrome (ITBS), shin splints, lower-back pain and other muscular issues. On the other hand, if your pelvis is stable, your legs spin beneath you like wheels, your energy is directed forward, and your stride is light, efficient and biomechanically correct.

The good news: you can get there with targeted training. The following routine engages your transverse abdominals (the deep abs that stabilise the spine and pelvis) and your gluteus medius (the muscle on the side of your glutes that minimises side-to-side rotation). The regime begins with simple exercises that focus on abdominal bracing – pulling your belly button up and in – and get progressively harder. Be sure to do them in order and maintain braced abs as you progress.

Do this 20-minute routine at least three times a week before a run, so you reinforce the correct muscle engagement before you're in motion. The results you feel as you run (and run and run) will be dramatic.

CENTRE OF ATTENTION
Work the right muscles to avoid injury

1 PRONE MARCH

WHY To imprint the feeling of braced abs and a stable pelvis, and to teach your muscles how to fire the deep core stabilisers before you engage your leg muscles.

HOW

❶ Lie on your back with your hands on your hips, both knees bent at a 45-degree angle, and your feet flat on the floor.

❷ With braced abs and lower back flat on the floor, lift your left leg until your calf is parallel to the floor, then return to the start. Repeat 15 times with each leg.

MAKE IT HARDER As you get stronger, lift both legs at once, then alternate lowering each leg.

❶

❷

2 PRONE DRIVE

WHY To lengthen your hip flexors without moving your pelvis.

HOW

❶ Lie flat on your back with braced abs and a neutral spine, and lift both feet off the floor so your knees are bent at 90 degrees and your calves are parallel to the floor. Then, keeping one leg stable, extend your other leg forward as though you were driving off it during a run.

❷ Tap your heel on the ground for an instant, then return to the start. Alternate legs for 15 reps on each side.

MAKE IT HARDER Maintain your form and gradually increase the speed of your drives.

❶

❷

3 | SIDE LIFT

WHY To promote a stable pelvis as the gluteus muscles engage and the hip flexors extend. This can help prevent pain in your knees and your IT band (tissue down your thigh).

HOW

❶ Lie on your right side, hips in line with your shoulders, right knee bent 60 degrees, left hand on left hip, head on right arm.

❷ Flex your left foot and raise your left leg, toes angled slightly off the ground, a few inches off the floor. With a stable pelvis – use your left hand to check it isn't moving – lift your left leg back and rotate it slightly (no more than 45 degrees) towards the ceiling. Repeat 15 times on each side.

4 | INVERTED BRIDGE

WHY To engage your deep core muscles and strengthen the gluteus medius, reinforcing correct muscle-firing pattern.

HOW

❶ Lie on your right side, with your head resting on your right arm and your left arm extended along your left side. Stack both feet on a block that is between eight and 14 inches high.

❷ Brace your abs. Keeping your hips in line with your shoulders, imagine pushing your right leg into the block as you raise your pelvis off the floor. Pause, then lower. Aim for 30 reps each side.

How to prevent injuries while you run

The plan detailed here can help you become injury free, especially if you apply it while you run. "Concentrate on your form until it becomes habit," says Dicharry. To help you, he offers the following tips:

MECHANICAL MUSTS

➜ As you run, check that your transverse abdominals, the muscles that stabilise the spine and pelvis, are engaged by putting your fingers lightly above your pelvic bones. The muscles should feel tight.

➜ A thunderous heel-strike will often presage an aching back. "You could be over-striding, which makes you overarch your lower back," he says. Instead, try to maintain a long, neutral spine. To do that, stop running

5 HIP HIKE

WHY To mimic proper gluteus function during touchdown while running, strengthen hip mechanics and improve balance.

HOW

❶ Stand on a step or box with your right foot on the edge and your left foot off it, arms by your sides, abs braced. Keeping your right knee bent slightly, lower the left side of your pelvis so that your left foot drops a few inches below your right. ❷ Then hike your pelvis up so that the left foot is above your right foot. Lift and lower for 30 reps each side. **MAKE IT HARDER** Do this movement before – and during – your runs by finding a curb. It helps remind you how your glutes should feel.

6 DRIVE THROUGH

WHY To teach optimal alignment and engagement for the propulsion stage of running, and to target all lower-body muscles and improve balance.

HOW

❶ Stand on your left foot, arms at sides, abs braced. Keeping your back flat and your weight over the ball of your left foot, assume a position as if you were running – bend your left knee and extend your right leg behind you, knee bent 90 degrees, your right arm bent in front of you. ❷ In one smooth motion, drive your right knee and left arm forward as you come up on the ball of your left foot. Pause, then repeat. Do 30 reps on each side.

and locate proper posture: put one hand on your belly button and the other on your breastbone, then lengthen your spine and engage your transverse abs to shorten the distance between your hands.

→ A heavy heel-strike also wreaks havoc on your muscles. Land with your foot directly underneath you to control your balance and stability.

→ Next time you huff up a hill, note your form: you probably had a natural forward lean, centred each footstrike underneath your body, and took small, rapid steps. Try to mimic this form on all kinds of terrain.

→ While running downhill, lean forward like a skier so your body maintains perpendicular to the hill. This prevents a damaging heel-strike.

→ When you hit a gentle downhill, focus on your transverse abs and your posture to keep strides short.

3 GOLDEN RULES

→ **THE LONGEST RUN OF THE WEEK**

Should never be more than half of your weekly total So if you're running 20 miles a week, your longest run is 10 miles, maximum.

→ **NO LIMPING**

Limping means you're compromising your form, and you'll eventually pay the price. If you feel minor pain – below three on a scale of one to 10, keep running. If the discomfort rises above three, stop.

→ **INCREASE MILEAGE**

No more than 10 per cent weekly. Push too hard too fast, and you'll get hurt. "There are exceptions," says Dicharry. "If you ran 80 miles but dropped to 20 to heal an injury, you can step up more quickly."

7 UPPER STAR

WHY To develop stability, strength and balance in each leg.

HOW

① Lay five objects in a semicircle in front of you (on a clock, they'd be at 9, 10:30, 12, 1:30, and 3). Stand two feet behind the 12 on your right foot, left calf bent 90 degrees behind you. Place your right hand on your hip.

② Bend forward from the hips, so that your right knee is over your toes. Reach out with your left arm toward the 9 – don't reach down, but to the side so your hand is over it – then return to upright. Reach towards 10:30, then return to standing. Repeat until you get to 3. Then start with your right arm at 3 and work toward 9. Switch legs, and repeat.

8 LOWER STAR

WHY Develops stability, strength and balance.

HOW

① This time, line up the five objects in a semicircle on one side of you (on a clock, they'd be positioned at 6, 7:30, 9, 10:30, and 12). Stand about two feet across from the 9 object, balancing on your right foot. Keeping your hands on your hips and your back straight, brace your abs. Bend your right knee so it is lined up over your toes. Then reach back with your left foot towards 6. Without touching your toe to the floor, stand back up.

② Aim for 7:30, then return to standing. Repeat until you get to 12, then go back to 6. Turn around and repeat on the opposite leg.

BITE BACK AT INJURY

When running begins to take its toll on your body, plate up and let food be your medicine

Injury is undoubtedly the most frustrating part of running. Tear your patellar tendon, and you are likely to miss several weeks of running, cycling and almost every other activity requiring knee movement. Not fun. If surgery is required, you will enter a rehabilitation programme that will include icing and physical therapy.

But what about a food-rehab programme? Surely feeding an injury such as a patellar tendon tear with the right foods will help nourish the knee and rebuild new, healthy tissue? Given your regular exercise programme is on hold for several weeks, you do of course want to heal as quickly as possible. Well, take heart because the foods you choose to eat, and those you omit, can significantly influence your rate of recovery.

Although different injuries, and the fact every runner has a unique physiology mean no nutrition programme fits all, we've highlighted five remedies that should help keep you healthy, keep the weight off and have you back in your running kit before you can say, "A glucosamine-fortified kiwi fruit juice please?"

ANTIOXIDANTS

You can blame much of the swelling and soreness you feel when injured on substances called free radicals. These highly reactive molecules damage tissue as they search for missing electrons. Antioxidants, such as vitamin E and betacarotene, stop this damage by providing free radicals with the electrons they need,

thus ending their destructive search. This, in turn, prevents unnecessary swelling and pain.

To be sure of consuming a complete array of antioxidants, including flavonoids and carotenes, eat several daily servings of fruits and vegetables, such as kiwis, apples, oranges, winter squashes and dark leafy greens. You might also want to consider taking vitamin E supplements every day, because it's difficult to consume enough from food alone.

GLUCOSAMINE

In the past few years, sports doctors and other physicians have increasingly advised patients to take the amino acid glucosamine to ease the inflammation and pain of osteoarthritis, a degenerative joint condition caused by overuse, traumatic injury or simply old age. One of the hallmarks of osteoarthritis is an erosion of the cartilage that cushions your joints.

Chondrocytes (the cells in your joints that make up cartilage) need glucosamine to function optimally. According to several studies, supplemental glucosamine – about 1,500mg daily – helps soothe pain, possibly by stimulating cartilage growth. Animal studies suggest supplemental glucosamine may speed up the healing of injured joints as well.

Glucosamine also helps produce glycoproteins, which are substances in ligaments, tendons and joint fluids. So it may speed healing in those areas as well, though research has yet to test that theory. "I find that glucosamine does work in some of my patients who

GO GREEN
Leafy greens such as
spinach pack a powerfully
healthy punch

AN APPLE A DAY...
The antioxidants in fruit
and veg help fight pain

are active, giving them better mobility," says Eric Heiden, an orthopaedic surgeon and former Olympic speed-skating gold medalist.

If you want to give glucosamine a try (it's sold over the counter), then consult your GP. Glucosamine is considered safe, though long-term use has not yet been evaluated.

PROTEIN

Every day, your body busily makes millions of new proteins to replace worn-out proteins in your muscles, red blood cells and connective tissues. When you damage your muscles, tendons, ligaments or joints, many of these proteins break down more rapidly than usual. Your body struggles to pump up production by forming new proteins from dietary amino acids (the building blocks of protein). To do so, however, your body needs these amino acids in abundant supply. Without them, you slow the repairing process, just as a Tarmac shortage would slow a road project.

As a runner, you need about 60-100g of protein daily – a bit more than a non-athlete – to keep up your body's normal protein-building schedule. Once you throw an injury into the mix, you need to concentrate on protein even more. As you recover, keep your protein intake in the 80-100g range.

Also, don't skimp too much on calories. Many of us cut calories to avoid gaining extra weight during couch-bound recovery, but this may actually delay your recovery. If your muscles, brain or other organs don't have enough fuel to function, they will raid your body's protein stores, dwindling those supplies. So if you start losing weight, be wary. It could mean you're not feeding your body enough protein to heal.

Feed your injury top-quality protein by using eggs (or egg whites), soy products, lean meats and non-fat or low-fat dairy products in your meals. These foods contain all the amino acids your body needs. Beans also provide protein, but you must combine them with a grain (such as lentil soup with bread) to produce a complete supply of amino acids.

VITAMIN C

When you're injured, an adhesive-like protein called collagen forms scar tissue which glues your cells back together. Without adequate vitamin C, your body can't make this important substance.

In a classic study conducted more than 30 years ago (such studies aren't done today for ethical reasons), a group of men were fed a vitamin C-deficient diet, with no fruit and vegetables, for several weeks. The researchers then made a small incision on one leg of each man and monitored his healing process. Scar tissue failed to form because little collagen was present. Fortunately the men recovered from their disastrous diet – and their cuts – as soon as they resumed their vitamin C intake.

While this experiment is extreme, it shows the value of vitamin C for optimal healing. The recommended daily requirement (RDA) for vitamin C is 60mg, but that amount is widely regarded as being too low. Aim for 100-250mg. Taking in extra vitamin C is easy, as just one orange supplies 80mg. Other fruits and many winter vegetables, such as broccoli, cabbage and even potatoes, are also good sources. Or take a supplement.

ZINC

Your body needs this mineral to manufacture healthy bone cells (osteoblasts), and cartilage cells (chondrocytes). If you suffer a stress fracture or tear some cartilage, these cells work overtime to repair the damage. Without enough zinc, your body can't make enough osteoblasts and chondrocytes to do the job.

Unfortunately, many runners are already zinc-deficient. If you don't eat meat or don't take a multivitamin, you're probably not consuming the daily 15mg your body needs. Besides red meat, zinc-rich foods include clams and oysters. Good vegetarian sources include wheatgerm, whole-grain cereals and breads, and zinc-fortified cereals. Along with loading up on zinc-rich foods during your rehab, multivitamin that contains 100 per cent of the recommended daily dose of zinc.

WHICH INJURY SPECIALIST?

If you're unlucky enough to get injured, here's how to find the right expert to have you back on your feet fast

Runners pick up injuries. There's no point denying it and no reason to hide it. That's the bad news. The good news is most running injuries are soft-tissue injuries you can resolve yourself with ice, rest and perhaps a dose of cross-training.

Other injuries prove more stubborn. They don't clear up; or if they do, they swiftly recur.

AN ARRAY OF SPECIALISTS

If this happens you may start to think about seeing a medical specialist. But which one? There's a range of specialists all claiming they can help runners. Chiropractors, osteopaths, sports doctors, physiotherapists, podiatrists and sports masseurs can all lay claim to expertise in treating running injuries.

"It can be extremely confusing," admits John Betser, an osteopath who runs sports injury clinics in Dunstable and Bedford. "There are no absolute guidelines as to which word to use for which treatment. There are seven osteopaths and three physios in our practice, and when we sit down and discuss things we fight a constant battle with nebulous language. It's impossible to pin down exactly what frequently used terms such as 'manipulation' or 'adjustment' actually mean."

So where do you start? We suggest you start with your family GP. Although they are by definition generalists, your doctor may be able to cure many of the simpler running problems. If they are unable to help you with your particular problem, they can usually refer you to other medical specialists within the NHS who can; or, depending on the GP, they could also recommend an alternative in the private sector who will see you more quickly. A GP referral is also often required by private medical insurance companies before they will cover treatment costs.

Independent of your GP, you could also seek out a sports injury clinic through your existing running contacts. Often, practitioners work in close contact with one another, so if you have a club physio they might be able to recommend an osteopath or a chiropractor familiar with running problems. The staff at your local running shop may have information, and each month *Runner's World* provides details of doctors and specialists all over the country who frequently treat runners.

THE RIGHT ONE FOR YOU

When you visit a specialist, don't be afraid to ask questions. Specialists can be a great source of advice, not just about clearing up injuries, but about preventing problems in the future. Then, as you gain more knowledge and experience, you'll have a more precise understanding of how to avoid injuries and, if you do pick one up, of which practitioner to consult for which injury.

Although the advice that follows should help you gain a better understanding of the medical professionals available, with a rough guide to their area of specialisation, medicine is invariably a broader subject than its clinically defined terms suggest. Many

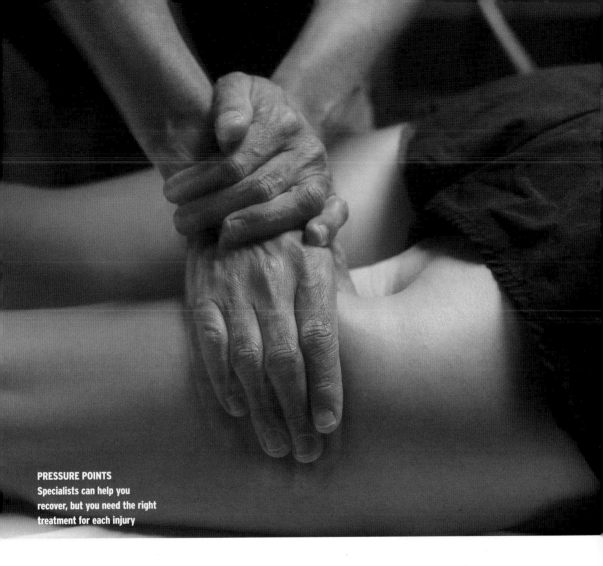

PRESSURE POINTS
Specialists can help you
recover, but you need the right
treatment for each injury

of these medical professionals work together and
complement each other, rather than compete with
each other for your custom. Indeed, many of them
cross over into the same areas and may prescribe
a similar type of treatment for the same injury.

Finally, it is difficult to assess one medical
professional against another, even among those
belonging to the same professional body. So, the
best practitioner for you is the one that keeps you
running injury-free.

PHYSIOTHERAPISTS

The most common variety of specialist in the UK is the
physiotherapist. In fact, a recent poll commissioned by
the Chartered Society of Physiotherapy (CSP) revealed

88 per cent of people will happily self-refer by taking
themselves straight to a physio, bypassing the doctor's
surgery altogether when they're suffering from a
musculo-skeletal injury.

COVERING COSTS: FUNDING YOUR TREATMENT

Of course, at between £40 and £60, trips to private
physios can quickly burn a hole in your pocket. So
medical insurance might not be a bad idea. And it's not
that expensive. "It varies according to your age, where
you live and so on," explains Ben Falkner at AXA PPP
Healthcare. "But a healthy, 30-year-old male runner
living somewhere like Brighton could get insurance for
about £36 a month. That would include £800-worth of

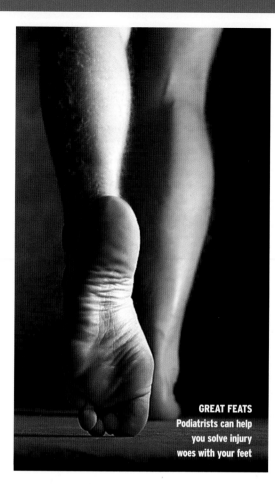

GREAT FEATS
Podiatrists can help
you solve injury
woes with your feet

RESCUE REMEDIES

To help you when you're injured, physiotherapists focus on reducing pain and inflammation, and speeding tissue healing. Effective options include:

➔ CRYOTHERAPY
A fancy term for ice or other cold treatment, cryotherapy is used in the initial injury phase to relieve pain and swelling by reducing blood flow and nerve conduction. Ice is often used after other rehab treatments to reduce swelling.

➔ DEEP-TISSUE MASSAGE
Although there are specialist sports masseurs out there, many physios use rigorous stroking and kneading of muscles and connective tissue. "When you injure your tissue, collagen is like a superglue that heals it," explains Jon Lewis, physio and strength coach at Balance Physiotherapy. "But sometimes the collagen can bind the healthy fibres with adhesions. Then every time you move, it hurts, even though the injury is healed. Massage breaks up the adhesions. It hurts, but it works."

➔ INTERFERENTIAL TREATMENT Sometimes called "e-stim", this treatment sends low-voltage electrical impulses to the injured area via electrodes. For the sake of a mild twinge, it relieves pain in the injured area and helps heal bone and tissue.

➔ IONTOPHORESIS
Iontophoresis is a non-invasive method of delivering healing medication. The drug (usually an anti-inflammatory) is transmitted to the tissues via an electrode with an absorbent pad.

➔ ULTRASOUND
The use of sound waves to produce a deep heat to warm muscle tissues. A wand attached to the ultrasound machine massages tissue around the affected area.

outpatient care, which is what physiotherapy is classed as, as well as hospital care in the event of something major going wrong." This would be subject to a referral from your GP. Though in truth, as Andrew Caldwell, a chartered physiotherapist at the East Midlands Physiotherapy Clinic in Loughborough explains, "most of the time it's simply a case of popping into your GP, telling them what the problem is and that you need a referral for insurance purposes, and they'll write one for you fairly happily." It's also worth remembering that expensive scans, such as MRI and bone scans, would be covered in full with a policy such as that quoted by AXA.

THE LORES OF PHYSICS: TREATMENT AND REHABILITATION

So, you're going to the physio. What will they do? The building blocks of physiotherapy are anatomy, physiology, kinesiology and biomechanics, not medicine and surgery. They can't yet prescribe medications, and not all are able to give injections themselves. And, in addition, most physios can't even order diagnostic exams such as MRIs, bone scans or X-rays (though they should be able to tell you when such things are needed, and may be able to organise them for you. And there are a growing number of extended scope physiotherapy practitioners who can inject and order scans and other tests.)

But what physiotherapists do have is a deep knowledge of the way we move. In truth, the level of specialist knowledge is incredible. As Jennie Edmondson of the CSP explains, "In addition to the obvious areas of sports physiotherapy, back-pain specialists and so on, there are physios whose expertise is treating cancer patients or people with learning disabilities." Whatever your specific problem, there will be a physio for you.

And a good physio will do more than ease your pain. In order to fully cure the overuse injuries that plague runners (tendonitis, runner's knee, shin splints, plantar fasciitis and muscle strains) most physios will first treat the symptoms, and then try to determine the cause. "Physios probably have the best understanding of the mechanics of human movement out of any group of therapists," says exercise physiologist Janet Hamilton, author of *Running Strong and Injury Free*. "They're also one of the best sources for understanding the 'why' of injury onset. Just about any overuse injury will respond to rest and ice, but when you resume running, you may get injured again unless the factors that led to the injury are corrected."

That's why visits to a physio typically involve a lot of detective work. Once the initial healing treatments reduce your pain, the physio will probably watch you run on a treadmill (and videotape it) to analyse your stride and biomechanics. They may also measure muscle strength and efficiency throughout the body in order to detect imbalances that can pull a stride out of alignment.

After the cause of injury has been determined, a physio can prescribe various steps to correct the root cause of the problem – a stretching and strengthening programme for certain weak or tight muscle groups, for example. A physiotherapist might also check the runner's shoe and add arches, heel lifts or refer them to a podiatrist for customised orthoses.

OTHER SPECIALISTS

Chiropractors are best known for manual manipulations of the spine and neck joints to cure back and neck injuries. However, most chiropractors treat the extremities as well. They concentrate on applying pressure to the bones and joints, characterised by clicks and crunches.

Sports doctors treat the musculoskeletal system – ligaments, joints, bones, tendons, muscles and nerves. Some treat the entire human body, others specialise in specific areas of the body.

Osteopaths are different from chiropractors, who are likely to crunch and click the bones, because they are more likely to apply pressure to the soft tissue: the muscles, the ligaments, and the tendons.

Chartered physiotherapists use a variety of treatments to help muscles and joints overcome injury and work to their full potential. These treatments include: exercise programmes to improve mobility and strengthen muscles; manipulation and mobilisation to reduce pain and stiffness; electrotherapy such as ultrasound to break down scar tissue; acupuncture; hydrotherapy; and sports massage.

Podiatrists have, in the past, fallen victim to the myth that they won't give you a second thought unless you're laid low with foot pain. In actual fact, although podiatrists do specialise in the lower body, podiatry is essentially the treatment of gait and posture problems, which could be located anywhere from your neck to your toes.

Sports masseurs knead and stroke the muscles with their hands to relieve muscle tension and improve circulation. Massage can improve flexibility and, for some runners, help to prevent injury, but one of the main benefits is simply relaxation.

TOP TIPS

➡ When looking for a sports doctor, seek a recommendation from a fellow runner to help find a practitioner who specialises in running injuries.

➡ Don't assume that because a friend has the same symptoms as you they have the same injury – obtain a professional diagnosis.

➡ Don't be tempted to take a pain-killer and keep on running – you'll exacerbate the injury, and could turn a short-term problem into a long-term one.

➡ A simple way to check you are running evenly when you come back from injury: count 1, 2, 3 with each footstep, so the 1 falls on alternate sides. Maintain this rhythm and you know you aren't subconsciously altering your gait to protect a vulnerable knee or ankle.

➡ Ask the specialist what has caused the injury – if it's an imbalance in muscle strength, or tight ITBs she'll be able to give you exercises and stretches to do after it's healed to make sure it doesn't reoccur.

RUNNER'S RELIEF

How to beat pounding headaches, sudden allergy attacks and other woes that can strike on the road

Four years ago, Dutch duathlete Huub Mass was competing at world level in shorter events, but suffering diarrhoea and vomiting when attempting longer races. He approached sport and exercise nutritionist Asker Jeukendrup for advice.

"He was convinced he was better suited to the longer events, and had tried everything to fix his problem," says Jeukendrup, who is based at University of Birmingham School of Sport and Exercise Sciences.

Luckily, Jeukendrup was able to uncover the culprit: intolerances to fibre and lactose, which meant they weren't sufficiently absorbed. After cutting his intake of dairy products and fibre before events, Mass went on to become a world champion.

When common health issues such as allergies, headaches or acid reflux strike mid-run, as they did to Jeukendrup's patient, it is sometimes hard for you – or your doctor – to figure out and fix the problem. Here, experts offer simple solutions to six symptoms that strike runners.

THE SYMPTOM
A BURNING SENSATION IN YOUR CHEST OR THROAT

➡ **THE DIAGNOSIS** Acid reflux – or heartburn – is the bubbling up of stomach acid into the esophagus. "Vigorous exercise can cause reflux even in people who don't normally have a problem with it," says Jeukendrup. "Running jostles the contents of the stomach, and in certain people the pressure relaxes the valve that normally keeps acid in its place – the oesophageal sphincter – allowing acid to come up."

➡ **THE FIX** Avoid common trigger foods – caffeine, chocolate, mint, onions and citrus fruits – at least two hours before you run. "I have noticed that red fruits and vegetables in particular can be a common cause in some runners," says Jeukendrup. Also, loosen your waistband and fuel belt: if they're too snug, they can squeeze open the valve that keeps stomach acid down.

THE SYMPTOM
YOU FINISH A RACE AND YOUR HEAD IS POUNDING

➡ **THE DIAGNOSIS** An exertion headache, which is essentially a tension headache. "This occurs when the upper back and neck muscles tighten, with this tension transferring to the head and face," says Greg Whyte, from the Research Institute for Sport and Exercise Science at Liverpool John Moores University.

➡ **THE FIX** Warm up your neck and upper back with self-massage, as well as doing neck and shoulder rolls. This will help prevent the fatigue and cramping in those areas that can lead to headaches, says Whyte. Also, keep your shoulders relaxed throughout your run – once per mile, shake out your arms.

THE SYMPTOM
YOU FEEL SLUGGISH AND DRAINED DURING RUNS

➡ **THE DIAGNOSIS** If sleep deprivation or overtraining isn't to blame, your iron stores may be low. Iron is necessary for the production of haemoglobin, the protein of red blood cells that carries oxygen to your muscles. Low iron means less haemoglobin – and less energy to run.

THE FIX If you think you might have an iron deficiency, your first stop should be your GP for a blood test. "What's normal for a non-runner might be too low for runners," says Jeukendrup. "Even a relatively mild deficiency can cause symptoms." The best nutritional sources of iron are beef, fish and poultry, which your body absorbs better than the plant-based iron found in fortified cereals, soya beans and kale, says Jeukendrup. "For optimum absorption, include some vitamin C in your meal," he adds. Your doctor may also recommend an iron supplement.

THE SYMPTOM
POST-RUN COUGHING

THE DIAGNOSIS Exercise-induced asthma, a condition that's brought on by the constriction of the muscles surrounding bronchial tubes. At rest, you breathe more through your nose, which warms and humidifies air. "When you're running and breathing through your mouth, the air that hits your lungs is colder and drier," says Andy Jones, chair of Applied Physiology at University of Exeter's School of Sport and Health Sciences. This causes coughing, wheezing and shortness of breath.

THE FIX "Walk for five minutes before picking up your pace to give your lungs time to adjust to the effort of running," says Jones. When your lungs are warmed up gradually, they can handle a heavier breathing rate. "Wearing a face mask or scarf can increase the humidity and warming of the air before you breathe it," adds Jones. A vitamin C supplement may help, too. An Indiana University study found that participants who took 1,500mg of vitamin C for two weeks cut their asthma symptoms in half.

THE SYMPTOM
ITCHY BUMPS, WHEEZING, FEELING FLUSHED OR TINGLY

THE DIAGNOSIS Exercise-induced urticaria (hives) is a mild allergic response (to food, medication, clothing, detergent or pollen) that's set off by physical activity. "It's the combination of the allergen and exercise that causes the reaction – although we're not sure why," says Whyte.

THE FIX Seek medical attention if you have these symptoms. Anaphylaxis, a more severe – and frankly, rare – reaction can cause facial swelling and difficulty breathing, says Whyte. To help your doctor pinpoint the cause, keep a log of where you ran, what you were wearing and what you ate beforehand. Once you

identify your allergen, limit your exposure to it within two hours of running. Taking an antihistamine such as Claritin before running can also help.

THE SYMPTOM
ABDOMINAL PAIN, BLOATING

THE DIAGNOSIS Gas. During an intense bout of exercise, blood moves from the digestive tract to the legs, leaving less blood to help with digestion.

THE FIX Fruits, beans and vegetables – great foods for runners – contain fibre and sugars that commonly lead to gas. Dairy and wheat can also cause trouble, especially if you're intolerant or allergic. Eliminate these foods from your diet one at a time for a week to see if your symptoms ease. Then avoid the offenders at least three hours before you run, says Jeukendrup. "This will ensure they are completely absorbed." But you don't have to miss out on energy foods forever. "You can train your gut by starting to eat smaller amounts before a run and building this up over time. You'll find your gut is surprisingly adaptable."

GAIN FROM PAIN

Injuries happen to all but the very luckiest of runners, so here's how to be best prepared if a niggle comes your way

I f you do pick up an injury – and if you run for long enough, you almost certainly will – it can be a miserable experience. It's easy to become bogged down in a funereal gloom at the injustice of it all. Which, of course, does you no good at all – just the opposite, in fact. Recovery is your goal, and what you need is an effective way to bridge that depressing gap between the day you're forced to stop running and the day you can start again.

It's up to you. You can wallow in self-pity, lose your aerobic base, put on weight and make yourself and everyone around you miserable – or you can keep in shape so you're ready to go as soon as the niggle clears. Here's the plan...

1 NO WHINING

Keep your running injuries in perspective. Most are relatively minor and will heal in due time. It may seem catastrophic when you can't run, but don't moan – no one wants to hear it. Not your partner, not your children, not even your running friends. Besides, complaining is counterproductive to regaining your health and fitness.

The gain You'll stay positive during the lay-off, thus speeding your recovery.

2 BE PATIENT

There are very few runners who haven't been injured at one time or another, and the vast majority of those runners – even one 72-year-old who broke his hip – was able to run again. Unfortunately, no magic pill will cure you instantly. Instead, be confident that regardless of how bad your injury may seem, it's only temporary. You will run again, if you're patient enough.

The gain You'll give your injury time to heal.

3 EAT PROPERLY

When you're running, it's easy to go on a "see-food" diet. Any food you see, you eat – in large quantities. So when you stop running it's easy to stack on the pounds unless you exercise a little dietary control. It doesn't mean going on a crash diet; reduced nutrition lessens the body's ability to repair itself. But by focusing on low-fat goodies, fruit and veg, rather than beer and crisps, you can assist your body's mending process and avoid porking out. When you resume running, any weight gain will come off quickly.

The gain Staying lean will keep self-confidence up.

4 IF YOU HAVE A ROUTINE, STICK TO IT

That is, if you normally run at lunchtime, continue with some sort of exercise at lunchtime. If you're an early morning runner, go for a walk early in the morning.

Try walking one of your favourite routes, maybe a trail, and take the time to enjoy the landscape. A two-hour walk followed by typical post-run rituals will deliver recuperation benefits while keeping your morale at healthy levels.

The gain By sticking with some semblance of exercise ritual, you'll reap many of its mood-boosting benefits.

5 DO IT OUTDOORS

Fresh air is never better than when you're injured. You can scoop up a lot of it on a bike ride. Processing lungfuls of oxygen is one of the things that make you feel good when running, and you'll achieve a similar effect by doing just about any outdoor activity.

The gain Checking out the world around you will take your mind off your injury, and you'll be revitalised by a daily dose of fresh air, scenery and (hopefully) sunlight.

ILLUSTRATION: EDEL RODRIGUEZ

6 STAY CONNECTED

One of the worst aspects of being injured is not being able to run with friends. The only time you may see some of them is when you run together. So when you're out of action, make an effort to stay in touch and at least feel like you're part of the running scene. One way to do this is to volunteer to help at races.

Take the opportunity to spend more time with your family and non-running friends; you've got no excuse for dropping out of things such as playing football with the kids or going to a late-night party.

The gain Instead of becoming too self-absorbed, you'll keep lines of communication open with your friends, family and the running community.

7 LIFT WEIGHTS

Since you're going to be at the gym anyway, riding a stationary bike or on the stairclimber, it's not a big deal to spend another 20 minutes with weights. And, because you're not running, you're doing more legwork than usual, along with some abdominal and upper-body stuff.

The gain You'll burn calories and maintain overall fitness and muscle tone.

8 SWEAT

If you normally run 45 minutes a day, make sure you do some activity vigorous enough to keep you aerobic for 45 minutes. It doesn't matter too much what you do, as long as it doesn't aggravate the existing injury. Hit the exercise bike or use some sort of indoor trainer: a cross-country ski machine, a treadmill, or a stairclimber. More importantly, several studies suggest that if you do these alternatives with enough intensity, they can maintain and even increase your fitness level.

The gain You'll end up with a puddle of sweat and soggy T-shirt – evidence you've done something to burn calories and retain your aerobic base.

9 MAKE A DAILY EFFORT

While injuries can be markedly different, most of them respond extremely well to rest and self-treatment. If there are things you can do – see a chiropractor or podiatrist, have a massage – do them. If all you need to do is ice the injury or take anti-inflammatories, do it religiously. If muscle inflexibility or imbalance may have contributed to the problem, stretch carefully twice a day.

The gain By taking action, you'll speed recovery and achieve peace of mind.

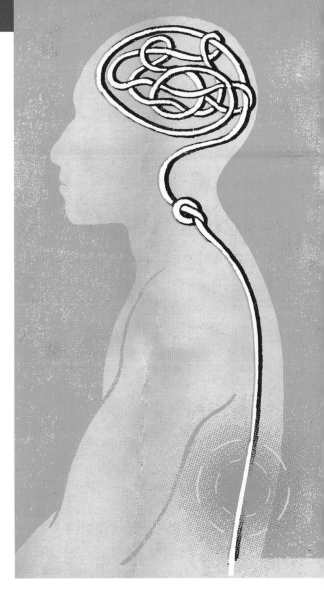

10 FOCUS ON TODAY

Don't set an arbitrary deadline for when you'll be ready and then start, whether you're healthy or not. With any luck, you'll only be out of action for a few weeks at the most, but you never know how quickly you'll heal. It doesn't follow that an injury that took four days to heal last time will do so again. As you age, it takes longer for your body to heal.

The gain By not setting strict deadlines, you won't become frustrated when you miss them. More importantly, you won't start running before you're ready.

RUN LIKE A DREAM

Make sleep the sharpest training tool in your box to take your running to a new level

Better sleep. That's all that could be standing between you and a new PB. Too good to be true? Not according to British marathon runner Mara Yamauchi. "Sleep is one of the most important elements of my routine, because it's crucial for recovery, when the body adapts to the stimulus of training and repairs itself."

Eight or more hours' sleep a night and two-hour afternoon naps aren't realistic for most recreational runners. But you too should up your sleeping game, says Professor Jim Horne from the Sleep Research Centre at Loughborough University.

'The sleep-deprived athlete responds poorly to training both in the short term and over the course of a season'

"Consistent, regular, good-quality sleep is vital when training for any endurance event," says Horne. "Besides just feeling more rested and ready to tackle the day ahead, adequate sleep – at least seven hours – can make a big difference in your recovery."

Sleep is divided into five stages – the first four are characterised by non-rapid eye movement, while stage five is marked by rapid-eye movement (REM). Depending on age and how rested the individual is, REM and non-REM patterns cycle throughout the night about every 90 minutes. When brain waves are measured in sleeping subjects they show a slow wave during stages three and four.

"When it comes to fitness, slow-wave sleep is the most important of the night, as this is when human growth hormone (HGH) is released by the pituitary gland at the base of the brain," says Horne. "It's necessary to build and repair muscles and bones, and it causes us to use more fat for fuel." Loughborough University studies revealed that when sleep is restricted over several nights, HGH release is markedly reduced. "Without the right amount of HGH in the blood, recovery from workouts is hindered, prolonging the time it takes the body to build a strong aerobic engine," says Horne. As a result, the sleep-deprived athlete responds poorly to training.

As HGH decreases, another hormone, cortisol (the 'stress hormone'), increases. "Too much cortisol can

TO NAP OR NOT TO NAP?

PAULA RADCLIFFE
swears by her 2-4pm nap
"If I have a nap I find I can manage much better quality training in the night-time." But do we normal runners need the same? Probably not, says Mark Blagrove, sleep psychologist from the University of Wales. "Unless you're putting in over four hours of intense training every day, I wouldn't advise napping as it can inhibit your night-time sleep quality. But listen to your body."

prohibit the body from recovering fully and interfere with the repair and growth of soft tissue," says Horne.

A study published in *The Lancet* medical journal showed that decreased sleep over only a few days can disrupt in glucose metabolism – a process responsible for storing energy from food, and why marathon runners carbo-load before a big race or long run.

"With impaired glycogen synthesis, runners can't get their glycogen stores as high, which means they may hit the wall sooner during longer runs or races than if they were well-rested," says Horne.

'If you lie awake with anxiety the night before a race, Don't sweat it; it's the sleep two nights before that matters'

Other studies have revealed that people suffering from sleep deprivation often make poor decisions, can't focus and become unmotivated. Lack of sleep can also compromise your immune system, which is already vulnerable during training: those who get six hours or fewer of sleep have 50 per cent less immunity protection than those who get eight hours per night.

QUALITY COUNTS

While most people need seven to nine hours of sleep a night to feel fully rested, the number of hours varies by the individual. To find your magic number, try this: "Go to bed at the same time every night and wake up naturally," says Mark Blagrove, sleep psychologist from the University of Wales. "By the fourth day, you'll have paid off your sleep debt, and should wake up refreshed." Take note of how many hours you slept – that's your goal, he says.

While you may feel the need to sleep a little longer when training for a half-marathon or marathon, the key to full recovery is not just how many hours of sleep you get, but the quality of your sleep. "For the highly trained athlete, sleep becomes more important, but the hours might be less because their sleep is more effective," says Paul Martin, author of *Counting Sheep* (Flamingo). And the fitter you become, the more likely the quality of your sleep will also improve. "Most people find that when they are in the midst of their training and they're feeling good, their sleep is much more sound compared with the tossing and turning that, unfortunately, a lot of people do."

One thing that most runners, coaches and doctors agree on is being well-rested leading up to a race. "I tell all my runners that, in the final weeks of training – and during the taper – you can do more by sleeping than you can by running," says coach Richard Holt. "That's when sleep should really become your primary training component and biggest focus."

And if you lie awake tossing and turning with anxiety the night before a race? Don't sweat it. The *Journal of Sports Medicine and Physical Fitness* reports that it's the sleep you get two nights before a race that matters. The study found that athletes' VO2 max wasn't adversely affected after one sleepless night; it was lowest two days after sleep deprivation.

"One bad day won't have much effect, but days of poor sleep could play havoc with your training," says Holt. "The key with sleep, as with all aspects of your training, is focus and consistency."

NO-NONSENSE NAPPING

➔ HAVE A CUPPA
To feel daisy-fresh after a nap, keep it to less than 45 minutes, when you'll hit the slow-wave slumber. Drink coffee before you hit the pillow – caffeine takes 30 minutes to take effect, so you'll wake up alert.

➔ LOAD UP
Heard that eating turkey and other foods rich in tryptophan can help you nod off? Not true, says Catherine Collins, chief dietician at St George's Hospital in London. Eat carbohydrates – a bowl of porridge with honey should hit all your sleep buttons.

➔ POP SOME PILLS
Not sleeping pills, but vitamin B5 – an antidote to cortisol, the stress hormone. Wash it down with some Gatorade about an hour before

getting horizontal. In tests at Lyon University, France, athletes and couch potatoes alike who downed a high-carbohydrate drink enjoyed a sleep-inducing lower cortisol spike.

➔ CHILL OUT
Part of the reason exercise helps you sleep has to do with its effect on body temperature, which rises when you run, then drops afterwards. "It's that drop that promotes sleep," says Dr William Dement. He advises having a warm bath half an hour before bedtime to induce the drop in body temperature.

➔ AND... RELAX
Seal the deal by thinking about a calming waterfall or tranquil beach, which Oxford University researchers found helped insomniacs fall asleep 20 minutes sooner.

Run the world in 2010

Put a spring in your step in 2010 and book the running holiday of a lifetime! Sign up for a week's spring training holiday in the Algarve to focus your running programme, or book yourself an adventurous running event overseas. There's a comprehensive list of amazing destinations to choose from and there's nothing like setting a goal to motivate you and your training.

SPRING MARATHON TRAINING BREAKS

What better way to dedicate time to your running than under the warmth of the sun away from the stresses and distractions of everyday life?

Join veteran London Marathon winner, Mike Gratton, and his team of experts in Portugal's Algarve for a week of tailored training. Sharpen your regime with indispensable advice and help from some of the world's finest coaches. Reach your peak performance with long training runs, stretching sessions and relaxing yoga, not to mention socialising with your team mates!

NEW YORK MARATHON

RUN NEW YORK

Make the world's largest marathon your goal for 2010. Join the Runner's World team for one of the most sought-after marathons and ensure your place on the start-line of the famous streets of the Big Apple.

GLOBAL RACE CALENDAR

Plan your year – Runner's World and 2:09 Events will be at the following races in 2010 – join us for the experience of a lifetime:

May 15
Great Wall Marathon, China

May 16
Source of the Nile Marathon, Uganda

July 25
San Francisco Marathon

July 31
Swiss Alpine Marathon

September 11
Medoc Marathon, France

September 18
Algarve Summer Training Week

September 25
Petra Marathon, Jordon

September 26
Berlin Marathon

October 10
Chicago Marathon

October 23
Polar Circle Marathon, Greenland

October 24
Venice Marathon

October 24
Beijing Marathon

October 24 Health & Fitness Bootcamp, Cyprus

October 31
Athens Classic Marathon

November 7
New York City Marathon

November 25-28
Cyprus 4-Day Challenge

November 28
Florence Marathon

November 28
Shanghai Marathon

2:09 EVENTS LIMITED

For full details visit www.209events.com or call 01252 373 797

RAVE RUN

Deep Dale, Derbyshire

GET UP AND GO

Have you lost your motivation? Don't fret. We picked the brains of the experts and gathered top coaching tips to help you jump-start your drive

I t's not always easy to lace up your running shoes and move yourself out of your front door. Tiredness, a lack of time and little niggles can all contribute to making you run less than you might want to. And when your trainers do hit the Tarmac, not every run is going to leave you feeling great. It pays to understand how your mind responds to certain kinds of motivation so that you can use how you think to your advantage.

The first thing to understand about motivation is that it's not a switch that's either on or off, but is a moving target. And motivation isn't just about getting out the door. It influences your running performance. It affects your concentration during running, your emotions and how hard you try, which in turn affects how often you run in the future and how you see the sport itself.

There are three forms of motivation, all of which work in different ways but operate at the same time. This means that there isn't a 'magic moment' when you switch from being demotivated to being motivated – you need to work at it constantly.

At one end of the spectrum is amotivation, where you have trouble getting out of bed in the morning. One way to counteract this is to reward yourself for achieving a basic goal, such as going running, with a treat – this is the second type: extrinsic motivation.

"This happens in response to an outside force such as money, fame or being shouted at by your partner," says Dr Costas Karageorghis, a reader in sports psychology at Brunel University.

"Finally, there's intrinsic motivation, which you get from experiencing running as sheer pleasure," he adds.

1 GET THE BALANCE RIGHT

So what is the ideal state of motivation that you should aspire to and how can you get it? "Intrinsic motivation combined with extrinsic motivation gives the best results. However, if the rewards for running end up dominating, this motivation breaks down," says Karageorghis.

An example of a good balance of motivations would be the intrinsic motivation of doing your favourite run, combined with the extrinsic motivation of losing an amount of weight in a month. But if you started to dislike the run and focused purely on losing another kilo of fat, your motivation would tail off – you would start to think negatively about running and that would make it harder to achieve your goal.

You might have found it easy to fall in love with running, but like any relationship, staying the course needs care and attention. The best way is to keep a positive mindset.

"It sounds easy enough, but it takes work to develop a consistently positive attitude," says sports psychologist Andrea Firth-Clark. "Anyone who has felt dejected after failing to beat a PB time or run through atrocious weather knows how true this is."

ILLUSTRATIONS: DONGYUN LEE

2 EMBRACE THE CHALLENGE

Rather than being relentlessly cheerful, there is another route to positive thinking. "You can programme yourself to be positive," says Rick Pitino, athletic coach at the University of Louisville, USA. It might sound like a paradox, but you can learn to think positively and increase your motivation by putting yourself in challenging situations. "You have to embrace adversity because every time you take on something outside your comfort zone and get through it, your self-belief increases," agrees Firth-Clark.

You can structure this quest for a positive state of mind by drawing up a performance profile. List 10 things that you think are important to running (such as discipline or fitness) and that you admire in a running role model, such as Paula Radcliffe.

"Give yourself a score out of 10 for each point. This will give you your strengths and weaknesses," says Firth-Clark.

Identifying your weaknesses makes their improvement a goal. Tracking your progress by amending the numbers as you improve will push you on to the next success.

3 GET FOCUSED

Knowing how your mind can motivate your body can make the difference between improving your performance and getting caught in a de-motivating spiral. The most important thing you can do to maintain your focus is set a long-term goal that you work back from, identifying what you need to do to achieve that goal and when, right down to the purpose of the particular run that you're about to do.

Then within each run it's a good idea to develop a focus plan, based on what you want to achieve at certain stages of it.

"This will help you focus on the positives, and disregard irrelevant issues that could lead you into a negative mindset. Hitting focus goals also increases motivation and your satisfaction with the performance," says Firth-Clark.

"Lots of people use running to clear their minds, which is fine until your focus wanders and your motivation starts to flag. Use the first 15 minutes of your run to clear your head, then switch into your focus plan with its intermediate goals," she says.

If you're heading out for a long training run, a focus plan can break it up into manageable chunks. You may not know how long it will take, but you can still set time and distance goals such as: hold my pace at 60 per cent

of maximum effort for 20 minutes at minute 40; drink 750ml of water by 60 minutes; or, concentrate on my stride length and form during mile six.

"Each time you achieve a focus goal you're one step closer to achieving your overall goal," says Firth-Clark. Focus goals can be used on your training runs as much as during an event, but there are specific things you can do during a race to help you run faster. The first thing is to avoid fixating on the finish line.

"Research has shown that focusing excessively on a specific outcome such as beating a PB can be disruptive to your performance," says Karageorghis.

This doesn't mean you have to give up all thought of your final goal, but if you trust in your focus plan for the race, which you'll have perfected in training, then you know that on a good day you can achieve the result you want.

"You need to have confidence in your plan, and this is why it needs to be measurable and repeatable," says Firth-Clark. "Race-day routines are crucial to performance because they help you to stay relaxed, concentrate and disregard negative thoughts."

Rehearse your routine so you know exactly what needs to be done before and during the race. This includes everything from putting your kit out the night before, to doing a structured warm-up. You should also

5 ENTER THE ZONE

While you can't be perfectly motivated all of the time, you can work towards being highly motivated. There is a further state of motivation that even the most focused of people can only achieve for a temporary but glorious moment during a run. This is when your mind and body move into the motivational state called "the zone".

"During this state, the mind works in perfect harmony with the body, performance seems effortless, concentration is total, time seems to stand still or speed up and the runner is totally absorbed in the actions of their running. It is an extremely pleasurable, highly focused experience," says Firth-Clark.

Unsurprisingly, this state is the one in which athletes perform at their very best, so it's highly sought after for its competitive advantage. Research has been done to find out how you can enter it.

"We've found that focusing on processes such as regulating your breathing and stride pattern, or trying to use good form, tend to bring the zone on more than focusing on the potential race result," says Karageorghis.

Some of us do have a natural advantage. "Having an autotelic personality means engaging in an activity for its own sake and not caring about the outcome. People who can lose themselves in an activity are more likely to experience the zone," he adds.

But the problem for the rest of us is that humans are hardwired to focus on things like achieving success and receiving rewards. "Getting into the zone relies on you immersing yourself in the moment. If you speak to athletes like Usain Bolt, they focus on immersing themselves and getting the processes right rather than what athlete A, B or C is doing," says Karageorghis.

know what you're going to do if you lose your focus and practise maintaining a positive mindset if things don't go according to plan.

"This allows you to control the controllables and not waste energy worrying about what other runners are doing or things you can't do anything about," adds Karageorghis.

4 MIND GAMES

There are techniques you can use to 'trick' your mind back into a focused, internally motivated state if your attention wanders.

"Try to develop a trigger word that you say to yourself to get back into a positive mindset. This can be as simple as 'let's go'. When things get tough, use visualisation to see yourself achieving your goals or imagine how your running hero would behave in the same situation," says Firth-Clark.

It's good to keep an eye on your pace during races if you're aiming for a certain time, but checking your watch every minute will get in the way of an efficient running style and will cost you dearly.

"Instead try to learn to experience running as a series of moments by focusing on what your body is doing at that moment," says Karageorghis. A state that is sometimes referred to as getting "in the zone".

6 THE PAY-OFF

So good motivation lies in learning to love running as a long-term partner. It won't always be easy, but remember that it's not just about what you can get out of it.

"Focusing on outcomes that you then don't achieve can cause motivation to plummet," Karageorghis says.

But learning to experience running as a series of moments by focusing on what you're doing and thinking positively about yourself as a runner can allow you to grow old and content with each other. Get this much right and running faster, beating your PB, running for longer and achieving your ultimate goals will come naturally to you.

WHY DO WE SUFFER?

Running can hurt. This is runner Christie Aschwanden's quest to understand the bittersweet symphony

The wheels were coming off, and all I could do was watch them roll away. This was my third straight August running the Pikes Peak Ascent in Manitou Springs, USA, and I'd begun the day confident, ready to put hard-won lessons to work. My first year, I'd entered on a whim and lumbered to the finish line, 13.3 miles and 7,815 feet above the start, thoroughly spanked. The next year, I'd upped my mileage and practised running above 14,000 feet, but still I'd limped home after aggravating an old Achilles injury. Today I was ready for a charmed third try. I was fit, healthy and confident of a top-10 finish. Maybe I'd even break three hours if all went well.

I'd begun at a moderate pace as planned, but as I neared five miles, where I'd intended to start pushing, my body refused to follow the script. My quads and hamstrings tightened, my chest constricted, my arms went all noodley. It was slow-motion agony.

My confidence evaporated and I was wallowing in dread at the many miles I had left to plod, when a spectator pumped her fist at me and shouted, "Looking great! You're in eighth place!"

> **'Your expectations about pain going into a race come from your training. You have to train your pain threshold just as you train your lactic threshold'**

In an instant, my world changed. The weight in my legs lifted, my breathing relaxed, and my spirit crawled out of its hole. Suddenly I didn't just look great to my anonymous fan, I actually felt great, too. So great that I picked up the pace and finished the race sixth overall. My time, 3:08:21, wasn't quite what I'd hoped for, yet I'd turned a disaster into a solid performance.

But how? As I sat at the finish, watching runners trudge up the final switchbacks like a swarm of ants, I wondered: what exactly was that misery I'd experienced early on? Why had the pain evaporated with one tidbit of positive information? Is suffering a psychological phenomenon that can be overcome like a bad mood, or a danger signal that can't be ignored?

NO PAIN, NO GAIN?

To better understand the nature of pain, I started talking to scientists. And the short answer, say these experts, is that the discomfort associated with a hard effort is sort of like the "check engine" light in your car – serious enough to warrant attention, but more of an early warning than a beacon of death. While you run, your brain gauges the factors that determine the pace you can maintain – your fitness level, the heat, your fuel levels, the course profile – then adds physiological feedback it receives to devise a feeling of perceived effort, says exercise physiologist Jonathan Dugas, co-author of the blog *Science of Sport* (sportsscientists. com). Researchers call this sensation a rating of perceived exertion (PE). You feel it as fatigue in your legs, tightness in your chest, soreness in your muscles, aching in your feet and heat on your face.

ILLUSTRATIONS: MARK MATCHO

WHERE IT HURTS

Ten ways a runner can feel the burn – and then deal with it

❯ DEHYDRATION

OUCH You're parched and your heart races.
SCIENCE Plain and simple: You've lost too much fluid.
CURE Drink! Water is best to quench the thirst, but drink what you crave.

❯ HITTING THE RED ZONE

OUCH Your muscles burn – everything's on fire.
SCIENCE Many call this "going anaerobic," but there's little evidence that the pain arises from too little oxygen (or too much lactic acid). Rather, your brain recognises that you're too close to your limit and forces you to slow down.
CURE Ease up soon – or it's game over.

❯ LEG CRAMPS

OUCH Your muscles are seizing up big time.
SCIENCE Electrical impulses in the muscles have gone haywire, causing rapid contractions.
CURE Stop and stretch.

❯ SHIN SPLINTS

OUCH Your shins are beyond sore.
SCIENCE Pain is likely due to overtraining, wearing worn shoes, or uneven surfaces.
CURE Walk it out. Avoid relapses by doing stretching and strengthening exercises.

❯ HITTING THE WALL

OUCH You're out of energy.
SCIENCE You've depleted your liver's supply of glycogen, and it can't maintain blood glucose.
CURE Begin long runs with full glycogen stores and down carbs when runs top 75 minutes. Aim for 30g to 60g per hour.

❯ SIDE STITCH

OUCH A stabbing pain pierces your side.
SCIENCE Theories abound. The most popular: cramp in your diaphragm muscle.
CURE Focus on breathing with your diaphragm by pulling your stomach in as you exhale and pushing out as you inhale.

❯ CHAFING

OUCH Feels like burning.
SCIENCE Friction between skin and skin (or skin and clothing) rubs you raw.
CURE Avoid clothing with stitching in chafe-prone areas and apply lube to potential hot spots.

❯ LEG LOCK

OUCH Your muscles feel like they're filled with cement.
SCIENCE You've run in the red zone too long and damaged muscle fibres. Your brain is slowing down your muscles to protect you.
CURE The damage is done – just slow down.

❯ BLISTERS

OUCH Your feet burn.
SCIENCE Friction rubs skin raw. Moisture makes it worse.
CURE Try preventive taping, or lube problem areas and keep feet dry. Wear socks of moisture-wicking material, or thin, double-layer socks.

If you try to push yourself to perform beyond your body's physiological limits, "your brain will always protect you, and it does that by adjusting your PE", says Dugas. "It's your brain's way of saying, 'Hey stupid – you can't keep this up.'" In my case, I was running a strong race, but it required more physical stress than I'd expected so my brain stepped in.

The spectator's positive cue had changed my interpretation of the discomfort I was feeling, says Alan Utter, an exercise physiologist at Appalachian State University, North Carolina, USA. "Nothing changed physiologically; it was purely psychological," he says. The news that I could attain a top-10 finish had altered how I viewed my muscle fatigue and other signals that had been driving my pain perception up to that point. Instead of taking my discomfort as a sign I was exploding, I now saw it as a symptom of success. "Your brain received an external cue, and it sent commands down to your muscles to keep going," Utter says. "This is why coaches shout from the sidelines."

CHEER YOURSELF ON

Just as important, the cheering helped me shut down my negative self-talk, according to sports psychologist Stephen Walker, editor of *Podium Sports Journal*. The knowledge that I was running within my goals had refocused my mind from thoughts like "I feel crappy" to ones like "I'm on target". "How you talk to yourself in that situation can really define your race," he says. "You need to focus on exactly how you want your body and muscles to feel."

Experience plays a major role in how we interpret pain, says Utter. The year after my turnaround at Pikes Peak, I returned and finished within six seconds of my previous year's time – and this time it felt easier. My experience illustrates a component of pain perception that Utter calls teleoanticipation. "The pace you set at the beginning of a race and throughout is based on prior experiences," he says. "Your brain remembers the last marathon that you ran and how you felt, and uses that as a benchmark to set your intensity by."

Teleoanticipation explains why it's easier to speed up in the final mile of a race than early in a 10K. "When you only have a mile left, you can usually handle more pain, because you know where your endpoint is," says Utter. "When that anticipatory response kicks in, you can often pick up the pace."

Your expectations about pain going into a race come from your training experiences, says Mark Tarnopolsky, a professor of neuromuscular and mitochondrial disorders at McMaster University Medical Centre, Ontario, Canada, and an accomplished runner. "You have to train your pain threshold just as you train your lactic threshold," he says. In fact, the same kinds of intervals that up your lactate threshold also improve your pain tolerance, because they teach your brain what it feels like to approach your limit and keep going. This is both a physical and psychological process – your body adapts to the exercise, while your mind learns to cope with the discomfort and develop confidence that you can handle the pain.

Another way to boost your pain threshold is to join what Michael Atkinson, a runner and sports sociologist at Loughborough University, calls a "pain community" – a running club, workout group or training partner that pushes you to run harder. A pain community can teach you to handle suffering by guiding you through a set of intense physical rituals,

'You want to feel your lungs burn a little, to feel your quadriceps get fatigued. It's part of feeling that you're alive out there on a run'

whether they are Tuesday track workouts or a weekly long run. "One of the biggest things separating runners who can come to enjoy pain and suffering from those who don't is that they've been opened up to the possibility that pain can be a source of pleasure and enjoyment," says Atkinson. "So often in everyday life, we're taught that for any kind of physical discomfort or pain you just negate it, you try to medicate it, you do everything in your power to avoid any suffering. The more you learn to embrace the process, the better you'll deal with it over time."

Ultra-marathon runner Andy Jones-Wilkins sees his acceptance of pain as a competitive advantage. "The person who knows the suffering is coming, who expects and embraces it, will do better than someone who's scared of it," he says.

That may be true, but Utter is convinced that not everyone feels pain the same way. "If you put two different runners on a treadmill at 70 per cent of their max, one might say they're at six or seven on a 10-point perceived exertion scale, and the other might be at nine." Fitness levels and training influence how

RUNNER'S WORLD *Online*

Do you want to be a part of Britain's largest and most informative running community?

With more than half a million members, more than 3,000 events and thousands of daily forum posts, we have so much to offer any runner, whatever your level.

Here's a snapshot of what you'll find on runnersworld.co.uk:

Fresh, Focused Running Content
Read thousands of articles covering training, nutrition and injury, written in our friendly, authoritative style.

Interactive Tools
Use our personalised schedules, Garmin-compatible downloads and online training log to get the most from your running.

Events Diary
Browse details of more than 3,000 races taking place across the UK, hundreds of which you can enter via our secure credit-card system.

Gear Reviews
Enjoy expert assessments and hundreds of user reviews on the latest gear releases, then buy direct through links to online stockists.

Forum Community
Tap the collective knowledge of thousands of fellow athletes, find a local training buddy or arrange a post-race social.

Regular E-Newsletters
Opt to receive information about what's new on the site, what events are coming up in your region or marathon-training bulletins straight to your inbox.

Great Competitions
Win fantastic prizes each month - recently, we've given away expert coaching sessions, state-of-the-art equipment and overseas travel packages.

Subscriber Offer - Save up to 50%
Make the most of our online subscription offers and enjoy a significant saving on our newsstand prices.

Plus, following a phenomenal year for triathlete's world magazine, we've launched the online arm – triathletesworld.co.uk – to complement the number one triathlon title on the newsstand. The site is standalone but is also housed within the runnersworld.co.uk framework, meaning runners are only a click away from the world of triathlon. Triathletesworld.co.uk already houses the second largest triathlon forum in the UK, as well as event listings and editorial, so there's no better time to join the community!

Visit triathletesworld.co.uk to find out more.

RUNNER'S WORLD
Runnersworld.co.uk

Triathlete's World
Triathletesworld.co.uk

difficult a given effort level feels, but pain tolerance also is an inherent component, says Tarnopolsky. "I see it in the clinic all the time: some people find the tiniest little thing uncomfortable, and others can tolerate a muscle biopsy with very little anesthetic." All elite runners have talent, he says, but "when it comes time to separate the top athletes, the differences may be from the neck up".

"When I am running well, pain is just another feeling, as in: am I hot or cold? Is it quiet or loud in this room?" says Justin Freeman, a 14:52 5K runner and former Olympian in cross-country skiing. "Pain becomes an indicator of whether I have the fitness to continue at a given pace, not something that controls me."

Many successful runners say their very best performances seem to transcend pain, according to running coach Ric Rojas (ricrojasrunning.com). "It's a common misconception that peak performance requires you to feel maximum pain and suffering," Rojas says. "Top athletes will tell you their peak performance hits a sweet spot. They don't feel pain and suffering as much as the exhilaration of the running experience." In interviews with runners after an Olympic Marathon, "the words pain and suffering very rarely come up", says Rojas. "What comes up is 'I relaxed', 'I focused', 'I stayed calm'."

But why seek that pain at all? "It's an amazing thing for people outside of running to get their heads around: why would you put yourself through something you know is going to hurt?" says Atkinson. "A lot of runners say pain is not just a necessary evil; it's a fundamental part of the process," he says. "It's part of the reason you go out there. You want to feel your lungs burn a little, to feel your quads get fatigued. It's part of feeling that you're alive out there on a run."

For many runners, the urge to suffer represents a turning away from society's obsession with numbing pain or medicating every discomfort. "Many people are coming to running at a point in our cultural history where they're saying, 'I'm not satisfied with this anesthetised way of living,'" says Atkinson.

Long-distance races can also serve as rites of passage. "You go into a race with a sense of self, and in the process of encountering this really uncomfortable pain and suffering, you're forced to look in the mirror and find out, what defines me? Am I a person who perseveres? Can I endure?" he says. "You may emerge at the end as a qualitatively different person, and that's something you carry over to the rest of your life."

OUTSMART PAIN
How to mentally fight suffering

① BELIEVE YOU CAN HANDLE THE HURT
Like most runners, you probably realise when pain is coming, so plan for how you'll react. If you know that your legs will burn in the last mile, anticipate this feeling and turn it into a cue that the finish is near and you're on target. Your physiology sets limits on how fast you can go, but self-confidence can nudge your brain into allowing you closer to that limit before it cranks the pain to make you stop, says exercise physiologist Jonathan Dugas.

② TRY RELAXING
If you're hurting, don't fight the feeling – relax and listen to what your body is telling you. "Digging deeper will just get you deeper in a hole," says coach Ric Rojas. Instead, try relaxing the muscle groups that you're not using in order to save energy and run more efficiently, says William Gayton, a sports psychologist at the University of Southern Maine, USA. "Your forehead muscles don't need to be tense."

③ CHALLENGE NEGATIVE SELF-TALK
Seize your power to reframe your pain. "If you find yourself focusing on how tired you are, you might turn that around and say, 'So what? Tiredness is normal, it comes in waves, and it's not going to last forever,'" says Gayton. "The thought 'my legs are killing me' might be countered by telling yourself, 'That's a good sign. I must be really working it. Keep it up!'"

④ DIVIDE AND CONQUER
You can tolerate more pain when you know the end is near, says exercise physiologist Alan Utter. Use this to your advantage by breaking a race into manageable chunks, focusing on intermediate landmarks. Tell yourself that you just need to tolerate the pain until the top of the next hill instead of focusing on the far-off finish.

THINK TOUGH

A strong mind makes an even stronger runner, so it's time to break the mental barrier that's holding you back

It's an all too common story: runner sets achievable goals; runner puts in the necessary physical training to meet goals; runner falls short on race day. So, what's the problem? Could it be that you're spending too much time becoming a stronger runner on the road, and precious little on becoming a stronger runner in your mind? Big mistake. To achieve your true potential, it's essential to train mentally as well as physically.

"The athlete who ignores the mental element of training quite simply won't enjoy their running or achieve as much, and might even give up altogether," explains sports psychologist Jamie Edwards (trained-brain.com). "As a runner you really get to know yourself and what kind of mental toughness you have inside – once you've realised what you're capable of, and can block out the negative voices, you become not just a stronger runner, but a stronger person." With the help of the UK's premier sports psychologists, we've come up with solutions for the most common mental hurdles standing between you and the happier, stronger runner fighting to get out.

I CAN'T HANDLE THE PAIN BARRIER

● **What's happening** The brain always gives up before the body, according to Simone Lewis, sports psychologist at Bath University. "Unless you're used to pushing yourself to the limit, the only credible option to improve the situation you're in appears to be stopping."

● **Your strategy** "There are two essential strategies for handling the pain – dissociating to externalise it and distract yourself away from it, and associating to actually focus on the feeling," says Lewis. To associate, start from the head and work down, assessing each area or group of muscles. "Keep your pace in line with the information you gain from your body monitoring, from heart rate to basic breathing, not being afraid to increase the pace if you feel good."

'The brain always gives up before the body. The only credible option to improve the situation appears to be stopping'

To dissociate, focus more on your surroundings – the sounds, sights and smells – and let them distract you temporarily. "The most successful runners switch between the two," says Lewis, "using association during the more crucial sections of a race and dissociation at times where you can give yourself a break from the tough mental demands – associating for long periods simply isn't possible, because the mind is going to wander."

PRE-RACE NERVES RUIN MY PERFORMANCES

● **What's happening** You've got textbook "what if" syndrome. "The reason you're so nervous – burning huge amounts of precious glycogen, as well as being

away from the calm zone from where athletes are able to perform at their best – is that you're panicking about what might happen in the future, rather than dealing with the present," says sports psychologist Jamie Edwards.

⊃ Your strategy Try Edwards' principle technique: structured belly breathing. Inhale through your nose to a count of three, pause, then slowly exhale through your mouth for a count of four. How does this help? "Short, staccato breathing floods your respiratory system with carbon dioxide, which means your brain and muscles aren't getting the oxygen they need to function properly," says Edwards. "Deep, long breaths activate the parasympathetic nervous system, slowing down your heart rate and reducing anxiety."

MY LAST RACE WAS A SHOCKER – AND NOW I'VE LOST MY MOTIVATION

⊃ What's happening That brick wall standing between you and the starting line is your pride. "Not long after you started running, being a runner probably became a part of your self-identity – and pivotal to your identity in your peers' eyes," says Dr Dan Bishop, a sports psychologist at Brunel University, and sub-three-hour marathon runner. "You're 'The Runner' that your friends know, which is a very brittle concept – and one that is easily shattered in your own mind through one bad performance."

'Until those negative memories about old injuries are replaced with the confidence that your injury is fully healed, you'll always be holding back'

⊃ Your strategy "Without the disappointments, the successes simply wouldn't be as sweet," says Bishop, who advises first getting to the root cause of your poor performance – the weather, a poorly executed race plan – and venting your frustration about it. "Moan to as many people as will listen to get it out of your system." Now congratulate yourself for having the courage to take risks. "Accept and savour your mistakes as learning experiences." If that still doesn't help, take a break from running competitively and only lace-up for pure pleasure, says Bishop. "You'll know deep down when you're ready to come back."

I ALWAYS CHOKE WHEN I SEEM TO BE PERFORMING WELL

⊃ What's happening While many people leap ceiling-high at the sight of a spider, yours is a different kind of fear: success. "Many of us find something frightening about surpassing our own or others' expectations – and that can be enough to keep us from doing so," says Bishop. "For some it's lacking the confidence to challenge the status quo, while others fear that if they're successful they'll have to take the sport too seriously; that too much will be expected of them; or even that they'll be resented."

⊃ Your strategy Acknowledge that your fear exists – then pump yourself up with positive affirmation. "See yourself accepting success," says Bishop. "While nobody likes a big-head, modesty in runners all too often leads to self-deprecation." Take your lead from athletes in post-race TV interviews, he suggests.

stopwatch and rekindle your running desire by throwing some variety into your training, advises Lewis. "Try shorter distances, take different routes, enter a race somewhere you've never been to before or just do your usual run back to front."

WORRYING ABOUT AN OLD INJURY IS HOLDING ME BACK

⬧ What's happening Your brain is behaving like an over-protective mum. "People develop a defensive memory function to help prevent them from re-injuring themselves," says Paul Russell, sports and exercise psychologist at the University of Bolton and private consultant (thefifthspace.com). "Until those negative memories are replaced with the confidence that your injury is fully healed, you'll always be holding back." You'll also potentially be risking fresh damage. "Anxiety leads to muscle tension, which can result in new injuries," he adds.

⬧ Your strategy You must take your know-how of the injury up a gear to gain mental control. "Develop specific visualisation of problem area(s) by becoming familiar with anatomical drawings of the muscles of the body," says Russell. "Being able to 'see' those muscles widening and lengthening as you run will encourage them to relax, which in turn will ward off the tension that causes them to shorten, tighten and fatigue."

"When someone says 'Nice race', reply with 'Thanks, I worked hard for it' – rather than 'I was lucky' or 'I should've done better'." Building self-belief without over-selling yourself will pay dividends, says Bishop. "It will empower you to take the lead in the next race."

I FEEL COMPLETELY BURNT OUT

⬧ What's happening Quite simply, you're expecting too much of yourself physically, which means that mentally your main sail drops. "Too often runners get to this point and become dispirited," says Lewis. "The mind and body work as one, so your brain helps you overcome hurdles when your running is on the up, but can turn on you if you continually push yourself to chase new PBs without success."

⬧ Your strategy Know your limits. "Accept that consistent improvement simply isn't sustainable and that you'll have set-backs," explains Lewis. "Plan several scheduled time-outs a year – at least a week at a time – to rest, regenerate and develop that hunger for running again." Forget your times, unstrap your

I LOSE ALL FOCUS IN RACES

⬧ What's happening En route to the finish line, the racing environment bombards us with information, and we have the necessary tools (ears, eyes etc) to pick up the lot. "Being stressed can cause our focus to narrow, cutting out important information, such as the position of a competitor," says sports psychologist Ian Maynard from Sheffield Hallam University. "Or we can be so relaxed (or determined to shut out the stressor) that we begin to focus too much on things that are superfluous to our performance."

⬧ Your strategy Take your cue. Maynard recommends this tried-and-tested re-focusing technique: "I like the simple routine of 'breathe', 'talk' and 'race'," he explains. "'Breathe' is your cue to focus on the movement of your chest, which should instantly take you away from the distraction; the 'talk' element introduces an instructional cue word, such as 'relax', 'rhythm' or '100 per cent'. Lastly, focus on your 'race' – your splits, breathing, strategy. This process brings you back into the here and now, where good concentration always needs to be."

49 WAYS TO KEEP GOING

There are reasons but no excuses for losing motivation to run. We can combat them all, with tips, inspiring stories and more

1 START A BLOG
Post your daily mileage, then give out the url to your friends and family. Do you really want Auntie Susan or Uncle Bob asking why you skipped your four-miler on Wednesday?

2 FORGET TIME
Running coach Shane Bogan advises leaving your watch at home once in a while. "It's liberating not to be worried about pace," he says. Just enjoy a run for its own sake.

3 SIGN UP NOW...
...for a winter race or running holiday in a warm country. Every training mile you log takes you closer to that winter marathon in Bangkok (thailandmarathon. org), Las Vegas (las-vegas.competitor.com) or Sydney (sydneymarathon.org).

4 TREAT YOURSELF
That new running watch you're hankering after? Go ahead and buy it – after timing 10 more speed sessions with your old one.

5 LOOK TO THE PAST
Emil Zatopek, who won four Olympic gold medals in his career, was a tough-as-nails athlete known for his intense training methods, such as running in work boots. Competing with a gland infection and against his doctor's orders, the Czech won three distance events, including the marathon, at the 1952 Helsinki Olympics.

6 THINK FAST
The runners coach Christy Coughlin works with always get a boost from this simple negative-splits workout: run for 20 minutes as slowly as you want, then turn around and run home faster. "The long warm-up helps you feel great and run faster on the way back," says Coughlin.

7 BLAZE A NEW PATH
"If you do the same runs all the time, it can beat you down," says Alan Culpepper, an Olympic marathon runner. Try a GPS system, or check out mapmyrun.com to find new routes.

8 GET YOUR KIT ON
Don't think about running – just throw on the appropriate clothes. You can take them off again, after you've gone outside and sweated on them a bit.

9 ENTER A RELAY RACE
Either as part of a running team, or do the run leg of a triathlon with a cycling and a swimming friend. Don't let the team down by skimping on your training.

ILLUSTRATIONS: ADAM McCAULEY

10 DEVISE YOURSELF A RUNNING LOYALTY SCHEME

One mile equals one point. Start collecting today and soon you could have saved up enough points for a new pair of shoes, an afternoon at a health spa, a ticket to the big game or a small but guilt-free treat from a very expensive chocolate shop.

11 FEEL INSPIRED

In 1949, nine-year-old Wilma Rudolph learned to walk without leg braces after suffering from polio and spending most of her first years in bed. Rudolph went on to win three gold medals for the USA in the 1960 Olympics.

12 HAVE A DAILY GOAL

Scott Jurek, seven-time winner of the Western States 100-Mile Endurance Run in the USA, sets himself a variety of goals not just for big races but also for training sessions. "Maybe it is a technique goal, maybe a pace goal, maybe a goal of running faster at the end," he says.

13 SPOIL YOURSELF

Book a massage for the day after your long run. It's good for your muscles and an appropriate treat after all that hard running.

14 RUN WHEN IT'S TIPPING DOWN

Trust us – with rain hitting you sideways and the wind whipping your face, you'll feel wonderfully alive. Just make sure that you have a dry pair of shoes for tomorrow.

15 FOR EMERGENCY USE ONLY

Consider taking a short break from running if you think you've got the beginning of an overuse injury or you're truly fatigued. A couple of days of rest may be just the thing to reinvigorate you. Call this one instant running motivation for three days from now.

16 IT'S SUMMER!

Well, it may not be when you buy this book, but when it is, go outside and run now. Read the rest of this later.

17 YOU WANT TO LOOK GOOD IN YOUR SWIMMING COSTUME

Don't you?

18 IT'S NEVER TOO LATE

Mary Peters was 33 and near the end of her career when she defeated local favourite Heide Rosendahl to take gold in the pentathlon at the 1972 Olympics in Munich. Her victory brought temporary calmness to Northern Ireland with rival factions celebrating together the country's greatest ever sporting success.

19 PAY YOURSELF

Set a price for attaining a certain weekly mileage goal. When you hit it, pay up. Keep your mileage money in a jar, and once it accumulates, buy yourself that new running jacket you've been ogling.

20 IF YOU'RE REALLY IN THE MOOD...

...for a change, or if you just have nothing to wear, check out the list of clothing-optional races and other events at british-naturism.org.uk/events.

21 EXERCISE IMPROVES SEXUAL PERFORMANCE

According to research. Enough said.

22 WATCH THIS

Endurance – a 1999 docudrama which shows how Ethiopian Haile Gebrselassie became one of the best distance runners of all time.

23 ASK A FRIEND FOR A RIDE

Not for yourself. Just ask them to cycle alongside you if your running partner isn't available.

24 GET WET

If it gets too hot outside, coach Bruce Gross suggests logging your miles by running in the deep end of a pool while wearing a flotation vest. Gross tells his runners to break it up by going hard for five minutes, then resting for one minute. Build up to an hour.

25 RACE RESULTS STAY ON GOOGLE FOREVER

Well, until the end of either the internet or the world, anyway.

26 TURN THINGS AROUND

"A poor performance is a strong motivator for me," says elite marathon runner Clint Verran. "I can't wait to prove to myself that I'm a better runner than my last showing." Verran also says negative comments from his coaches fire him up. "For me, proving somebody wrong is key."

27 BEEN RUNNING MARATHONS FOR YEARS?

Maybe it's time to try an ultra. Or a mile.

28 BECOME A RUNNING MENTOR

Once you get your neighbour, colleague or significant other hooked on your favourite sport, they'll be counting on your continued support and guidance – and company.

29 IF YOU'RE STAYING IN

The Four-Minute Mile is a 1988 UK film that tells the story of how Roger Bannister became the first man to run the mile in under four minutes, despite conventional wisdom of the time insisting that such an achievement was physiologically impossible.

30 DUST OFF YOUR TRACK SPIKES

Some athletics clubs organise Olympic-style summer games where you can compete in events like the mile or the 400-metre hurdles. If you want a real change of pace, train for a field event such as the long jump.

31 REMEMBER THE SIMPLE TRUTH

That you almost always feel better after a run than you do before it.

32 MAKE A CONNECTION

Try logging on to dateactive.co.uk, a website that connects active people looking for love. Get in your run and go on a date at the same time.

33 DON'T EXPECT EVERY DAY TO BE BETTER THAN THE LAST

Some days will be slower than others, and some days might hurt a bit more than others. But as long as you're out running, it's a good day.

34 JUST... START!

If the thought of running your full session is too much to bear, just go out to run around the block. Chances are, once you're outside, you'll start to feel better and put in at least a few miles.

35 FOCUS ON THE COMPETITION

Shawn Crawford, the 2004 Olympic 200-metre gold medalist, says his two chief competitors are himself and his stopwatch, and they keep him heading out every day. "I want to break records, and you can't break records sitting at home."

36 FORGET ABOUT THE BIG PICTURE

every now and then. Put away your training manual and set aside your race calendar. Stop overthinking it all, and just run for today.

37 THINK ON... AND STRONG

Roger Bannister and John Landy (the only two men to have broken four minutes in the mile at the time) raced at the 1954 British Empire and Commonwealth Games in Vancouver in what was billed as 'The Miracle Mile.' Landy led for most of the race, but Bannister passed him on the final turn, proving it ain't over till it's over.

38 FILL THE BATH...

...with hot water, then head out for a three-miler on a freezing morning. The sooner you get back, the hotter your bath is.

39 BECOME A RACE DIRECTOR

If you live in a small town with no road races, start your own. Most towns have some sort of annual celebration in the summer, and you can tie the race to that. Work with local track and cross-country teams to help promote it.

40 STOP RUNNING IN CIRCLES

Andy Steinfeld, who coaches marathon runners, says group point-to-point runs are a fun way to add a new twist to training. His runners head out for 12 to 20 miles, then refuel at a local restaurant before hopping on the bus to ride back to the starting point.

41 LIVE IN THE NOW

Ultrarunner Scott Jurek focuses on the moment to get him through difficult patches on his long runs and races. "I tune in to my breath, my technique, and my current pace, and I stay away from what lies ahead," he says. This is an especially helpful technique when what lies ahead is another 99 miles.

42 GET SOME PERSPECTIVE

Meb Keflezighi, the Eritrean-born US runner and 2009 New York Marathon winner, listens to songs about his former country's struggle for independence from Ethiopia when he needs a boost. "The true heroes are the soldiers," he says. "Those are the real tough guys."

43 BUY A FULL-LENGTH MIRROR

Make sure you look in it every day. If you're running regularly (and eating well) you will soon see changes to your body composition that make you want to carry on.

44 TRY A TRI

Doing a chunk of your weekly miles in the pool and on the bike for a triathlon can reinvigorate your mind and body, as well as your running.

45 INVEST IN GOOD GEAR

For beginners, this may mean a good pair of running shoes to avoid injuries and technical clothes made of fabric that wicks away moisture and prevents chafing. For others, experimenting with the latest GPS unit or footpod can be a fun way to track training progress and stay motivated.

46 IGNORE THE DIRTY DISHES

They can wait till the sun goes down. Your tempo run can't. Okay?

47 BE CREATIVE

If the idea of going on your regular four-miler just sinks you further into the sofa, remember that there are other ways to put in some miles – like a game of five-a-side football. A midfielder runs up to six miles in a 90-minute football game.

48 BRING HOME SOME HARDWARE

Okay, so you're not going to win the London Marathon, but that doesn't mean you can't score a trophy. Find a few small local races where you might be able to compete for the top spots in your age group.

49 LET US HELP

We've got more where these came from. Visit runnersworld.co.uk for pages of ideas and inspiration.

RAVE RUN

Bolton Abbey, North Yorkshire

6 Cross Training

192 CROSS ROADS
Don't ignore other sports such as cycling
and swimming – they can make you a
better runner

196 CENTRE OF ATTENTION
This core workout will give you abs that
boost performance, not just appearance

202 BALANCING ACTS
Alternative techniques to prolong
your running life

206 BAND AID
A resistance-band session that builds
strength – no gym required

212 THE X FACTOR
This no-gym, outdoor workout will get you
in tip-top shape for race day

CROSS ROADS

Good cross-training can be the best way to run faster

Cross-training can be a tough concept for many runners to grasp. It's not that we don't believe that a variety of workouts is good for us. It's just that we can't work out where the time is going to come from. A 30-minute run is often difficult enough to fit in, so how are you going to swim and bike and row and all that other stuff?

Maybe we feel under pressure to put more effort into cross-training because of thae increasing interest in triathlons and other multi-discipline events. To be an elite triathlete, some people spend hours every day training. Who needs it?

Fortunately, no one but an elite athlete. The rest of us can benefit from more realistic doses of cross-training. Still, it's hard to work out how to begin, how much and what kinds of cross-training to do.

Life used to be simple. Runners ran, and swimmers swam. Cyclists pedalled and weight-lifters grunted. Then everything got mixed up. Runners started cycling, swimmers lifted weights, cyclists start running. Now, it's not unusual to see athletes climbing stairs that go nowhere, or cross-country skiing over a gym floor.

These activities may look odd but they're very good for you. You'll stretch certain muscles, strengthen others and burn plenty of calories, but what exactly can cross-training do for runners? And, given all the cross-training choices, which are the best ones for you?

THE DO MORE, GET FITTER THEORY

Proponents of this position believe that runners should cross-train with exercises and activities that are as close to running as possible.

THE LOGIC The stronger you make your running muscles, the better you'll run.

THE REST THEORY

According to this approach, runners should cross-train with sports that are as different from running as possible.

THE LOGIC You can burn calories and get a good workout, and, at the same time, you'll be resting your running muscles and won't be creating the one-sport muscle imbalances that often lead to injury.

THE SPECIFICITY THEORY

Specificity advocates believe that runners shouldn't cross-train – and that's the end of it. It's a waste of time and will only tire you for your next run. When you need a day off from running, take a day off from everything.

THE LOGIC Training is sports specific, so the best way to train for running is to run.

No wonder so many runners are confused. Who are they supposed to believe, and which theory should they follow? "All of the approaches make sense and could work," says Dr Mike Flynn, an exercise physiologist and one of America's leading researchers in cross-training.

The trick to optimising your training programme, he explains, is to pick the approach that best fits your current running and fitness goals.

To make your decision easier, we've designed cross-training programmes for five different types of runner. Simply find the category that best describes you over the page and follow the suggested advice.

TWO WHEELS GOOD
Cycling gives your running
muscles a rest but the
variety keeps you motivated

BEGINNERS

This is for runners who do 5-15 miles per week.

THE BASICS If you're running to get into shape, the first thing you need to do is build up your cardiovascular system. A strong heart and lungs will supply more fuel to your working leg muscles and allow you to run without constantly feeling out of breath.

If you're switching to running from another sport, you're probably fit enough to run a few miles without much problem, but don't overdo it. Running involves more pounding than most other sports, and it takes time for the muscles, tendons and ligaments to adapt.

THE PROGRAMME The best cross-training programme for beginners is one that mixes running and cross-training in equal amounts. If you're running twice a week, try cross-training twice a week as well. This will allow you to build your cardio system and muscle strength without undue risk of injury. Another idea: if you can't handle more than one hard run a week, split your hard workouts between running and cross-training.

'A strong heart and lungs will supply more fuel to leg muscles and allow you to run without constantly being out of breath'

THE EXERCISES As a beginner, almost any aerobic activity will help to increase your cardiovascular strength. The best exercises are those that also strengthen as many of your running muscles as possible. These exercises will improve the co-ordination of your running muscles and teach them to process and store fuel more effectively.

INTERMEDIATES

This is for runners who do 15-40 miles per week.

THE BASICS You have developed a strong cardio system through your running so easy cross-training workouts won't improve your running performance. You need to choose cross-training activities that either provide a very high-intensity cardiovascular workout or specifically target your running muscles.

THE PROGRAMME Run two to three times as much as you are cross-training. Run for two or three days, and then do cross-training. If you are doing two hard

runs a week, select cross-training workouts that allow you to exercise at a moderate pace. You should be using these workouts just to give your running muscles some extra training without extra pounding. If your body can handle only one hard run a week, then one of your cross-training workouts should be hard.

THE EXERCISES Cross-training exercises that provide high-intensity cardio workouts are cross-country skiing, stair climbing and high-cadence stationary cycling. Grinding away in a high gear on a bike will slow your turnover, but using a high cadence (over 90rpm) will keep you quick and allow you to get your heart rate up.

ADVANCED RUNNERS

This is for those who run more than 40 miles per week.

THE BASICS You have probably maximised your cardiovascular conditioning, as well as the strength of your leg muscles, so cross-training won't directly do you much good. To improve your running performance, you need more quality in your runs. Running coaches and exercise physiologists generally recommend at least two hard runs a week – a shorter interval session on the track and a longer tempo run.

THE PROGRAMME Since both hard running and high mileage can increase your injury risk, your best bet may be complete rest rather than cross-training. This will allow your muscles to recover completely for your next run. If you don't want to take days off, you can consider low-intensity cross-training with a sport that doesn't tax your running muscles. This will burn calories, and the variety will keep you mentally fresh.

If you choose to cross-train, replace one or two of your easy runs – preferably the ones that come a day after a hard run – with a cross-training activity.

THE EXERCISES Cycling, pool running, swimming and rowing will all give your running muscles a break and let them recover for your next hard run.

INJURY-PRONE RUNNERS

This is for runners who experience two or more running injuries per year.

THE BASICS Surveys show two out of three runners will be injured in the course of a year. Cross-training can help in two ways. First, it can keep you healthy by allowing you to stay fit without the constant pounding of running. Second, cross-training can help forestall the

HIT THE WATER
Swimming is a great way
to boost fitness while taking
the load off your legs

performance losses that come when an injury keeps you from running. Studies have shown that runners can maintain their running times for up to six weeks by cross-training alone if it is done at the proper intensity.

THE PROGRAMME The best cross-training programme for injury-prone runners includes two to four runs per week (depending on how much your body can tolerate) and two cross-training workouts. Both cross-training workouts should target running-specific muscles in order to increase their strength and efficiency without subjecting them to more pounding.

The extra training of these muscles through cross-training rarely produces injuries because high impact is the main injury cause, but if you're unsure, ask your doctor. And to reduce the risk, don't do more than one high-intensity workout per week.

THE EXERCISES So, injury-prone runners should keep their cross-training workouts as specific to training as possible. In-line skating, stair climbing, rowing and cross-country skiing are good choices. Unfortunately, some injuries – stress fractures in particular – don't allow many cross-training options. In these cases, cross-training in the pool by swimming or deep-water running is the best alternative. These are non-weight-bearing activities that don't hurt the legs.

GENERAL RUNNERS

This is for low- to mid-mileage runners more concerned with overall fitness than racing.

THE BASICS Look at any elite runner, and you'll notice that running doesn't do much for the upper body. It also neglects quadriceps in favour of the calves, hamstrings and buttocks. Furthermore, after the age of 30, all the muscles in bodies begin to lose strength. Fortunately, exercise can cut the rate almost in half.

THE PROGRAMME For total-body fitness, run twice a week and do a complementary exercise on one or two other days of the week. In addition, 20 minutes of circuit weight training twice a week will help you condition any muscles that you may have missed.

THE EXERCISES General-fitness runners need exercises that target the upper body and quadriceps. The best choices are rowing, swimming, cross-country skiing and cycling on a stationary bike that has attachments to work your upper body.

CENTRE OF ATTENTION

Forget crunches. If you want to get faster, fitter and stronger, you need to train your core like a runner

In the past you'd have been hard-pressed to find elite runners paying attention to their abs. Today, it's mandatory. "It's so important. The stronger the core, the more likely you are to hold your form and less likely to get injured," explains marathon world record holder Paula Radcliffe. You simply can't run your best without a strong core: the muscles in your abdominals, lower back and glutes. They provide the stability, power and endurance that runners need for powering up hills, sprinting to the finish and maintaining form mile after mile. "When

your core is strong, everything else will follow," says running coach Greg McMillan, who has worked with scores of elite and recreational runners. "It's the foundation for all of your movement, no matter what level of running you're doing."

The key is to train your core like a specialist. Quality core work isn't easy, but it doesn't require much of your time, says running coach Nick Anderson. "You don't need to put in more than 15 minutes a few times a week." It's an investment that will pay dividends on the road.

KNOW YOUR CORE

A close look at the muscle groups that make up your core

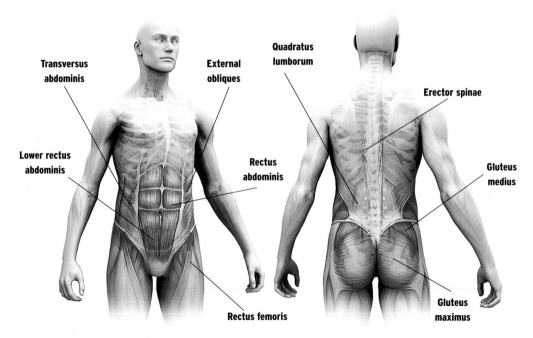

Transversus abdominis

External obliques

Quadratus lumborum

Erector spinae

Lower rectus abdominis

Rectus abdominis

Gluteus medius

Gluteus maximus

Rectus femoris

HERE'S HOW YOUR CORE WORKS FOR YOU ON THE ROAD

A strong midsection will help you maintain form, avoid injury and finish races faster. This is why...

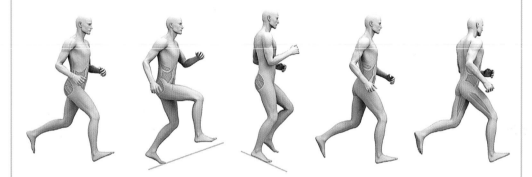

SPEED

➔ As you extend your stride or quicken the rate of your leg and foot turnover when you're trying to pick up the pace, the lower abs – including the transversus and rectus abdominis – and lower back are called into action. The stronger and more stable these muscles are, the more force and speed you can generate as you push off the ground.

UPHILLS

➔ The glutes and lower abs support the pelvis, which connects to the leg muscles needed to get uphill. If the core is strong, the legs will have a stable plane to push from, for a more powerful ascent. When you swing your leg forward, the hip-flexor muscles, such as the rectus femoris, pull on the pelvis. As you push off the ground, the glutes and hamstrings are engaged.

DOWNHILLS

➔ When you're flying down a slope, you need strong gluteal muscles to help absorb the impact and counter the momentum of the forward motion. As fun as it may be to zoom down, without the core strength to control your movement, your quads and knee joints bear the extra pounding of your body weight, which can lead to fatigue, pain and injury.

ENDURANCE

➔ As you near the end of a race, a solid core helps you maintain proper form and run efficiently, even through fatigue. With strong lower abs and lower-back muscles, such as the erector spinae, it's easier to stay upright. If your core is weak, you may end up shuffling, slouching and putting too much stress on your hips, knees and shins.

LATERAL MOVEMENT

➔ Whenever you have to suddenly move to the side – to turn the corner on a track, dodge a pothole or navigate undulating terrain – the obliques provide stability and help keep you upright. If your core is weak, then you may end up leaning into the movement, which can put excess weight and strain on the joints in your legs and feet.

BEYOND CRUNCHES

The 15-minute workout designed just for runners

Fortunately, quality core strength work doesn't require a great deal of time or equipment – just 15 minutes three times a week, a few feet of floor space and some key moves done correctly and consistently. This workout is designed by Greg McMillan, a running coach and exercise scientist, who has worked with many recreational runners and world-class athletes. The workout is devised to strengthen the specific muscles runners need for bounding up hills, sprinting to the finish, enduring long distances and preventing common running injuries. Try doing two sets of these moves right before or after your run, three times a week.

◆ SUPERMAN

WHAT IT HITS Transversus abdominis (deep abs) and erector spinae (lower back).
HOW Start face down on the floor, with your arms and legs extended out in front. Raise your head, your left arm, and right leg five inches off the floor. Hold for three counts, then lower. Repeat with your right arm and left leg. Do up to 10 reps each side.
GET IT RIGHT Don't raise your shoulders too much.
MAKE IT HARDER Lift both arms and legs at the same time.

◆ BRIDGE

WHAT IT HITS Glutes and hamstrings.
HOW Lie face up on the floor, with your knees bent 90 degrees, your feet on the floor. Lift your hips and back off the floor until your body forms a straight line from your shoulders to your knees. Hold for five to 10 seconds. Lower to the floor and repeat 10 to 12 times.
GET IT RIGHT Squeeze your glutes at the top of the movement, and don't let your spine sag.
MAKE IT HARDER Straighten one leg once your hips are lifted.

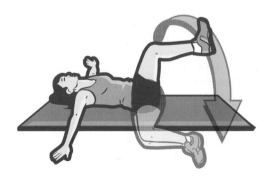

◆ METRONOME

WHAT IT HITS Obliques.
HOW Lie face up with your knees bent and raised over your hips, with your shins parallel to the ground, your feet lifted, and your arms out. Rotate your legs to the left, bringing your knees as close to the floor as possible without touching. Return to the centre, then rotate your knees to the right. Do 10 to 12 reps on each side.
GET IT RIGHT Make sure not to swing your hips or use momentum; start the movement from your core and continue to move slowly from side to side.
MAKE IT HARDER Keep your legs straight.

ALL THE RIGHT MOVES A few quick fixes will pay off on the run

⊙ THE MISTAKE
You're doing the wrong exercises

"The biggest mistake that runners tend to make is to take strength-training moves, such as crunches, straight from the fitness industry," says running coach Greg McMillan. For most runners, standard crunches aren't helpful because they don't work the deep core muscles that provide the stability to run mile after mile.

⊙ THE FIX
Do workouts that hit the muscles and movements that runners need. Try exercises like the side plank or plank lift (opposite) that strengthen the obliques, on the sides of the trunk, and the transverse abs, the deep core muscles that wrap around the trunk like a corset. These muscles stabilise the core, help counter rotation, and minimise wasteful movement so that you run more efficiently.

⊙ THE MISTAKE
You're a creature of habit

Even if you've moved beyond crunches, you may find you have slipped into a routine. "You need to constantly challenge your muscles to get results," says running coach Sam Murphy.

⊙ THE FIX
Mix it up. Fine-tune your workout to make it more difficult. Try balancing on one leg or changing your arm position. At the gym, use devices like a stability ball – an unstable platform that forces your core muscles to work harder to keep you steady. And as a rule, McMillan says, change your routine around every six weeks or so.

⊙ THE MISTAKE
You whip through your workouts

If you're flying through the moves in your workout, you're using momentum, not muscles.

⊙ THE FIX
Slow it down. Exercises like the plank, which require holding one position for 10 to 60 seconds, force you to work your muscles continuously. Even in exercises that involve repetitions, make steady – not rapid-fire – movements. "It takes intention," says Paula Coates, running coach, physiotherapist and author of *Running Repairs: A Runner's Guide to Keeping Injury Free* (A&C Black Publishers Ltd).

"Don't rush through them, and make sure you're doing them properly."

⊙ THE MISTAKE
You ignore what you don't see

Runners often have weak backs because they just forget about them, says running coach Nick Anderson. "But when you're running, especially if you're running for a long time, those muscles in the lower back are crucial for providing stability and support."

⊙ THE FIX
Include at least one exercise that hits the lower back and glutes in each workout. Moves like the bridge and superman (previous page), build muscles that support and protect the spine.

PREHAB YOUR PROBLEM AREAS TO RUN INJURY-FREE

Your core is like a power plant. If it's not working efficiently, you'll waste energy, says Tim Hilden, a physical therapist, coach and physiologist who specialises in running. "You'll see too much unwanted movement, which decreases performance or sets you up for injury." Here are three areas that can be injured as a result of a weak core.

➡ LOWER BACK

As your legs pound the pavement, your vertebrae absorb much of the force. That shock worsens if your core is weak, which will produce lower-back pain. Build those muscles with moves like the superman (previous page).

➡ HAMSTRINGS

When your core isn't stable, your hamstrings often have to work extra hard, says running coach and physiotherapist Paula Coates. The added work can leave them shorter, tighter, and more vulnerable to injury. To strengthen them, as well as your glutes, try exercises like bridges, lunges and squats.

➡ KNEES

Without a stable core, you can't control the movement of your torso as well, and you risk putting excess force on your joints each time your foot lands. This can lead to pain under the knee (known as 'runner's knee'), patellar tendinitis (a sharp pain in the bottom of the knee), and iliotibial-band tendinitis. The plank (below) strengthens the transversus abdominis, which help steady the core.

➡ SIDE PLANK

WHAT IT HITS Obliques, transversus abdominis, lower back, hips and glutes.
HOW Lie on your right side, supporting your upper body on your right forearm, with your left arm at your side. Lift your hips and, keeping your body weight supported on the forearm and the side of the right foot, extend your left arm above your shoulder. Hold for 10 to 30 seconds. Switch sides and repeat.
GET IT RIGHT Keep your hips up; don't let them sag.
MAKE IT HARDER Support your upper body with your right hand, not your forearm.

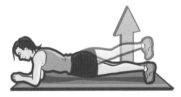

➡ PLANK LIFT

WHAT IT HITS Transversus abdominis and lower back.
HOW Begin face down on the floor, propped up on your forearms, with knees and feet together. With your elbows under your shoulders, lift your torso, legs and hips in a straight line. Hold for 10 seconds. Raise your right leg a few inches, keeping the rest of the body still. Lower and repeat with your left leg.
GET IT RIGHT Pull in your belly and don't let your hips sag.
MAKE IT HARDER Extend the time of the exercise.

FLAT OUT
The metronome works your obliques

BALANCING ACTS

Try these alternative approaches to ensure you have a long and satisfying running life

YOGA

In the early to mid-1990s, Uta Pippig (pictured opposite) was one of the best marathon runners in the world, winning Boston three times in a row. But by 2000, things had changed. "I was stuck in a rut, exhausted and mentally tired," she says. Her saviour? Yoga. "It helped me to regain my energy, improve my breathing, and find inner peace and satisfaction."

Yoga has been credited with everything from helping people to reach a higher spiritual sphere to creating Madonna's muscles (nothing to do with running and resistance work, then?). Meanwhile, runners and their coaches are divided about how much difference it will make to your performance, but as people like Pippig will testify, it offers mental space and a good stretch – which can't do any harm.

"Yoga teaches you to be in an intense situation – perhaps deep in a back-bending pose – and to bring awareness to your form and your breathing to make the situation manageable," says coach Sage Rountree. "This skill is invaluable at mile 18 of a marathon. You'll learn ways to cope that benefit you as an athlete and in life."

There are dozens of types of yoga. Treat intense classes (Ashtanga or power yoga) as hard sessions and fit them into your training accordingly. Classes in Hatha yoga are very popular and should offer a more gentle stretch. It's best to start with an instructor, but Rountree recommends developing a home-based practice that you can adjust to your running schedule: poses that stretch your muscles post-run; others that strengthen your core three times a week; and a longer routine that works the whole body on a rest day.

TRY THIS

PYRAMID
WHY Promotes stability, stretches hamstrings.
HOW Stand tall and relaxed with your right leg in front of you. Hinge forward from the hips, tilting the pelvis forwards and keeping the back straight, with your knee slightly bent. Interlace your fingers behind your back and stretch them up and away from you. Repeat on the other side.

REVERSE TABLE
WHY Strengthens your abs and back.
HOW Sit with your knees bent, feet on the floor, hands directly under your shoulders with your fingers spread. Push up through your hands and feet until your torso and thighs are parallel to the floor.

LUNGE WITH TWIST
WHY Stretches the hips.
HOW Step your left foot back; lower down so your knee and toes rest on the ground and your front knee is just beyond a

right-angle. Put your palms together and keep your shoulders down. Twist from the waist and rest your left triceps on your right quad. Look over your shoulder. Repeat on the other side.

PILATES

Core strength is a popular term these days – you've probably seen it in the papers – but the idea of strengthening your back, abdominal and pelvic muscles to benefit your whole body isn't new. Joseph Pilates called the core the 'powerhouse'. Pilates was a German-born sportsman and fitness trainer, and began developing his method while training other inmates in a prisoner-of-war camp during the First World War. Afterwards, he moved to New York where, with his wife, he set up his first studio, teaching 'Contrology', the system now known as Pilates.

Runners are often advised to take up Pilates to prevent injury, but you'll need patience because Pilates is meant to be performed slowly.

There are different approaches to Pilates, but all of them can benefit runners. It can be performed using special equipment, or on a mat. Your pelvic floor should be contracted throughout, but not strongly. Breathe "laterally" into the sides of your chest (use a mirror to watch your chest expanding, or have a partner check with their hands on your ribs), so you can hold your tummy in through the exercises. Perform movements on the exhalation.

TRY THIS

PLANK AND V
WHY Works core, stretches calves, hamstrings and back
HOW
1 Start in a plank – face down in a press-up position, supported by your forearms and toes. Your back should be straight, tummy in and pelvic floor lightly contracted.
2 Push your hips and bottom up and let your heels drop so you're in an inverted V position. Return to the plank. Repeat 10 times, slowly, without resting.

REVERSE CRUNCH AND V
WHY Works core and back
HOW
1 Start on your back with your arms by your side and pull your tummy in and use your stomach muscles to pull your hips up and legs over your head. Take your legs apart, then together.
2 Roll down and up into an upright V position. As you come up, bring your arms up and lightly hold the outside of your legs to help you balance. In the V position, take your legs apart and together again, roll back down to the floor and start the movement again. Repeat 10 times.

SIDE KICKS AND FIGURE OF EIGHT
WHY Works the core, glutes and outer thigh muscles
HOW
1 Lie on your side with a rolled towel between your head and bottom arm for support. Contract your abs and lift both legs slightly. Move one leg forward and one leg back, then switch.
2 When you've completed 10, keep your legs off the floor and raise your upper leg slightly. Point your toes and draw a sideways figure of eight, keeping your upper body still. Build up to 10. Repeat on the other side.

ALEXANDER TECHNIQUE

You may have heard that it's best to "run tall", but few of us know what it means. You can force it, but you'll probably stick your chest out. A trained teacher in the Alexander Technique can help you find the position that frees up your legs and arms.

Frederick Alexander was an Australian performer who specialised in monologues, but he suffered from hoarseness. He noticed that he tensed up when performing, and set about letting go of the habits that were affecting his voice. The result, now known as Alexander Technique (AT), is used to help everyone from musicians to sportspeople. AT teacher and sportsman Malcolm Balk has applied it to running, working with Shields to describe an approach to the sport that uses elements of the Pose and Chi running methods but centres on the principles of AT, including the relationship between the head, neck and spine.

You'll need patience and hands-on guidance to follow this approach so should forget about times while you're learning. One of the main principles is avoiding 'end-gaining' – you think, "I'm going to run 20 minutes for 5K and if I don't I'll feel terrible." Which is rubbish – don't set yourself up for failure."

TRY THIS... RW DID!

THE ART OF RUNNING WORKSHOP

Bad running techniques are picked up over years, so you might wonder how much you can learn about running well in three hours. The answer is: a lot. I've been running for nine years but snatch PBs between bouts of injury. I spend my day slouched over a desk and carry my bad habits with me on every run, so I was interested to find out what Malcolm Balk and Liz Dodgson, both AT experts, would make of my gait.

Video analysis showed that I used an up-and-down, heel-striking gait. Balk explained the problems with this: striking in front of the body causes braking, while the exaggerated push off the ground wastes energy.

The rest of the workshop was aimed at re-learning how to run, beginning with some AT basics: Balk and Dodgson helped me find a comfortable, aligned position lying down. Moving outside, we paired up to support each other's necks, to give an awareness

of walking with a long spine and balanced head. We ran through some drills designed to encourage a more efficient running action: swinging each leg to engage the hamstrings and glutes; lightly pawing the ground to learn the 'wheel-like' action of the correct gait; and lightly bouncing then jogging on the spot on the midfoot. Then it was time

to put this together into a new, momentum-aided run.

Few of us got it right first time. Physically, it was easier than I expected but mentally it felt strange. "If it doesn't feel weird, something's wrong," said Balk. "That would mean you're slipping back into your old habits."

So, no-one came away with a set, super-efficient stride,

but a second video analysis showed improvements. Balk himself admitted he still has to think about running well every time he goes out. What the workshop gave me was the tools to give my own running that consideration, instead of pounding out step after injury-inducing step.

Find out more at theartofrunning.com.

GET THE PICTURE
Balk holds his own style up for analysis

STRETCHING OUT
To help find the right gait

STARTING POINT
The importance of proper alignment

A HELPING HAND
Learning how to walk tall

BAND AID

Running's your thing. Pumping iron isn't. But strength training can toughen you up, so we've come up with a solution: a fast, simple routine that'll improve your running – no iron required

Strength training is a bit like flossing: we know it's good for us, but we don't do it as often as we should. But successful runners do more than just run – they lift and lunge to build strong muscles for climbing hills, maintaining perfect form and preventing injuries. But it can be hard to run well when you're recovering from a weights workout. Plus, squeezing running into your schedule can be tough enough as it is. And you probably don't want to join a gym; after all, one of the reasons you're a runner is that you can do it wherever you are.

Well, enough excuses: Tom Sheehan, director of strength and conditioning at Columbia University in the US, has designed a resistance-band programme for

'Bands boost core stability, balance and power – all of which improve performance'

runners that provides all the benefits of lifting weights with none of the hassles. The bands put constant tension on the body, which produces a challenging cardiovascular workout. Also, the resistance provided by the bands doesn't overload joints like a dumbbell can. As a result, there's less risk of injury, more work that can be performed in a single session, and faster recovery between workouts.

"Your knees, shoulders and back won't hurt the next day," says Sheehan, "so there's minimal impact on your running." Several of the exercises in the band programme require multiple muscles to work simultaneously to perform a single move. "The bands work on synchronising the lower and upper body,

which helps provide core stability, balance and muscular power – all things that can improve a runner's performance," says Sheehan.

GETTING STARTED

Here's how you can jump on the bandwagon: get hold of some bands (try fitmag.co.uk, where you can also get interchangeable handles and clip tubes), and a bench. Two or three times a week, put in your miles first, and then do one of the workouts below, alternating between them. Each takes 20 to 30 minutes. Except where noted, do three sets of 20 reps. Increase the reps each week until you get to 50, then increase the resistance.

FULL-BODY WORKOUT OPTIONS

WORKOUT 1
- Overhead press and squat
- Two-leg squat
- Overhead tricep extension
- Abs/lower-back extension
- Bench press

WORKOUT 2
- Overhead press and back lunge
- Single-leg squat
- One-arm row
- Shoulder press
- Overhead tricep extension
- Abs/lower-back extension

⊖ OVERHEAD PRESS AND SQUAT

Attach two bands to the handles, then stand on the bottom band with both feet. Holding the top band, press your arms up and out to a 45-degree angle so your body looks like a 'Y'.

Bend your knees and squat until your thighs are parallel with the floor – go lower if you can. Return to standing, then lower your arms to your shoulders. Repeat.

BENCH PRESS

1 Wrap the band around the back leg of the bench. Lie back on the bench with your feet flat on it. Hold the handles with your elbows bent and your hands in line with your chest.

2 Press your arms straight up until your hands are over mid-chest. Lower and repeat.

TWO-LEG SQUAT

1 Secure the band underneath the bench. Holding the handles, stand on the bench with your arms straight down at your sides. Feet should be shoulder-width apart, chest over midfoot, hips back, knees behind toes.

2 Bending at the knee and hip, lower yourself down for a three-second count until you get to a quarter-squat position. Pause for a moment, then, pushing through your midfoot, drive upwards to full extension. This three-seconds down, pause, up-fast should be one continuous movement. Repeat.

➲ OVERHEAD TRICEP EXTENSION

① Using two bands attached to the handles, stand on the lower band with your right foot and pull the upper band up behind your head so your elbows are bent at 90 degrees. Your elbows should be near your ears.

② Maintaining tension on the band, press your arms overhead by extending at the elbows only. Return to the starting position and repeat.

➲ ABS/LOWER-BACK EXTENSION

① Lie flat on your back with the band under the bottom of your feet. Grab the band under the handles and hold it at your hips with your arms fully extended on the floor.

② Keeping your arms and legs straight, jackknife your arms and legs up until the body is in a 'V' position with just your upper buttocks on the floor. Push back down to full, flat extension on the floor. (Note: a more resistant band places emphasis on the lower back; a lighter band makes the abs work harder.) Do two sets of 30 to 50 reps.

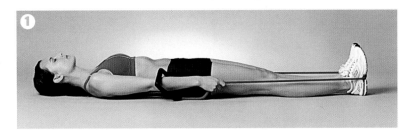

⮕ ONE-ARM ROW

① Secure the middle part of the band under the front leg of the bench. With your left foot on the floor and your right knee on the bench, hold the handle in your left hand. Your right palm should be flat on the bench under your right shoulder and your back should be straight.

② Leading the move with your elbow, pull the handle into your waist. Lower and repeat, doing all reps on the left side, then switch sides and do the same on the right side.

⮕ OVERHEAD PRESS AND BACK LUNGE

① Attach two bands to the handles, then stand on the lower band with your left foot while holding the upper band at a 45-degree angle so your body looks like a 'Y'.

② Maintaining tension on the bands, step your right foot back two to three feet and drop your right knee down until it almost touches the floor and your left thigh becomes parallel with the floor. Keep your weight on your front foot – your back leg is for balance only. Pushing up through the front foot, return your feet to the start position, and lower arms to shoulders. Do 20 reps lunging back with right foot, then switch sides.

⊖ SINGLE-LEG SQUAT

① Secure the band underneath the bench and stand with your left foot on it, holding the handle in your left hand. Your right leg should be straight and hanging off the bench, even with your left leg.

② Push your hips back and down just as in the two-leg squat, into the quarter-squat position. Push through your left foot to full extension. Repeat.

⊖ SHOULDER PRESS

① Sit on the bench with the band secured under the front leg. Hold the handle in your right hand and bend your right elbow 90 degrees so your hand is facing forward at eye level.

② Press your arm straight up so your bicep is close to your right ear. Lower and repeat. Then do another complete set on the opposite side.

THE X FACTOR

Forget Simon Cowell – Crossfit will help you run faster, stronger and longer so you always hit the right note come race day

Looking for a performance booster that will slap on running-specific muscle and kick you into your best race shape? Try Crossfit, a blend of resistance exercises and intense running sessions. The best bit: everyone uses the same programme. These three sessions from Andrew Stemler of Crossfit London (stemlerfit.com) will help you clock faster times without going near a gym. Perform a few sessions a week. Treat each as a quality workout, so bookend with a day of easy running.

2 PRESS-UPS (x100)

A Lie face down on the ground. Support your body with the balls of your feet and position your hands slightly wider than shoulder-width apart. Keep your arms straight.
B With a straight back, lower yourself to the floor. Push back up. To make it easier, keep knees on the ground – this reduces the lifting load by about half.

3 BODYWEIGHT SQUATS (x200)

A Standing with your feet shoulder-width apart, keeping your back straight and looking forward, bend your hips and knees to lower yourself until the bottoms of your thighs touch your calves. Keep your knees in line with your feet.
B Rise to the start position and imagine you're pulling the ground apart with your feet to involve your glutes.

1 Run 2km at whatever pace you feel comfortable with.

BOOST ENDURANCE

"Perform the circuit once, as fast as you can," says Stemler. "Take as many rest periods between the exercises as you need to. You tire out all your muscles and keep running – this teaches your body to push through fatigue and builds incredible stamina."

2 PULL-UPS (x20)

A Grab a pull-up bar with an overhand grip that's shoulder-width apart. Hang at arm's length so your elbows are completely extended.
B Bend your elbows to pull yourself up until your chin crosses the plane of the bar. Pause, then slowly lower yourself to the starting position without allowing your body to sway.

5 Run 3km at whatever pace you feel comfortable with.

ILLUSTRATION: ACUTE GRAPHICS

1 Run 400 metres at whatever pace you feel comfortable with.

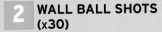

BUILD POWER

"Perform this circuit as many times as you can in 25 minutes and you'll get legs that'll carry you anywhere," says Stemler. "It builds lower-body strength to power you up hills."

2 ### WALL BALL SHOTS (x30)

A Positioned 4ft away from a tall wall, with your feet shoulder-width apart and a medicine ball (or football) in both hands in front of your chest, sink into the deepest squat you can.

B Explode upwards. Straighten your arms, letting the ball fly to a target on the wall about 10ft up. Catch it, then return to the start position and repeat.

3 ### BOX JUMPS (x30)

A With your feet shoulder-width apart in front of a 24-inch box or park bench, bend your knees until the bottom of your thighs are parallel to the floor.

B Jump up onto the box, landing with both feet together. Fling your arms above your head to generate momentum. Step back down and repeat.

1 Run 400 metres at your fastest pace.

IMPROVE PACE

"Perform the circuit five times," says Stemler. Scribble down the time it takes you to complete, then try to beat it next time. "In time you'll be able to run faster with less effort."

2 ### OVERHEAD SQUATS (x15)

A Stand with your feet shoulder-width apart and hold a medicine ball above your head. Your arms should be directly above your shoulders.

B Keeping your back straight, squat until the bottoms of your thighs touch your calves. Stand up, imagining that you're pulling the ground apart with your feet.

3 ### BODYWEIGHT LUNGES (10 ON EACH LEG)

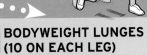

A Take a giant step forward with your left foot and bend your left knee until the bottom of your left thigh is parallel to the ground. Your back should remain straight throughout.

B Reverse the motion, stepping back into the starting position. Repeat with your right leg.

RAVE RUN

Sugar Loaf Hill, Kent

7 Weight Loss

FAREWELL FAT

Run faster, eat better and lose 10 pounds in the next month

You're either a runner or you want to be one. And you would like to be in good shape. But even if you are not clinically obese that doesn't mean you're entirely satisfied with your current weight and that you're not interested in losing a few pounds in order to become healthier, feel better and run stronger.

To demonstrate how easy that could be, we've set out a plan. The goal: lose 10lb this month. The modus operandi: run a series of fat-burning workouts each week; then watch what and how much you eat.

Now let's look at the numbers. To lose a pound, you have to burn roughly 3,500 calories. Ten pounds a month is 2.5 pounds a week. So you need to create an 8,750-calorie deficit each week – or 1,250 calories a day.

Wait! Before you throw up your hands in despair over these impossible-sounding targets (and reach for the Haägen Dazs for comfort), remember that daily calorie input and output is a big numbers game.

Your body burns thousands of calories each day just sitting around. For instance, a 12-stone man burns 1,850 calories a day at rest and another 1,600 through normal daily activity. That's a total of 3,450 calories per day. Then, if he runs 30 minutes at seven-minute mile pace he burns another 540, which brings the total up to 3,990 a day. If he follows the weight-loss guidelines in this chapter to create a 1,250-calorie deficit each day, he can still consume 2,740 calories. All these principles apply to women too, but on a smaller scale. Because women weigh less and have slower metabolisms, they burn fewer calories than men over the same activity. Now the numbers aren't so daunting, let's take a closer look at how to lose those pounds.

RUNNING STRATEGIES THAT BURN CALORIES

Running is the most efficient way to shed weight. For our 12st man, running for 30 minutes at 10-minute mile pace will burn about 385 calories. Of course, there's the time-proven long run, which puts the body in the fat-burning zone, but these days, the shift is towards faster sessions, which burn calories and fat much more efficiently. A study at the University of Texas showed that fast running burns 33 per cent more fat per minute than slower running. That can be a big help when you're trying to lose weight and are pressed for time.

We've selected some of the best calorie-consuming, fat-burning training sessions. Do two or three a week. On the other days, run easy for 20-30 minutes or do some relaxed cross-training such as cycling, swimming or stair-climbing.

LONG RUNS Run slowly for at least 45 minutes to an hour; one and a half to two hours would be ideal. The slow pace – which puts your metabolism in the fat-burning zone – coupled with the long period of time

WHEN IS THE BEST TIME TO BURN CALORIES?

If you're trying to lose weight through running and gym workouts, is it better to burn calories by working out before eating, or afterwards?

The timing of your meals won't change the number of calories burned during a workout (for running, that's about 100 calories per mile).

However, timing will affect how you feel and perform when you train. If you're not properly fuelled up, a workout can leave you feeling tired and shaky, and this will compromise the intensity and duration of your exercise.

To make sure you have plenty of fuel in the tank, eat two to four hours before your workouts. Include easily digested foods that are high in carbohydrates – such as pasta, cereal, yoghurt and fruit and veg. To speed recovery, refuel immediately after your workouts with more carbohydrate-rich foods, plus a bit of protein from foods such as lean beef, chicken or fish and skimmed or soya milk.

For optimum weight loss, it's also important to balance calorie intake with physical activity level throughout the day. Eat more when you are more active, and less when you are less active.

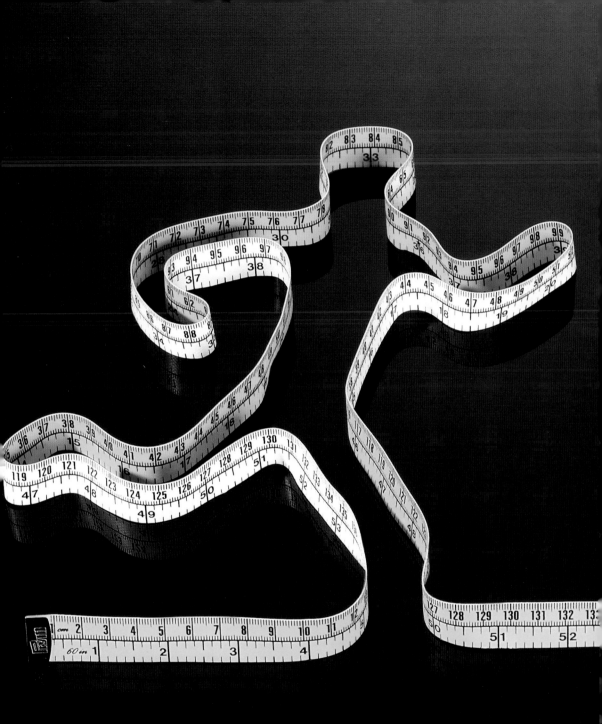

TALE OF THE TAPE
The right mix of running
and nutrition will
reduce your waistline

maximises total fat burning. A 90-minute long run for a 12-stone man can burn more than 1,000 calories.

TEMPO RUNS If you have just 20-30 minutes to run, your best bet is to pick up the pace. The faster you run in those 20-30 minutes, the more fat you'll burn, because your total energy cost is up. A 12st man on a tempo run of 30 minutes can burn more than 450 calories.

SPEED SESSIONS After a five-minute warm-up, try running one to three minutes at 85-95 per cent effort, then walk or jog for recovery. Do five to 10 of these fast intervals in a session, then finish with a five-minute cool-down. Speedwork also produces an "afterburn" effect. That is, you keep burning calories at a high level even after you've stopped running. This can sometimes amount to as much as 200 extra calories, and fast running suppresses your appetite for an hour or two, so you'll eat less and lose more.

A speed workout that includes 8 x 2 minutes at 90 per cent effort (with a five-minute warm-up and cool-down) can burn more than 700 calories (including afterburn) for a 12st man.

SCALE DOWN
Eat smaller portions
and the scales won't lie

PUMP UP THE WEIGHT LOSS

By adding a once- or twice-weekly weight-training session to your schedule, you not only burn more calories when you are working out (115 every 30 minutes for our 12st runner) – but also when you are just sitting around. That's because as you add muscle, your resting metabolism rises. A good workout is circuit training – laps around the weight room, doing all the standard machine exercises, one right after another. When you can lift a weight 15 times easily, set it at a higher level. Five pounds is a good increase for upper-body exercises; 10lb for the lower body.

EATING STRATEGIES THAT BURN CALORIES

While you're revving up your running, ease back a little on your eating. Don't worry – you don't have to starve yourself. In fact, taking in too few calories slows your metabolism and makes it harder to lose weight. By simply making a few adjustments to your usual diet, you can cut calories quickly.

You don't need a calorie counter to plan low-fat meals, just some common sense. Eat less, on the basis that your battle isn't against food, but against too much food. Learn to be polite but firm at Sunday lunch when

your mum passes the roast potatoes the second time. When you eat at home, cut your serving size. "It's the number one way to cut calories," says John Allred, co-author of *Taking The Fear Out Of Eating: A Nutritionists' Guide to Sensible Food Choices* (Cambridge University Press). If you usually have two slices of bread with dinner, eat one. If you have 170g of pasta, have 110g.

Allred also suggests using smaller dinner plates. "That way, you still have a full plate of food in front of you, but you'll be eating less," he says.

The flipside is to eat more often. Many sumo wrestlers skip breakfast on purpose. They want to drive up hunger and slow their metabolism so when they dive into a fat-filled lunch, it sticks to their ribs (and bellies and sides) like glue. You, of course, don't want to look like a sumo wrestler. By eating three small meals a day, plus healthy snacks, you keep hunger on an even keel (avoiding overeating, the real enemy), and your metabolism runs at an even burn.

First, don't skip breakfast. Nancy Clark, author of *Nancy Clark's Sports Nutrition Guidebook* (Human Kinetics), says a good breakfast is one of the most potent weapons for losing weight. It keeps your metabolism turning over, prevents hunger and overeating at lunch, and makes you more likely to eat high-quality foods during the day. A good breakfast and afternoon snack will give you energy to burn.

You almost certainly know your weak spots (ice cream, croissants, pizza, whatever). Set up a defence. If you crave ice cream, don't have it in the freezer. It's okay to indulge once in a while, but try the low-fat treats available, and consume them in moderation. But remember, despite the "healthy" labels, these snacks do still have plenty of calories, so eat them sparingly.

MAKE NEW HABITS

There are plenty of little things you can do with your diet that will make a big difference in your weight-loss efforts. Here are five of them...

DON'T MIX FAT AND SUGAR A burger, large fries and cola is a bad combination to begin with, but it's doubly unhealthy because it acts as a hidden invitation to your body to pack on fat. The simple sugars in carbonated drinks cause a release of insulin into your bloodstream, which makes fat cells more prone to storing fat.

MAN CANNOT LIVE BY CARBS ALONE Protein and a little fat help to keep you satiated for longer and prevent you from overeating. "Fat and protein stay with you longer," says Clark. For example, if you have a plain toasted bagel and a fruit juice for breakfast, you'll be hungry again an hour later, but if you spread a little peanut butter on the bagel, you'll be fuller for longer.

EAT A COMPLEX DIET So you want loads of energy to burn all day? Eat lots of complex carbohydrates: fresh

fruits, veg, whole grains and legumes. Complex carbs take longer to burn than simple sugars, giving you energy and staving off hunger at the same time.

HOLD THE MAYO Fish is a healthy option, right? But mixing tuna with mayonnaise adds hundreds of fat calories to a tuna salad sandwich. Instead, try mixing the tuna with chilli sauce, lemon juice or mustard.

ONE STEP AT A TIME According to sports nutritionist Kris Clark, you'll have the most success changing a dietary habit if you take the simplest approach. "When I spot a problem in an athlete's food record, I have my clients stay with one dietary change for as long as it takes to become habit. "Once we are successful with the first change, we can go on to the second."

It's like the way you learned to run. First one mile, then two... It's the same thing with your diet. Take your time. Don't set unattainable goals. Stay focused on the task and let patience and discipline work their magic.

11 SHORTCUTS TO FASTER FAT LOSS

Read on to reach your fat-loss finish line in the fastest way

1 GO LONG

Increase your total training mileage to 20 miles a week, and you'll lose abdominal fat even without decreasing your calorie intake, according to a report in the *Journal of Applied Physiology*. This is backed up by another study that found that substantial weight loss didn't occur unless running distances were more than 15.5 miles (25K) per week for men, and 29.8 miles (48K) per week for women.

2 LOW-FAT, SCHMO-FAT

Want to stay niggle-free throughout your fat-shedding quest (and beyond)? Give low-fat diets a wide berth. Studies have revealed that runners who got less than 30 per cent of their calories from fat were 2.5 times more likely to suffer injuries. Researchers believe this is down to a lower intake of vitamin K, deficiencies of which can increase the risk of bone fractures.

3 GO SOLO (IF YOU'RE A WOMAN)

Surely teaming up with your partner will spur you on to greater losses? Not according to one 16-month study reported in the *Archives of Internal Medicine*. Examining exercise for weight loss, and how it affects the genders, researchers discovered that with the same amount of exercise, the male participants lost 11.5lbs while the women only managed to maintain their weight.

4 BUY BELLY BLITZING KIT

Using a pedometer to track your mileage can motivate you to stay on your feet for longer – and lose extra pounds – according to a study published by the *Journal of the American Medical Association*. A survey at Stanford University School of Medicine revealed that pedometer users tended to walk an extra kilometre and half a day compared with those you exercised without.

Nike+ Sportband measures distance, time, pace and calories burned

MONDAY	TUESDAY	WEDNESDAY	THURSDAY	FRIDAY	SATURDAY	SUNDAY

5 RUN STRONGER IN 1 WEEK

Shifting just 2.2lbs – an average loss in the first week of a new regime – can give your running a real boost, physically as well as mentally. "A 2004 study found that aerobic demand increases by one per cent for every 2.2lbs carried on the trunk," says Stan Reents, author of *Sport and Exercise Pharmacology*. While aerobic demand doesn't correlate directly with decreased performance, Reents says there's enough of a relationship to suggest that losing extra pounds can make a difference to your running performance.

6 STICK TO IT

Don't give up. Weight gained during off weeks can't be lost by simply resuming a previous routine, according to studies at the Lawrence Berkeley National Laboratory, USA. Researchers say weight gain among those who decreased their weekly running distances was significantly more than weight loss among those who increased weekly distances by the same amount.

7 DO ONE MARATHON A WEEK

Calm down – you don't have to run a 26.2-miler every week. You can still feel the burn at a much slower pace. According to a study at the US Institute of Medicine, people who walk 60 to 90 minutes a day – equivalent to covering a marathon a week – tended to shed at least two stone in total and kept the weight off for six years.

8 8 IS THE MAGIC NUMBER

Running intervals? Eight-second blasts of effort are fat melters, say researchers at the University of New South Wales, Australia. They found that participants who followed a 20-minute cycling regime, in which they sprinted on a stationary bike for eight seconds followed by 12 seconds of cycling lightly, lost more weight than those who cycled at a steady pace for 40 minutes.

9 FINISH FAST

Want to torch a few extra calories at the end of your training run? It's simple: finish fast. "Choose a distance appropriate to your fitness and goals. Complete all but the last five minutes at a comfortable aerobic pace, then run at approximately your 5K race pace," says coach Nick Anderson. A 68kg runner will burn around 390 calories for a 30-minute run.

10 LOVE HILLS

OK, they can be tough. But hills are most certainly a fat-burning ally. "Generally, you can count on a 10 per cent increase in calories burned for each degree of incline," says Dr. Jana Klauer from St. Luke's-Roosevelt Hospital in New York. "So, running at a five per cent incline will burn 50 per cent more calories than running on a flat surface, and running on a 10 per cent incline doubles your calorie burn."

11 KNOW YOUR BURN

When losing weight, the best way to keep up with your progress is by finding out how many calories you burn when you run, using your pace and weight, below:

PACE	59KG	73KG	86KG
12 MIN/MILE	472 cals/hr	582 cals/hr	691 cals/hr
11 MIN/MILE	532 cals/hr	655 cals/hr	734 cals/hr
10 MIN/MILE	591 cals/hr	727 cals/hr	864 cals/hr
9 MIN/MILE	650 cals/hr	800 cals/hr	950 cals/hr
8 MIN/MILE	709 cals/hr	873 cals/hr	1,036 cals/hr
7 MIN/MILE	827 cals/hr	1,018 cals/hr	1,209 cals/hr
6 MIN/MILE	945 cals/hr	1,163 cals/hr	1,382 cals/hr

THE RUNNER'S GUIDE TO WEIGHT LOSS

Conventional dieting wisdom doesn't work for runners.
It leaves you hungry, tired, and... overweight. So
we updated seven popular weight-loss strategies
to help you drop pounds for good

DIETER'S STRATEGY	DEVELOP A RUNNING ROUTINE AND STICK TO IT
RUNNER'S STRATEGY	**MIX UP YOUR ROUTINE WITH NEW TYPES OF WORKOUTS**

Anyone trying to lose weight knows that he or she needs to work out on a nearly daily basis – and that's not easy. So to stay on track, dieters develop a workout routine (that often includes lots of steady, slowish runs) and then stick to it no matter what. "People are comfortable doing what they know," says Pete McCall, an exercise physiologist with the American Council on Exercise. "If you're a runner, you feel comfortable with a specific pace or distance."

Sticking to that routine brings dieters security. While running an easy three-miler a few days a week is better for weight loss than sprawling on the sofa, there is a smarter approach. Break out of your routine by boosting your intensity and doing different types of workouts (like a weekly long run or a day of cross-training) to challenge your body and burn more calories.

"It's a lot like city driving versus motorway driving," says McCall. "When running a long, slow distance, your body becomes really efficient at using oxygen. The more times you do the same distance, the easier it gets and the fewer calories you burn. Sprinting is like starting and stopping a car, which uses more petrol."

REAL RUNNER

GAVIN WREN,
31, Twickenham
I promised myself I'd give
up smoking before my 30th
birthday, and I did it with
a month to spare. I was
already quite heavy, but
after quitting I piled on more weight, and I was up to 16
stone (101kg) by March 2008. I didn't want to have to
start buying the next size up in jeans so I decided to do
something about it. I joined a gym, but just didn't get on
well in that environment. By comparison, running is such
an easy thing to slip in to. I'm asthmatic, so I couldn't go
far at first. To supplement my running I rowed 5,000m
on my ergo twice a week and biked five miles to and
from work twice a week. In seven months I lost nearly
four stone (25kg). Now I'm running about 45 miles a
week. I'm training for a sub-40 minute 10K. I've also
done a 1:30 half-marathon.

BREAK OUT OF A RUT

A 10.7 stone (68kg) runner doing four miles at nine-minute-mile pace burns about 480 calories. But you can torch more calories by swapping that four-miler with one of these high-intensity workouts one to three times a week.

RUT BUSTER	WHAT	WHY	HOW	CALORIES BURNED
INTERVALS	Alternating sprints of a certain distance (such as 400m) with recovery laps; often done at a measured track.	Sprinting at high speeds makes your body work harder and burns up to 30 per cent more calories to keep up with the demand.	➡ 4 x 400m hard, separated by an easy 400m recovery lap. ➡ 8 x 200m hard, separated by 200m easy. ➡ 4 x 100m hard, walking back to the start between sprints.	700
FARTLEK TRAINING	A less formal version of intervals; the term actually means "speed play" in Swedish.	Like interval workouts, fartlek sessions make your body burn more calories to match the demand of running faster.	On a 45-minute run, pick a tree about 50m away. Run hard until you reach it, and then slow down until recovered. Carry on alternating between landmarks.	540
HILL RUNS	This workout is exactly what it sounds like: running uphill for a period of time.	Hills require more force to overcome the angle of the incline, leading to a challenging cardio workout; it's also a great way to strengthen the larger muscles of the legs.	Find a steep hill of 40m to 80m. ➡ Start with 10 reps, building to 20. Run up and jog back down. ➡ 5 runs at 50 per cent max. ➡ 2 to 3 runs at 80 per cent max; 1 sprint at max speed.	600

DIETER'S STRATEGY — EAT LOW-FAT FOODS
RUNNER'S STRATEGY — EAT THE RIGHT FATS

Though the fat-free craze peaked in the 1990s, many dieters still avoid oils, butter, nuts and other fatty foods. Their logic: if you don't want your body to store fat, then don't eat fat. Many dieters also know that one gram of fat packs nine calories, while protein and carbohydrate both contain just four calories per gram.

But the logic of having fat in your diet has risen to the fore again. "I think it's a pretty antiquated thought now that we need to eliminate fat to lose weight," says Jonny Bowden, author of *The 150 Most Effective Ways to Boost Energy Naturally* (Fair Winds Press). In fact, eating moderate amounts of fat can actually help you lose weight. The key is to make sure you're eating the right kinds.

Saturated and trans fats are unhealthy because they raise your levels of LDL (so-called 'bad cholesterol'). Trans fats may also lower your HDL (or 'good cholesterol') levels and increase your risk of heart disease and weight gain. But unsaturated fats (which include the mono- and polyunsaturated varieties) have important benefits. For example, they...

1 KEEP YOU SATISFIED

Unsaturated fats promote satiety, reduce hunger and minimally impact blood sugar. That's important because if your blood sugar dips too low, you may experience cravings, brain fog, overeating and low energy, making it "fiendishly difficult to lose weight", according to Bowden.

2 PROTECT HEART HEALTH

Monounsaturated fats found in vegetable oils (such as olive and canola oil) and avocados have the added power to help lower LDL and reduce your risk of heart disease.

3 REDUCE INJURY

Eating unsaturated fats can actually help stave off injuries, such as stress fractures. A 2008 study in the *Journal of the International Society of Sports Nutrition* found that female runners on low-fat diets particularly are at increased risk of getting injured – and of course a sidelined runner can't burn as many calories.

REAL RUNNER

ALYSON KNOWLES, 49, Cumbria In September 2006, I weighed 13.7 stone (87kg). Around that time my dad had a major heart operation. With heart disease being hereditary, I really wanted to slim down. I'd tried all the fad diets with little success. Then I started nutritionist Rosemary Conley's plan and I became more aware of what I was putting into my body, keeping saturated fats like cheese and cream out of my diet. The more training I've done, I've been able to reintroduce healthier fats – such as avocado and nuts. These days I'm much fitter, my energy levels are up and I'm 10 stone (63.5kg).

DIETER'S STRATEGY   CUT OUT CARBS TO LOSE WEIGHT

RUNNER'S STRATEGY   HAVE QUALITY CARBS IN EVERY MEAL

In the past decade, the Atkins diet and other low-carb spin-offs have become as popular as 100-calorie snack packs. It's understandable why dieters would find these plans attractive – just eat high-protein, high-fat foods, and shun carbs – to drop pounds. "The theory behind reducing carbs is that it helps control blood-sugar and insulin surges," says Jonny Bowden, author of *The 150 Most Effective Ways to Boost Energy Naturally* (Fair Winds Press). "When you eat a high-carb food, insulin carries the sugar to muscles. But if your muscles don't use the energy, it gets stored in fat cells." This is what leads to weight gain.

It's a different story for runners, however. We need carbs because they're our main source of glucose, a sugar that our brains and muscles use as fuel. Most glucose is stored in muscles and the liver as glycogen and used as energy when we run. But the body can only store a limited amount of glycogen, so if you haven't eaten enough carbs, you'll literally run out of fuel.

Keeping carbs in your diet will have a domino effect, says sports nutritionist Barbara Lewin. Your energy levels will stay high, your workouts will improve and you'll have more zip throughout the day. All this leads the way to a greater calorie burn and weight loss. Just keep in mind that "the kind of carbohydrates you eat makes all the difference in the world," says Bowden. Here's a quick guide to choosing the right ones for the right times:

1 SLOW-BURNING CARBS

These are high in fibre and are slowly digested. They keep your blood-sugar steady, provide long-lasting energy, and should be a staple of your diet. Get them in oatmeal and other whole grains, beans, lentils, fruit and vegetables.

2 FAST-BURNING CARBS

These carbs are digested quickly, are low in fibre and have a greater effect on your blood sugar. They also provide a quick hit of energy that's useful to runners right before working out, but they should be eaten in moderation. Get them in pasta, white rice, white flour, potatoes and cornflakes.

REAL RUNNER

DAVID WHYTE, 30, West Dunbartonshire
At 26 I weighed 24 stone (152kg) and had no energy. My boss kept badgering me to join jogscotland, which uses gentle walk/jog programmes to get people active. I gave it a bash. At the same time I cut the junk out of my diet –and introduced good energy-giving carbs, including whole grains. I started seeing the benefits straight away, the weight was dropping off and I had more energy all the time – which meant I didn't feel like I'd made any sacrifices, and was inspired to keep running. I've lost eight stone (51kg).

IMAGE: DOM BOWER

DIETER'S STRATEGY | CUT 500 CALORIES A DAY TO LOSE 1 POUND

RUNNER'S STRATEGY | REDUCE CALORIE INTAKE BASED ON PERSONAL NEEDS

You've probably heard of the 500 rule: slash 500 calories a day to lose one pound a week. "It's a nice, clean rule," says Lewin, and can help weight loss – at least for a while. The problem for runners, though, is that slashing that many calories can be too much. "You might not be able to work out as well or maintain muscle mass," says Lewin. So rather than cutting 500 calories, runners should work to identify the number of calories they need to eat to lose weight. Here's how...

1 COUNT CALORIES

Track your intake by keeping a food journal for one week. Write down everything you eat and note your energy and hunger levels on a scale of one to 10 (nutritiondata.com has calorie counts for most foods).

2 TRIM, DON'T SLASH

Start by cutting 300 calories a day. If you're running, you'll still hit a 500-calorie deficit per day.

3 TWEAK IT

If you cut 300 calories but the scales haven't budged, it's time to reduce your intake gradually. You can also adjust according to your training.

SMALL CHANGES, BIG REWARDS

You don't need to make drastic adjustments to your calorie intake to start dropping pounds. Small substitutes here and there through the day can add up and lead to significant and sustainable weight loss. Nutritionist Kim Pearson suggests these simple food swaps for a day of meals to help cut calories while keeping your energy levels high.

SWAP OUT	SWAP IN
 Bagel with cream cheese **360 calories**	½ whole grain bagel with peanut butter and a pot of yoghurt **325 calories**
Starbucks Grande Latté **190 calories**	Starbucks Grande Skinny Latté **130 calories**
Snickers **313 calories**	Spurilina Ginseng Bounce Ball **169 calories**
Subway six-inch roast-beef sandwich on white with mayo, cheese and veggies **400 calories**	Subway six-inch roast-beef sandwich on wheat with mustard, cheese, extra veggies and apple slices on the side **340 calories**
4oz pork chop and salad with apples, walnuts and goat's cheese **485 calories**	4oz of pork tenderloin and a mixed green salad with apples and walnuts (no cheese), and 100g of brown rice **380 calories**
170g of vanilla ice cream **290 calories** 	85g of vanilla ice cream with a handful of raspberries **205 calories** 
Original daily intake: **2,038 calories**	New daily intake: **1,549 calories**

TOTAL DAILY SAVING 489 CALORIES

RUNNER'S STRATEGY EAT REAL FOOD

People think they need diet products for them to be successful," says Elaine Magee, author of *Food Synergy* (Rodale Press). But all too often, the opposite is true. Runners can accomplish the same weight-loss goals while eating whole, real foods that taste better, provide more nutritional value and are more satisfying.

"When you go for healthy whole foods, such as lean proteins, vegetables, fruits, whole grains, nuts and seeds and low-fat dairy, you tend to get satiated on the right amounts," says Joy Bauer, author of *The Life Diet: Four Steps to Thin Forever* (Collins). The right real foods will help you lose, not gain, weight.

THREE REAL MEALS

Many diet foods are low in carbs, fibre or protein, and won't keep you satisfied for long. Here, Magee offers a real, whole-foods recipe for each meal of the day in place of a "diet" choice. "While these are higher in calories than the diet options, they will help sustain your energy levels between meals," she says.

LUNCH

Curried chicken salad sandwich
(Makes four sandwiches)
- 420g skinless chicken breast, shredded
- 3 tbsp dried cranberries
- 3 tbsp toasted pine nuts
- 1 chopped apple
- 55g light mayonnaise
- 60g fat-free sour cream
- 1 tbsp honey mustard
- 1 tsp curry powder

- 60g spring greens or fresh spinach
- 8 slices multigrain, wholewheat, or sourdough bread, or 4 wholewheat pitta breads

➡ Toss together first four ingredients. Whisk mayonnaise, sour cream, honey mustard and curry powder. Combine and serve.

BREAKFAST

Melon mango breakfast smoothie
(Serves one)
- 125g frozen mango chunks
- 75g (1 small or half a very large) banana, sliced
- 80g (wedge of a medium-sized melon) cantaloupe, diced
- 80g low-fat vanilla yoghurt
- 60ml vanilla soy milk (or semi-skimmed milk

with a tsp of vanilla)
- 30g low-fat granola for topping

➡ Place all of the ingredients (except the granola) in a food processor or blender and purée until thick and smooth (or lumpy if that's how you like it). Spoon into a dish or glass and sprinkle granola over the top.

DINNER

Fish fillets with lemon sauce
(Serves four)
- 450g fish fillets (sole, halibut or flounder)
- 160g breadcrumbs
- 1 1/2 tsp ground sage
- 2 tsp seasoning (celery salt, mustard seeds, black and red pepper, cinnamon, ginger)
- 2 large eggs
- 2 tsp water
- 4 tsp extra-virgin olive oil
- 2 tbsp lemon curd

- 2 tbsp whole milk
- 400g steamed brown rice
- 310g steamed broccoli

➡ Combine breadcrumbs, sage and seasoning. Mix eggs and water in another bowl. Heat oil in a pan. Dip fillets in egg mixture, then coat in crumbs. Place in pan. Coat with olive oil spray. Flip when brown (about four minutes); cook other side. Boil lemon curd and milk. Serve with rice, sauce and broccoli.

IMAGES: MITCH MANDEL

DIETER'S STRATEGY — DROP POUNDS FAST

RUNNER'S STRATEGY — LOSE POUNDS SLOWLY AND HAVE A POST-LOSS PLAN

For many dieters, their sole motivation is to lose weight as fast as possible. But this strategy leads them down a dangerous path. Once they hit their goal weight, dieters go back to their old habits, and soon enough the pounds creep back on.

"We often say, 'Hooray, I hit my goal weight. I'm done,'" says Linda Spangle, author of *100 Days of Weight Loss* (Rutledge Hill Press). "That's the biggest mistake and stops you from maintaining it long-term." Just as you shouldn't stop training once you reach a running goal, keeping the weight off is a daily task. Here's how to be successful with your weight loss...

1 KEEP AT IT

Many "losers" continue high exercise levels and a reduced-calorie diet – two principles that got you to your new weight. "You can slowly increase your total calories if you remain very consistent with exercise – but do it gradually," says Spangle.

2 STEP ON THE SCALE

A review in the *International Journal of Behavioral Nutrition and Physical Activity* examined self-weighing and weight gain. The conclusion: people who weigh themselves daily lose more weight – and keep it off.

3 GET SUPPORT

Finding some social support helps keep off the pounds. A 2007 study in *Obesity* showed that an online, therapist-led behavioural weight-loss website led to greater weight loss than a self-help commercial site.

4 BEWARE EMOTIONAL EATING

This is the number-one reason people regain weight, says Spangle. Plus, according to a 2008 *Nature* study, emotional eating often triggers binges. Ask yourself: "Does a bowl of chicken and broccoli sound good?" If not, you're not hungry for food as fuel.

5 KEEP YOUR MOTIVATION HIGH

Create a list of the reasons you want to lose weight. "It feels so good to be comfortable in your new body," says nutritionist Bauer. "Even if every day is a bit of a struggle, it's a struggle worth fighting."

REAL RUNNER

SARAH HUMPHRIES, 29, London
In November 2007, having given birth to two girls, my weight ballooned to over 15.7 stone (100kg). So I took up running. I started off going around the block every night, but the moment I was able to run two miles in one go, I just wanted to keep doing it. Soon I was doing 15 miles a week. By December 2008, I'd run my first half-marathon and lost six stone. Running totally changes your body shape. My legs and bum are great now – I love being able to wear skirts and skinny jeans. Now, I run five miles five times a week.

IMAGE: CHRIS BROCK

RUNNER'S STRATEGY BALANCE RUNNING AND STRENGTH TRAINING

Dieters often shy away from strength training out of a fear it will make them bulk up. But for many dieters, the reason is simpler: they know one hour of intense cardio burns more calories than one hour of strength training.

Yet the truth is that taking the time to add strength training to your routine a few days a week has benefits that can boost your weight loss. Studies have shown that strength training can improve body composition and decrease your percentage of body fat, helping you look leaner and burn calories. Here's how it works...

1 MUSCLE BURNS CALORIES

"Fat burns almost nothing at rest," says exercise physiologist Pete McCall. "Muscle uses oxygen, so if you increase lean muscle mass you'll raise the body's ability to use oxygen and burn calories." Your body typically uses up to seven calories per pound of muscle every day. If an 11.7 stone (74kg) runner with 20 per cent body fat increases his muscle mass and lowers his body fat to 15 per cent, he'll burn an extra 36 to 56 calories a day at rest – simply by adding muscle.

2 YOU'LL BE MORE EFFICIENT

Strength training can help you run faster, longer and more efficiently. A study in the *Journal of Strength and Conditioning Research* found runners who add three days of resistance-training exercises to their weekly programme increase leg strength and endurance. Runners with better endurance can run longer – and burn more calories. You'll also be able to recover faster from those long runs because strength training makes your body more efficient at converting metabolic waste into energy. "It's like being able to convert car exhaust fumes into petrol," says McCall.

3 YOU'LL BE LESS INJURY-PRONE

"If you increase your strength, you'll also increase your joint stability," says McCall, citing a study in the *Journal of Strength and Conditioning Research*, which shows that doing squats, single-leg hops and abs work does not only prevent lower-body injuries, but improve performance as well. Leg exercises can also reduce injury.

REAL RUNNER

MARIE MINCHELLA, 31, Southampton
At 28, after a few years of overdrinking and too much junk food, I was 13.7 stone (87kg). I had to change. I started running with my dog, and to begin with it was lamppost to lamppost, and it took a while to build up my fitness. But I was starting to shift the weight and I loved it. Then someone said that combining running with strength training would boost my weight loss, so I started strength training in the morning, then running afterwards. Lifting weights definitely contributed to my 3.7 stone (24kg) weight loss – and improved my running performance.

POWERFUL STUFF

Ready to add strength training into your routine, but pressed for time? Exercise physiologist Pete McCall suggests adding the exercises here to your post-run routine. Start with one session per week and work up to three. Both exercises use a number of muscle groups, plus they're easy to do and take just a few minutes. "After 16 weeks, your waist measurement will shrink," he says.

➔ SQUAT TO ROW Strengthens knees, quads, glutes, hips, back, core, biceps

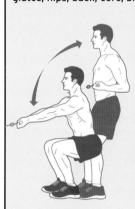

1 Stand two feet from a cable machine set at a weight that's hard but controllable.

2 Holding on to the cable handles with your arms extended, squat down.

3 As you rise up, pull your hands to your diaphragm. Do two or three sets of 12 to 15 reps.

➔ WOOD CHOP Strengthens hips, quads, glutes, shoulders, back, core

1 Stand with feet shoulder-width apart, holding a 5-8lb medicine ball in your hands.

2 Squat down with the ball held in front of you, keeping your heels on the floor, sticking your bottom out, and not letting your knees go more than a few inches over your toes.

3 Return to standing, raising the ball overhead, maintaining a slight bend in your knees. Keep your core engaged the whole time, as if bracing for a punch. Do two or three sets of 12 to 15 reps; increase weight of the medicine ball when you can do 15 in good form.

BREAKING DOWN (WEIGHT-LOSS) BARRIERS

That pesky number on the scale not budging yet? You may have encountered a few roadblocks. Here's how to get around them and back on the path to weight loss

ROADBLOCK

➔ YOU'RE NOT GETTING ENOUGH SLEEP

Research has found that people who get less sleep eat more snacks. Without enough sleep, says Heather Gillespie, a sports-medicine physician at the University of California, USA, your energy levels and immune system drop. But that doesn't mean you should cut out your morning runs to stay in bed. Routine is key for weight loss, so try going to bed earlier or switching your workouts to later in the day.

ROADBLOCK

➔ YOU EAT ENERGY-DENSE FOODS

A hamburger is an energy-dense food – so it packs more calories than less dense foods, such as vegetable soup or a turkey sandwich. Less dense foods have a higher water content than fats and carbs, and research has found that people who lower their energy density lower their weight. Those who eat a lot of energy-dense foods weigh more, have a higher intake of "bad" fats and eat less fruits and veg.

ROADBLOCK

➔ YOU'RE STUCK IN A COLOUR RUT

Many runners get the majority of their calories from carbohydrate. "I call it the flu diet," says nutritionist Lisa Dorfman. "Everything is bland and white." But research supports a colourful diet: eating berries twice a day for eight weeks helps lower your blood pressure. "Eat at least five different colours daily," says Dorfman, "so that you can be assured you're getting enough fibre and protein."

ROADBLOCK

➔ YOU ONLY RUN

Running 15 miles a week burns roughly 1,500 calories – but to lose a pound, you need to cut 3,500 calories a week. In a study in the American Journal of Physiology, Endocrinology and Metabolism, researchers found that adults who cut their calorie intake by 300 calories a day lost nearly 25 per cent of their body fat. People who only exercised lost just over 22 per cent. Both regimes worked, but your best bet is to combine the effort.

RUN IT OFF

Calorie-burning sessions to help you slim down and speed up

Cranking up the intensity is the best way to take your running to the next level. It's also an effective way to burn extra calories and shed body fat. A 68kg runner who picks up the pace from eight and a half minutes per mile to seven minutes per mile, for example, burns about 180 extra calories an hour. Should you speed up all of your runs that dramatically? No, but the following five sessions include segments of higher-intensity running to boost your calorie burn. Try one or two per week, and include a five-minute warm-up and cool-down.

1 JOE VIGIL'S ACCELERATIONS

Coach Joe Vigil designed this session for leg turnover and speed, but it also burns maximum calories in minimum time.

➜ **GO TO YOUR LOCAL TRACK**, or find a flat area where you can mark off 100 metres, and then every 10 metres after that up to 200 metres.

➜ **RUN 100 METRES** at roughly one-mile race pace. Note your time. Recover by walking from the finishing point back to the starting point.

➜ **RUN 110 METRES** slightly faster, so your 110-metre time is a second more than your 100-metre time.

➜ **CONTINUE** all the way up to 200 metres.

Estimated Burn: 340 calories

2 BRAD HUDSON'S MILES AND HILLS

Coach Brad Hudson, a former 2:13 marathon runner, likes to incorporate lots of short hill sprints into the sessions he prescribes. "They're great for developing running-specific strength," he says. Running hills also burns calories at a higher rate than running on flat terrain. This session combines hill sprints with 10K-pace mile intervals.

➜ **RUN 2 X 1 MILE** at 10K race pace. Follow each mile with three minutes' jogging for recovery.

➜ **RUN FOR 20 SECONDS** up part of a steep hill at maximum speed. Jog slowly for two minutes to recover. Do a total of five hill sprints.

Estimated Burn: 466 calories

3 MATT CENTROWITZ'S 10K RACE PREP

Cross-country coach Matt Centrowitz is a big believer in sessions that closely simulate the demands of racing. This session will prepare you for a peak 10K performance and incinerate a lot of calories.

➜ **RUN 800 METRES** roughly 20 seconds faster than your 10K goal pace. For example, if your 10K goal pace is eight minutes per mile, aim for 3:40. Walk or jog for two to three minutes for recovery.

➜ **RUN 800 METRES** roughly 10 seconds faster than your 10K goal pace. Recover as above.

➜ **RUN TWO MILES** at your 10K goal pace.

➜ **RUN 800 METRES** roughly 10 seconds faster than your 10K goal pace.

➜ **RUN 800 METRES** roughly 20 seconds faster than your 10K goal pace.

Estimated Burn: 520 calories

4 THE MONEGHETTI FARTLEK

Ex-Olympic marathon runner Steve Moneghetti developed a fartlek session that alternates short bursts of fast and slow running to boost overall calorie burn.

➜ **RUN TWO SETS** of 90 seconds hard (five to 10 seconds per mile faster than 5K pace), 90 seconds easy (45 to 50 seconds per mile slower than the hard runs).

➜ **RUN FOUR SETS** of 60 seconds hard, 60 seconds easy.

➜ **RUN FOUR SETS** of 30 seconds hard, 30 seconds easy.

➜ **RUN FOUR SETS** of 15 seconds hard, 15 seconds easy.

Estimated Burn: 400 calories

5 GREG McMILLAN'S SUPERFAST FINISH

Coach Greg McMillan has done this session since his days as a school cross-country runner. Choose a running distance appropriate to your fitness level.

➜ **COMPLETE** all but the last five minutes at a comfortable aerobic pace.

➜ **RUN THE LAST FIVE MINUTES** at approximately 5K race pace.

Estimated Burn: 390 calories for a 30-minute run (without including a warm-up or cool-down).

COMBAT THE FAT

Runners and readers offer their own tips on training to lose weight

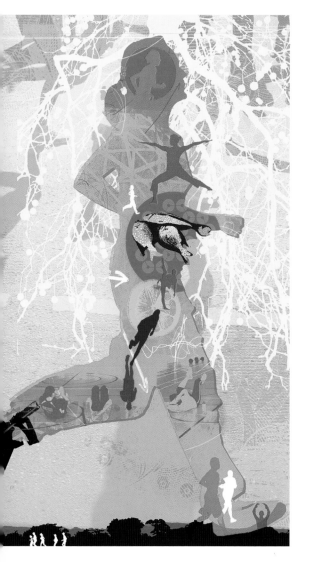

1 WALK AND RUN

Remember: miles are miles, as far as your belly's concerned. "Coming back from injury last year, I needed a plan to stop me piling on weight," says James Smith from Hemel Hempstead. "I stopped taking the bus and started walking to work and back instead. I was getting in six miles a day without even trying and the weight dropped off. I always start my runs with a walk until I'm ready to pick up the pace."

2 FAT IS YOUR FRIEND

"Certain 'diet' foods backfire because they leave you feeling unsatisfied, so you eat twice the amount," says Gina Kerr from the North West Triathlon Club in Londonderry. "After years of trying – and failing – with 'diet' foods, I cut out low-fat products, which were more often than not loaded with sugar, and focused on healthier fats, such as monounsaturates, dairy and fish oils. I'll have a full-fat yoghurt in the morning, which keeps me satisfied until lunch. I've lost 24 pounds in a year, so something has to be right."

3 FACE THE FACTS

"I decided to shock myself into losing the two spare stones I gained after my second child was born," says Helen Newton, member of the Black Pear Joggers in Worcester. "I pinned graphs and charts of my weight and body fat in the kitchen alongside photos of me before and after. Every time I reached for a biscuit I was reminded of the consequences."

4 GET WET

"I found that drinking water made a huge difference with controlling hunger pangs," says Himesh Gohil from Harrow. "Constantly sipping made me feel less hungry – I still eat as much as I want to, but I get

5 MIX IT UP

"The big mistake I made was thinking running held all the answers," explains Tom O'Shea from Cirencester. "But two years ago I injured my Achilles and was forced to take some time out. I went to the gym and did some weights work – I didn't put on one pound and my body fat actually went down, with not one bit of cardio. When I returned to running, I continued going to the gym twice a week to do a 60-minute circuit of low-weight high-rep full-body moves, such as squats, lunges and presses, and have lost almost three stone."

fuller quicker, and don't snack so much. I clock between two and three litres a day. It also gives me added energy. The best part is that it's not part of some faddish diet, so I've kept it up even after I've hit my target weight."

6 TELL THE TRUTH

The first rule about weight loss is to be true to yourself. "If snack foods are your weakness, don't buy them – it really is that simple," says Lorna Gold, a member of the Centurion Running Club in Birmingham. "People kid themselves into making excuses that crisps are for the kids' lunchboxes, or those chocolate biscuits are for their spouse's tea, when in reality it's for them. If you take temptation out of the equation you soon realise how quickly you don't need these things."

7 FUEL UP

As the saying goes, breakfast like a king, lunch like a queen and dinner like a pauper. "Last July I weighed in at close to 17 stone. I was eating too many treats and justifying that by skipping breakfast," says James McNeill, from Wallasey on the Wirral. "I was upping my mileage, but running on empty meant I never really enjoyed it. Now, I have a breakfast of porridge, toast and poached eggs, a jacket potato or pasta for lunch, and lean meat with salad for dinner. I've lost over two stone, and enjoy running more than ever."

8 TAKE 10 PER CENT

Small steps can lead to big changes. "One day I just decided I'd increase my mileage by 10 per cent each

week and see what happened," says Clare Brotherton from York. "It doesn't sound like much, but the extra calorie-burn accumulates faster than you think, and it wasn't so daunting a prospect – especially as I was starting on just 20 miles a week. Once I reached 50, I didn't have the time to do any more, so I started incorporating hills and fartlek sessions. Whatever session I did, I was absolutely spent by the end."

9 ANALYSE THIS

Controlling what you eat can be half the battle. "Ready meals are nearly always loaded with extra sugar, salt and fat to add flavour to what are pretty bad-quality basic ingredients," says Karl Andrews from Fife. "I was running a fair bit, but I was eating too much processed junk, so the extra weight I was carrying just wouldn't shift. I started to analyse what I was eating and took a real interest in cooking. I started using the *Collins Gem Calorie Counter* when going round the supermarket, sought out food at farmers' markets and kept a detailed food diary – seeing it in black and white really helps you understand where the problems are."

10 TREAT YOURSELF

Understand that it's OK to have the occasional treat. "If you're running regularly, you deserve it," says Lina Martino from Tipton Harriers in Stoke. "The reason why diets fail is because they're based on deprivation, and once you give in to that craving with one biscuit, you think 'Sod it' and demolish the whole packet. Focus on the foods you can eat rather than those you can't. The more you tell yourself you can't have something, the more you crave it. Experiment and find foods you like that are healthy. I love cereal, whereas others love toast – stick with those, if they're healthy."

RAVE RUN

Stoodley Pike, West Yorkshire

8 Women's Running

238 WOMEN'S HEALTH
Female runners are different from men –
these are the things every woman needs
to know before hitting the road

240 TIPS FOR
WOMEN RUNNERS
21 reasons to get out there

244 TWO FOR THE ROAD
Having a baby doesn't mean you can't
run. Here's how to keep going through
pregnancy and beyond

WOMEN'S HEALTH

The difference between men and women is not just visual when it comes to running – here are the things you need to know

Apart from the sort of injuries that can plague all runners – shin splints, black toenails, tendinitis – there are some health issues that are more prevalent in women runners, and some that are exclusively female.

MENSTRUAL PROBLEMS

Although some women complain of discomfort during their periods, it is generally accepted menstruation has limited impact on exercise performance. Women have run well, set records and won championships at all phases of the menstrual cycle. Clinical studies have shown no change in heart-rate, strength or endurance during the cycle. Exercise can improve your feelings of well-being before and during your period, and some doctors recommend exercise for women who suffer discomfort at this time of the month.

A potential problem for runners is the cessation of menstruation. Women who run strenuously may be at higher risk of having "athletic amenorrhoea", or irregular or absent periods. Training stress, performance pressure, low body fat and inadequate nutrition are all possible contributing factors.

One of the most serious consequences of amenorrhoea is osteoporosis, which happens because female hormones, which protect calcium in bone, are in short supply. An early onset of osteoporosis can lead to a greatly increased risk of stress fractures and acute fractures, and since decreased bone density is not easily reversed, it might last for the rest of your life.

An additional concern is lack of ovulation. Because women can menstruate even when not ovulating, the presence of a period does not guarantee a healthy menstrual cycle. A lack of ovulation can signal insufficient levels of progesterone, which can lead to over-stimulation of the uterine lining, putting you at risk of endometrial cancer.

A woman's body temperature is generally lower at the beginning of her monthly cycle and higher for the last two weeks. The increase in temperature occurs at the time of ovulation. To track this cycle, take your temperature first thing in the morning. If your conditions point towards any sort of irregularity, consult your doctor.

THE PILL

Researchers disagree about the impact of the pill on athletic performance. Though most studies have shown the pill has no effect on performance, some research indicates it may cause a slight reduction in aerobic capacity.

On the other hand, some runners feel the pill helps performance by reducing menstrual symptoms. These runners prefer taking the pill so they can control their cycle and don't have to race when they are having their period. Although it is safe to manipulate the timing of your period, experts generally agree this practice should be reserved for major competitions and done only a few times a year.

If you run recreationally, you probably don't have to worry about any athletic impact of the pill. But if you race and don't want to risk sacrificing aerobic capacity, consider another type of contraception.

OSTEOPOROSIS

Exercise can help build and maintain bone density levels in women, but women who have abnormal menstrual cycles, may not gain these benefits.

Several studies have shown women who have disrupted menstrual cycles suffer more stress fractures than their counterparts with normal cycles. These women typically exhibit lower levels of bone mineral density. Although it's generally accepted that hormonal disruptions and premature loss of bone density are linked in female athletes, the cause and effect relationship is not clear. For example, some researchers think the kind of woman drawn to intense exercise is more likely to exhibit stress in all areas of life, which could affect hormone levels even without exercise.

Experts agree women must act to protect themselves from early-onset osteoporosis. It's particularly important as once past the mid-thirties, a woman can no longer build bone mass, but only maintain her reserves. You should take every precaution to ensure you are not losing bone mass. That means eating a properly balanced diet – in addition to all the important nutrients, and calcium in particular, you should make sure you are consuming enough fat and calories overall to sustain your level of exercise. Monitor your menstrual cycle, and if there are any irregularities consult your doctor.

INCONTINENCE

Women are more prone to stress incontinence because of their anatomy. It's estimated that one in two women experience some level of urine leakage and it is annoying and disconcerting.

Although running does not cause incontinence, the activity can induce leakage in women who are already prone to it. Many women find relief by strengthening the muscles in the pelvic area with Kegel exercises. To do these, contract your pelvic muscles as if you are attempting to stop a flow of urine. Hold for a few seconds, and then release. There are also several devices that can be bought over the counter or with a prescription that help control leakage. Talk to your GP about what might work best for you.

ACNE

Women runners can be plagued by skin breakouts on their face, hairline, upper back, chest, upper arms and buttocks. Sweat production combined with hair follicles or friction from rubbing clothes is a formula for acne. Increased temperature and humidity exacerbate the problem, as do products such as sun screen and make-up, which sweat off on to the skin and clog pores.

LOOKING GOOD
Running is great, but women are more prone to certain problems than men

HOW TO FEND OFF ACNE

Minimise the use of make-up and hair-care products before running. Wash your face before running, and again before re-applying make-up.

Use a sunscreen specifically formulated for the face on your face and neck. Choose a gel or lotion for the rest of your body, rather than a cream.

Wipe acne-prone areas with an astringent pad or towelette immediately after running. Once your body's natural oils cool, they harden, which can lead to plugged pores.

Change out of sweaty exercise clothes straight after running, and shower as soon as possible.

Cleanse acne-prone areas thoroughly. Gentle exfoliation can help, but don't scrub to the point of aggravating your skin.

If you are prone to acne, consult a dermatologist.

21 TIPS FOR WOMEN RUNNERS

You shouldn't need an excuse to get out there, but there are plenty of very good reasons to slip those shoes on right now

Knowledge is power, in running as in any other pursuit. The more you know about training, nutrition and health, the better you'll be at maximising your running, whether that means fitness, weight loss, great race performances or just plain fun. In this section, you'll find loads of information to help you reach your goals.

These facts and tips cover health, psychology, weight loss, pregnancy and motherhood, training, racing and more, and address the specific needs of women to help you become the runner you want to be.

1 ANAEROBIC RESULTS

For female runners, controlled anaerobic training – intervals, hills, fartlek training – may lead to gains in strength and speed similar to those produced by steroids, but without the noxious side effects. Why? High-intensity anaerobic running is one of the most potent stimulators of natural human growth hormones – those that contribute to stronger muscles and, ultimately, enhanced performance.

2 FIRST THINGS FIRST

Running early in the morning means you can get the sweaty business out of the way before applying make-up and dressing for work. But perhaps more importantly, statistics show that women are more likely to be attacked later in the day. Don't be scared off, but do take precautions. More on that later...

3 RUNNING WITH CHILD

Doctors consider moderate exercise during a normal pregnancy is completely safe for the baby. Running should cause no problems in the first trimester and it should be fine for most people in the second trimester. Few women would run in their final three months, however. The most important precaution is to avoid becoming overheated; a core body temperature above 38°F could increase the risk of birth defects. So make sure you're staying cool enough, and if in doubt, take your temperature after a run. If it's over 101°F, you're probably overdoing it. Also, skip that post-run soak in a hot bath.

4 SHOE SELECTION

Women generally have narrower feet than men, so when buying running shoes, you're best off going for a pair designed specifically for women. That said, everyone's different, so if your feet are wide, you may feel more comfortable in shoes designed for men. The bottom line: buy the shoe that's best for you. If there's any question – or if you suffer blisters or injuries because of ill-fitting shoes – consult a podiatrist who specialises in treating runners.

5 REDUCE CANCER RATES

An American study found running women produce a less potent form of oestrogen than their sedentary counterparts. As a result, female runners cut

by half their risks of developing breast and uterine cancer, and by two thirds their risk of contracting the form of diabetes most common in women.

6 SISTERS UNITED

Having another woman or a group of women to run with regularly will help keep you motivated and ensure your safety. It's also a lot more fun than running alone. Women runners become more than training partners; they're confidantes, counsellors and coaches, too.

7 KEEP IT REAL

Women who run for weight control may lose perspective on what is an appropriate body size. A recent survey of thousands of women found while 44 per cent of respondents were medically overweight, 73 per cent thought they were.

8 CALCIUM AND IRON

The two minerals women runners need to pay the most attention to are calcium and iron (iron is especially important for menstruating women.) Good sources of calcium are dairy products, dark leafy vegetables, broccoli, canned sardines and salmon, while foods high in iron include liver, fortified dry cereals, beef and spinach.

9 GET TESTED

Women who train intensively, have been pregnant in the past two years or consume fewer than 2,500 calories a day should conduct more than routine blood tests for iron status, since these test only for anaemia, the final stage of iron deficiency. Ask for more revealing tests, such as those for serum ferritin, transferrin saturation and total iron-building capacity.

10 PERIOD GAINS

There's no need to miss a run or a race just because you're having your period. If you're suffering from cramps, running will often alleviate the pain, thanks to the release during exercise of pain-relieving chemicals called endorphins. Speedwork and hill sessions can be especially effective, but use a tampon and a towel for extra protection.

11 SKIN WINS

Running helps produce healthy skin. According to dermatologists, running stimulates circulation, transports nutrients and flushes out waste products.

All of this leads to a reduction in subcutaneous fat, making skin clearer and facial features more distinct.

12 IGNORE TAUNTING

It may not be much consolation, but men are sometimes verbally harassed and occasionally threatened while running, just as women are. Be sensible when you run, but don't let insignificant taunting limit your freedom.

13 DON'T OVERDO IT

If you run so much your periods become light or non-existent, you may be endangering your bones. Amenorrhoea (lack of a monthly period) means that little or no oestrogen, essential for the replacement of bone minerals, is circulating in your body. You can stop, but not reverse, the damage by taking oestrogen and plenty of calcium. If your periods are infrequent or absent, consult a gynaecologist.

14 STRONGER BABIES

If you were a regular runner before you became pregnant, you might have a bigger baby – good news,

one that stretches horizontally but not vertically. Most importantly, try before you buy. A sports bra should fit snugly, yet not feel too constrictive. Run or jump on the spot to see if it gives you the support you need.

17 LATE PREGNANCY AND BIRTH

If you ran early in your pregnancy, you might want to try switching to a lower-impact exercise during the latter stages and after delivery. Because of the release of the hormone relaxin during pregnancy, some ligaments and tendons might soften. This will make you more vulnerable to injury, especially around your pelvis. Walking, swimming, stationary cycling and aquarunning are good choices.

18 MONTHLY MOMENTS

"That time of the month" (or even the few days preceding it) is not the time when women run their worst. The hardest time for women to run fast is about a week before menstruation begins (a week after ovulation). That's when levels of the key hormone progesterone peak, inducing a much-higher-than-normal breathing rate during physical activity. The excess ventilation tends to make running feel more difficult.

19 MAKING TIME

Just because you're married and have young children and a job doesn't mean you don't have time to run. Running is time-efficient and the best stress-reducer on the market. You need this time. Taking it for yourself (by letting your husband baby-sit while you run, for instance) will benefit the whole family.

20 BREASTFEEDING

Some studies have suggested that babies dislike the taste of post-exercise breast milk, because it is high in lactic acid and may impart a sour flavour. These studies are not conclusive but you may like to either express milk for later feeding, or breast-feed before running.

21 WOMEN SWEAT LESS THAN MEN

However, contrary to popular belief, women dissipate heat as well as men. The reason: women are smaller and have a higher body-surface-to-volume ratio, which means that although their evaporative cooling is less efficient, they need less of it to achieve the same result. Nonetheless, be sure to drink plenty of water to prevent dehydration.

because, up to a certain point, larger infants tend to be stronger and weather physical adversity better. Researchers in the US found women who burned up to 1,000 calories per week through exercise gave birth to babies weighing five per cent more than the offspring of inactive mums. Those who burned 2,000 per week delivered babies weighing 10 per cent more.

15 IN THE INTEREST OF SAFETY

Women who run alone should take precautions. Leave a note at home stating when you left, where you'll be running and when you expect to return. Carry a mobile phone. Stick to well populated areas, and don't always run the same predictable route. Avoid running at night and don't wear jewellery. Pay attention to your surroundings and recurring faces. Carry identification, but include only your name and an emergency phone number.

16 CHEST SUPPORT

No matter what your size, it's a good idea to wear a sports bra when you run. By controlling breast motion, it'll make you feel more comfortable. Look for

TWO FOR THE ROAD

Becoming pregnant needn't mean your running has to fall by the wayside. It can benefit you both

"It was a beautiful winter day – snowy but sunny – and I felt great running on snow-packed roads. I was as pregnant as possible – that evening, I gave birth. I had gone out for a five-miler, but I felt I could have run forever. No matter how much time passes, I can still mentally put myself on that road. A perfect run on a perfect day."

Okay, you're not an Olympic champion like Joan Benoit Samuelson, from whose book *Running for Women* this quote is taken. But if you're a pregnant runner who wants to maintain her fitness, your running doesn't have to suffer. While adhering to certain principles to ensure your health and that of your baby, as an expectant mum you can enjoy running much the same as in your non-expectant condition.

First and foremost, it's crucial to listen to medical advice. A frank and open discussion with your midwife – about your overall health but particularly about your exercise programme – is essential.

A supportive midwife or doctor who recognises the benefits of an exercise programme will not only listen to your concerns, but should also address your individual needs, although you shouldn't hesitate to seek a second opinion if you're uncomfortable with

'Health benefits to women who exercise while pregnant include less back pain, less analgesic at delivery and fewer cases of post-natal depression'

your initial diagnosis. Your well-being and peace of mind, as well as the livelihood of your baby, are at stake, so don't be afraid to speak up.

If you've been given the green light to run, proceed with cautious enthusiasm, says Dr Rod Jaques, medical advisor to the British Triathlon Team at the British Olympic Medical Centre. The health benefits to women who exercise while pregnant have been well documented. They include: less lower-back pain; reduced amounts of analgesic at delivery; fewer instances of operative deliveries; and fewer cases of post-natal depression. What's more, women who exercise during pregnancy gain less weight, have improved mood and sleep patterns and lose weight more rapidly after giving birth. Although now is not the time to begin a running programme, if you're already a runner then there's no reason to stop – just modify.

HOW INTENSE IS TOO INTENSE?

Dr Jaques notes that concrete answers to the questions of "how much and at what intensity?" will never be found on the research block, since scientists will be hard-pressed to find a woman willing to subject her pregnancy to such experiments. But Dr Jaques advises women to keep their heart rate at or below 140 beats per minute (bpm) while exercising.

CHILL OUT AND RELAX

Some research shows an internal body temperature above 38°C may cause birth defects in the developing fetus; yet other studies fail to confirm these findings. Given such conflicting reports, however, most experts agree that a pregnant woman must keep her core body

LIFTING THE PRIZE
Paula Radcliffe won the New
York Marathon 10 months
after giving birth to Isla

temperature at a recognised safe level (below 38°C) to protect her unborn baby from potential birth defects, particularly to the fetus's central nervous system.

What can an expectant mother do to stay cool? In addition to keeping your heart rate at or below 140bpm, experts advise you to train outdoors, rather than indoors on a treadmill where the wind's cooling effect is eliminated. If you are inside, be sure the area is well ventilated; keep the windows open and consider investing in a fan or two. Avoid running in very warm and hot conditions. Pregnant women should never run to the point of breathlessness or exhaustion – it's important to work to a comfortable level and not overdo it. You should additionally ensure you remain very well hydrated before, during and after a run. Dr Jaques advises pregnant athletes to drink 100ml of water every 15 minutes during a run, and to keep pumping the fluids afterwards.

During pregnancy, a woman's body produces the hormone relaxin, which relaxes joints and ligaments. Loose joints and ligaments can make you more susceptible to injury, and the gradual widening of your hips will change your biomechanics and make your feet more likely to over-pronate. Easing gently into a run and stretching properly afterwards will help prevent injuries, as will choosing shoes with increased stability and cushioning.

According to the National Childbirth Trust, during the first trimester of pregnancy you may experience increased tiredness, nausea, breast tenderness, pressure on your bladder and constipation. Many of the side effects of pregnancy are due to the sudden rush of hormones in your body. Yet many women surveyed by Dr Jaques report having "a wonderful

time" when running during their first trimester. Be sure to map out toilet stops along your route, wear a supportive non-underwired bra and stop running if you feel too tired at this stage. Weeks 1-12 are crucial as far as your baby's development goes.

From weeks 12-28 your pregnancy begins to show, and your breasts grow as milk-producing cells develop. Many women experience lower-back pain at this time due to the increased pressure on their pelvis; this may contribute to other unexpected pain, such as knee strain. With the added weight, your running gait may change, so be alert to terrain and traffic while running.

BUMP IN THE ROAD

PAULA RADCLIFFE'S postpartum 2007 ING New York City Marathon win begs the question: Is there an athletic benefit to pregnancy? Although no definitive link has been proven, the biological tools needed to build a baby could boost a new mum's performance. During pregnancy, blood volume goes up by as much as 40 per cent. "Pregnancy makes you hypertrained. Your body becomes very efficient at circulating oxygen," says

Dr Nadya Swedan, author of *The Active Woman's Health and Fitness Handbook*.
"If you begin running within weeks of giving birth, you can capitalise on those... gains."

That said, right after giving birth, Radcliffe suffered a stress fracture in her sacrum. "Your bones can get leached of calcium, which makes them susceptible," says Swedan. What's more, the hormone relaxin, which causes joints and ligaments to loosen up so the hips can accommodate birth, doesn't depart the body until at least four months postpartum, making you more prone to sprains.

BACK UP AND RUNNING
New mums are short on time, but you can make your baby part of your workout

During the last lap of pregnancy your weight-gain – finally – will begin to slow down. You may experience a shortness of breath and your feet may swell, making running taxing. Dr Jaques notes: "It would take a heroic woman who would consider running during this stage of pregnancy. Physically, it's extremely challenging." Concentrated weight gain at the bottom of the sternum and pubic bone makes it difficult, biomechanically, to run.

Add to that the increased back pain, and running begins to seem a rather uncomfortable and painful – though not impossible – proposition. At this point it may be time to consider alternatives to running, such as swimming, cycling, low-impact aerobics or walking.

GETTING BACK IN THE SWING

Returning to your pre-pregnancy running form largely depends upon two things: the type of birth you experience and your fitness level. In a normal birth, a woman can most likely begin exercising again when she feels no pain. But it is advised to wait around six weeks before beginning any aerobic exercise.

If you have a Caesarean section, talk to your midwife. Residual scarring and bleeding may interfere with your ability to return to proper form as soon as you may like. Remember to take it slow. Low-impact exercises, such as walking and swimming, are good choices to ease you back into shape.

Dr Jaques explains that a woman may begin vigorous training from six weeks to three months following delivery – three months is more likely if there were any complications, but since everyone is different it's important to listen to your own body.

After pregnancy, the increased plasma volume in your bloodstream may spur recovery. After being mentally starved of running, you may have more appetite for it. With less time on your hands, concentrate on quality sessions, which lead to an improved running performance.

MILKING THE SYSTEM

If you've decided to breastfeed your baby, then here's some good news: it seems exercise does not affect the quality or quantity of a mother's milk.

It's been widely reported that breastfed babies are less likely to suffer from gastrointestinal problems, diarrhoea, respiratory problems, ear infections, pneumonia and food allergies, than formula-fed babies.

Some things to bear in mind: it's a good idea to breastfeed your baby before going out for a run. Keep note of your weight loss. If you're losing more than one pound a week then add nutritious snacks to your diet in between meals. And eat healthy, well-balanced meals and stay properly hydrated. For more information on breastfeeding, contact the La Leche League (laleche. org.uk), a support group for breastfeeding mothers.

TOP TIPS

→ **TALK TO YOUR MIDWIFE OR DOCTOR** Find out their attitude towards combining exercise with pregnancy.

→ **TRAIN, DON'T STRAIN** Forget about speedwork and long endurance runs. Pay attention to your level of exertion, heart rate and temperature.

→ **DON'T OVERHEAT** Run in the most temperate part of the day. Drink plenty of fluids before, during and after a run.

→ **KNOW WHEN TO STOP** Cease running if you begin cramping, gasping for air or feel dizzy. If you experience pain or bleeding or your water breaks, get medical attention immediately.

→ **CONSIDER YOUR OPTIONS** If running is becoming uncomfortable, try swimming.

→ **EAT WELL** Be sure you're getting enough iron, calcium, folic acid and other nutrients.

→ **GO EASY** Running to the point of exhaustion doesn't do you or your baby any good.

RAVE RUN

Barley, Lancashire

9 The Great Outdoors

OFF THE BEATEN TRACK

Ever wish running felt a bit more natural? Then try bounding
up the side of a mountain, messing about in mud or
tearing around on the trails. Here's how...

FELL RUNNING

You'd have to hark back to the 11th century to find the first recorded fell race. In a Middle Ages version of *The Apprentice*, King Malcolm of Scotland reputedly arranged a race to find a good runner to become his messenger. These days, runners take to the peaks around the UK in pursuit of the ultimate in running thrills. Ready to rock? Here's what you need to know:

THE SKILLS

➔ The climb "You just can't run some of the hills," says Keith Anderson, ex-British fell-running champion and running coach (www.fullpotential.co.uk). "It's like going up the side of a house." Fell runners have their own unique uphill walk. Place the heel of your hands above the knee, with your thumb on the inside of your leg and the little finger on the outside. Apply pressure with your hands in rhythm with your walking speed. This helps the legs lift the body weight up the slope.

➔ The descent Keep your eyes focused six to eight feet ahead of you, selecting the best ground. Land on the forefoot for more speed and greater control. On steeper hills, fell runners don't slow down – they actually put a jump into their running. "You launch off one foot into the air – straight up, not forward," says Anderson. Land on the same foot, using the other one for support. Take a transfer stride and jump again.

THE TRAINING

Build your own hill-charge workout: find a five to 10 per cent gradient that takes 60 to 90 seconds to ascend at hard pace; start with an easy 15-minute warm-up, preferably on rolling terrain to awaken your climbing muscles; try five to eight charges at hard pace, jogging slowly on each descent; cool down with a 15-minute jog.

NEED TO KNOW

It's important – particularly for road runners – to progress gradually to prepare muscles and ligaments before fell running, says Anderson. "Progress from cross-country to trail running, then to the lower fells before the higher fells." Solid map-reading and mountaineering skills will help. "You're not sticking to a set route," Anderson adds.

WHAT NEXT?

The Fell Runners Association has a comprehensive directory of clubs at the best spots around the UK. See fellrunner.org.uk for more info.

TRAIL RUNNING

There are good reasons why runners have been taking to the trails since Egyptian times: the scenery, tranquility and softer surfaces to name a few. Plus, going off-road on to the myriad footpaths found in the UK will make you a stronger, smarter runner, improving fitness, leg strength and coordination.

THE SKILLS

Mud There's a greater chance of slipping on wet mud – plus it sticks to your shoes, making them heavy. Always have a quick scan for dry and solid sections. But don't hang around and ruin your momentum. "You can spend more time trying to find the best line than the time you gain through finding it," says Andy Symonds, one of the world's top trail runners. "Just get your head down and plough through it."

Rocks When the terrain gets technical, use a higher leg lift to avoid tripping over. Be prepared to switch strides quickly. "Shorter, quicker strides are key for mastering trickier terrain," says top UK trail runner Natalie White.

Water When crossing streams, it's often easier than it seems to stay out of the drink. If you think you can clear it, take a running jump. "Taking off on one foot to land on the other is ideal," says White. Don't be afraid to run through. High-step as quickly as possible.

Navigation A compass isn't essential kit for trail running, but it's easy to get lost if you don't pay proper attention to your surroundings. Make a mental note of your route. "Keep looking behind you once in a while," says Symonds. "The scenery can look very different when you're heading in the opposite direction."

THE TRAINING

"A trail runner needs leg speed and trail speed," says Symonds. To boost both, alternate these two speed-training sessions every week:

Leg speed That flat-out turnover of your legs is best developed on the track. Increase stride efficiency, sense of pace and anaerobic threshold by doing a weekly set of 6 to 8 x 400 metres or 3 to 4 x 800 metres.

Trail speed To improve your pace over varying terrain, perform a 30- to 45-minute fartlek run.

NEED TO KNOW

Forget PBs. "Trail running is more about getting out there and enjoying it," says Symonds. It's not the same as a 10K – it's dependent on other factors, such as the weather and how muddy it is underfoot.

WHAT NEXT?
You won't have much trouble finding a route. But to meet others who enjoy trail running, and find about events across the country, see tra-uk.org.

FELL vs TRAIL

Which style is best for you? A devotee of each stakes their claim

'HOW I FELL IN LOVE'

KEITH ANDERSON
ex-British fell-running champion
and running coach
I arrived for my first race at Blencathra in the Lake District. Starting off gathered in a little group of runners ready to disappear into the mist was intimidating. I was convinced I would never be seen again. To get through it was mind-blowing. I was hooked. The rawness of the mountain, the spectacular views and the freeness of the sport were inspirational.

The spirit of fell running is unrivalled. Fell runners are always competitive, but they'll pick you up if you slip. There's a mutual respect; we've all got to get up and we've all got to get down. And runs usually start and finish at a pub, which is convenient.

There's an amazing sense of achievement at the top of a climb; not that you have long to appreciate it before you're throwing yourself back down. You never conquer a mountain; you can have a good day, but you'll never conquer it. The conditions are ever-changing. That's the thrill.

'WHY I LOVE TRAILBLAZING'

ANDY SYMONDS
one of the world's top trail
racers for Team Saab Salomon
You get a true feeling of being in the great outdoors on the trail. That's what it's all about for me – really taking advantage of everything the countryside has to offer. There's genuine exploration – you're not just aiming for the top of something.

The trail experience throws up variety with every step. The huge mix of scenery you take in on the trail gives you a buzz. It ups your energy levels and makes you want to keep going. Even the textures beneath your feet are constantly changing. You're not just pounding the same surface; it's grass, track, mud, rock, sand and more.

If you want a true all-weather sport, look no further. If it's raining, you might wear a different pair of shoes – but that's it. Anyone can do trail running. You don't need to live next to a mountain. Even in cities, you can head to a park and just go and get lost for a while.

TRAIL AND HEARTY

To build a strong, flexible body and an upbeat mental attitude, just let yourself run wild

Before you turn the page thinking we're about to con you in to some crippling cross-country sprint, stop. Trail running is a good thing – it's all about getting out into nature, for the sheer joy of running in gorgeous woodland or mountains, or even hidden corners of your nearest country park.

It's this that has been attracting runners to the trails since it became a defined category in the early 1990s – and before. "The term trail running was partly driven by marketing – shoe companies had this new off-road kit and needed a story to tell," says Paul Magner from Trailplus (trailplus.com), a company that organises some of Britain's toughest trail runs. "However, people had been running off-road for years, but just not thinking of themselves as trail runners per se. What drove it then as now is that, if you ask anyone what their favourite run is, it won't be a road route."

At the gentler end of the trail scale, running on soft, even ground is a good way to build miles without the repeated impact of crashing your foot down on to concrete, which contributes to overuse injuries. Don't restrict trail running to the odd joint-saving long run, though. Give yourself a total-body workout using the toughest trails you can find.

YOUR HEAD-TO-TOE WORKOUT

If you're completely new to off-road running, start with even, man-made trails (such as woodchip trails in the park) and work on your core strength and stability before you switch to the tough stuff. "If you are a novice, the chances are you will strain more muscles than you condition," says GB cross-coutry coach Nick Anderson. "It's a chicken-and-egg situation – off-road running will work on your core strength and balance, but you need to build them up before you go off-road." Try exercises such as the plank, single-leg squats and exercises on a wobble board to improve your stability.

STRONG FEET

Footwear has a huge impact on your trail experience, but if you can, spend some time on very soft trails so that you can wear minimal, light trail shoes. The soft ground makes up for lack of cushioning in the shoes,

and will help to strengthen the muscles in your foot and ankle, making you less injury-prone.

STURDY ANKLES

For many nervous novices, the potential for sprained ankles is the number one reason they won't stray off-road. In fact, heading off-road is a good way to prevent ankle sprains.

STRONG CALVES AND SHINS

Pushing through soft ground works your calves much harder than taking off from a firm surface. Be careful if you're prone to calf or Achilles problems, as soft ground stretches them more. Running downhill on trails also works the muscles down the front of your lower leg, as these provide some of the braking power.

STRONG QUADS, STABLE KNEES

Downhill and uneven running works your quads harder as they help to stop you falling forwards. Because you'll be changing your foot placement with every strike and running on different gradients, you'll be using all of your quad muscles, whereas road-running can overuse the larger, outer quads.

HAMSTRINGS AND GLUTES

Running uphill works the muscles at the back of your legs, and soft ground will make the exercise harder. "Bounding" up hills is a good way to toughen up.

CORE STABILITY

The core has several functions when you're running on trails. Strong abs, glutes and back muscles will help you balance on tricky ground, but a strong core also stops other muscle imbalances building up in the lower body which could lead to injuries.

MENTAL STRENGTH

Hitting the trails can be a strength-building exercise for the mind, or give it a good break, depending on the conditions. In the winter, it's perfect for giving yourself a bit of grit. On the other hand, a beautiful run in good weather can be just what you need to fire you up.

TAKE THE PLUNGE
Running off-road can
help prevent injuries,
rather than cause them

PEAK PRACTICE

It was an uphill struggle at first, but with stunning Alpine views around every corner it didn't take RW's Kerry McCarthy long to work out why mountain running is so rewarding

Mountain running: an oxymoron if ever there was one. That's a sanitised version of the vitriol pouring from my mouth as I stand at the foot of another ruinously long climb and look up at my running buddies disappearing into the distance. I'm 1,200m above sea level, my lungs feel like they're being scoured with a wire brush, my hamstrings are screaming bloody murder (the less said about my calves the better) and I'm only on kilometre four of a 13K run. I'm tempted – sorely tempted in fact – to return to my hotel, order a stein of lager and listen to the faint symphony of cow- and church-bells from a horizontal position on my balcony.

Before I have time to execute this plan though, my guide for the weekend, six-time world mountain-running champion Jonathan Wyatt, comes bounding back down the slope on a mine-sweeping operation and, with a few irritatingly chipper words of encouragement, chivvies me into a reluctant stagger.

I've come to Söll, in the Wilder Kaiser region of the Austrian Alps, for a short course in mountain running. It's a four-day trip with two runs on each day. This is the start of day two and I'm struggling.

The weekend is an official training trip for entrants of the Tour de Tirol, a multi-stage event taking place here in early October. It's a chance for the runners to get an advance look at different sections of the course and get some practice in ahead of time.

My companions, a mixture of Germans and Austrians, have all run at least one mountain race previously – and it shows. Some of them may have even more unathletic-looking frames than me but, as Wyatt explains, this is irrelevant.

"Mountain running, as with all forms of running, is easier if you're carrying less weight, but you can get round carrying a few extra pounds and still complete a race if you learn how to run the hills with the correct form," he says. "It's partly about stamina but also technique."

Partway through our run we stop at the foot of a conveniently steep slope and Wyatt puts each of us through our paces both up and down the hill, pointing out changes needed to achieve correct form of powerful arm backswing, economical stride and soft foot placement he's been drumming into us from minute one.

We continue on our way and there's no doubt the tips have made a difference; I now feel semi-conscious as opposed to half-dead. Kilometres seven to nine are the worst. I'm forced to walk up a narrow woodland track a quarter of a mile long – my calves just can't take any more and I'm being blinded by my own salty sweat – and am the second-to-last team member to reach the top (the last is recovering from some sort of major surgery, he later tells me. Great).

As I reach the top everyone comes hurtling back down past me, so without time for a breather I turn

IMAGES: BRIAN FINKE, WINFRIED STIMM ILLUSTRATIONS: ACUTE GRAPHICS

ONE WAY UP
Mountain running is hard on the way up, but there is an upside – it's the downside!

and follow. Running down a mountain is no easier than running up; the pain simply switches from your hamstrings to your quads – or so it seems to me.

Wyatt bounds effortlessly back up the track like a cross between Tigger and Zebedee, telling me to stop leaning back and digging my heels in and just to let the decline 'take me'. Easier said than done when you've put on road-running shoes that morning by mistake. *Runner's World* Gear Editor In Wrong Kit Shocker.

I somehow make it to the finish and, as I grab a proffered bottle of water and expend my momentum in the delightful coolness of a conveniently placed lake, a couple of German runners smilingly inform me in broken English that it will get easier. I'd snort derisively but I don't have the energy.

As I reflect on the morning's work, though, the tetchiness fades away as I remember the stunning views that I absorbed along the way – and there's no doubt that this is where mountain running comes into its own.

By definition it's going to be pretty special – you don't get mountains in the middle of urban conurbations – and no matter how much you're

'Running down a mountain is no easier than running up; the pain simply switches from your hamstrings to your quads'

feeling the burn you simply cannot help but discover all over again the raw beauty of nature.

On this one run alone I've trotted through flower-laden fields, up rocky crags, past lakes, along narrow, plunging forest trails, down valleys and through streams. You'd have to be pretty curmudgeonly not to be affected by it, and when I mention this to Wyatt later over a well-earned beer he agrees and claims the mountains are actually responsible for revitalising his running career.

A former New Zealand Olympic and Commonwealth 5,000m athlete, Wyatt, 37, became bored of the relentless grind of the training and the cut-throat nature of competing on the track. "After the Athens World Championships in 1998 my motivation was dipping and I was questioning my own will to compete when I wasn't enjoying it any more. Then I went out for a run off-road one day and it was a revelation. I remembered why I'd loved cross-country at school," he says. "It's the sense of freedom, of being in control, of running in surroundings whose beauty leaves you speechless, that make you remember why we do this sport.

"You can get that feeling with running off-road on the flat, but it's up in the mountains where the experience is at its purest. And if you're competitive it's a good challenge, which maintains your motivation through training because there's simply no winging it on the day. You have to put the work in – but when you get out on the trail, it's worth it."

It must have been, because by switching disciplines Wyatt was leaving behind him a well funded, well publicised sport for one that at the time had a long history but was best described as little more than an underground movement.

AS OLD AS THE HILLS

Mountain running pre-dates modern track and cross-country; the earliest recorded mountain race took place in 1068 when Malcolm III, King of Scotland, chose his messenger by having applicants race to the top of the nearest mountain and back.

The first recorded race in England was a 2.5K fell run in 1850 at Grasmere in the Lake District; and a race that was first run in 1895 – a 16K, 1500m climb to the summit of Ben Nevis and back – is still going today.

However, it was not until 1983 that a governing body, the World Mountain Running Association, was founded, and it took until this year for both the WMRA and its World Mountain Running Championship to be officially recognised by the IAAF – the overarching governing body for athletics.

As to what actually constitutes mountain running, well, that's open to interpretation. The WMRA says: "A common misconception surrounds the term 'mountain running' because immediate thoughts of running up the Matterhorn or other high Alpine mountains spring to mind.

"In fact, there are testing mountain races staged on hills no higher than 200m. We have often been challenged to define the difference between, say, cross-country running and mountain running. This has been resisted because the line between the two is blurred. What we can say is that mountain running involves considerable amounts of ascent and descent

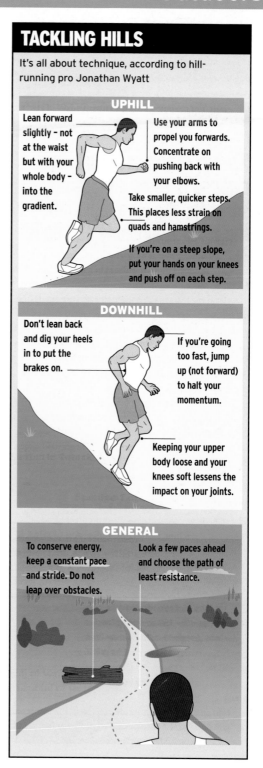

TACKLING HILLS

It's all about technique, according to hill-running pro Jonathan Wyatt

UPHILL

Lean forward slightly – not at the waist but with your whole body – into the gradient.

Use your arms to propel you forwards. Concentrate on pushing back with your elbows.

Take smaller, quicker steps. This places less strain on quads and hamstrings.

If you're on a steep slope, put your hands on your knees and push off on each step.

DOWNHILL

Don't lean back and dig your heels in to put the brakes on.

If you're going too fast, jump up (not forward) to halt your momentum.

Keeping your upper body loose and your knees soft lessens the impact on your joints.

GENERAL

To conserve energy, keep a constant pace and stride. Do not leap over obstacles.

Look a few paces ahead and choose the path of least resistance.

much in excess of that which would be contemplated for a cross-country race."

Jonathan Wyatt distinguishes between different forms of off-road running thus: "Cross-country or trail running can be anything off-road, even flat courses. Mountain running obviously has to have a decent element of ascent and descent," he says.

'Everyone thinks mountain running is some impossible sport for the elite only, but the truth is anybody can do it'

"Fell running is often taken as simply a British word for mountain running, but the difference there is that mountain races have the course marked out on defined pathways, whereas in fell races you can simply choose your own route between checkpoints.

"The mountain-running season is from May to October, cross-country from October to March, and fell running is done all year round. They're all part of the same family though."

Same family maybe, but even within just mountain running the challenge can vary from country to country. Austria, Switzerland and Germany have a strong tradition of uphill-only races; France and Spain favour long, technical, up-and-down rocky races, while Italy prefers brutal, sheer downhill runs.

REACHING THE TOP

The final day of the trip sees me standing outside our hotel awaiting a run of the uphill-only variety: a tough 12K with 1,200m of climb from the village of Söll to the top of the highest mountain in the region, HoHe Salve.

Some of my fellow runners look apprehensive but, rather surprisingly, I feel nothing but the urge to get underway.

My suffering on day two turned out to be a tipping point of sorts; by day three I'd made solid progress by keeping up with the mid-packers; and this morning I'd been able to get out of bed without first having to grease my joints with WD40.

I complete the first three kilometres at the head of the group, and have to be told to slow down and keep something in the tank for the increased gradient that is imminent.

Three kilometres further up the mountain I'm dodging nimbly past a stray cow, still at the head of the group and thinking: 'Increased gradient? Hah!' Despite the baking sun I wave aside the offer of water and put on a spurt to lead everyone to the 8K point where we will take a breather.

Not that I need one. I'm frankly amazed at how quickly I've adjusted in the space of a few days, but Jonathan Wyatt isn't. He grins knowingly as he says: "Everyone thinks that mountain running is some impossible sport for the elite only, but the truth is anybody can do it if they're already running to some degree. Your body needs time to adjust but it will do so quickly if you put the work in, and once you start to enjoy it even a little, it can become addictive."

He's not wrong. The final 4K section contains a scarcely credible 700m of climb. Everyone is forced to walk using the special hands-on-knees method we've been shown, but I do it with a grimace of masochistic pleasure on my face.

As I reach the top of HoHe Salve (1,800m above sea level) and look out at the snow-sprinkled mountain tops before me I discover that, yes I'm very tired, but I also feel energised and invincible. I'm not quite on top of the world but from up here it feels like it.

ONLY WAY IS UP
Our race reporter Kerry makes it look so easy

GROUP RUN
Enjoying a rare flat stretch to take in the surroundings

REACH THE TOP

Inspired to run a mountain race? Try this simple training programme

Here is a sample two-week programme (for runners who train five to six times a week) from Jonathan Wyatt. Typically it takes eight to 10 weeks for a novice hill runner to train for a mountain event from 10K to half-marathon distance, and 12-14 weeks for a mountain marathon.

In addition, aim for three to four cross-training sessions per week including some or all of these: stretching, core-stability exercises, massage, cardio cross-training and weight-training (especially lower limbs, including hamstring curls, leg press, lunges, barbells squats, dumbbell squats, calf raises).

EASY RUN 60-70% max heart rate (or 6/10 PE – rate of perceived exertion), STEADY RUN 70-80% max heart rate (or 7/10 PE)

WEEK	MON	TUES	WED	THURS	FRI	SAT	SUN
1	Easy 45-75-min run on the flat	60-min steady run followed by 6 x 3-min hill reps and 2-min jog back down in between	Steady 60-min run on flat terrain	75-min steady run on flat followed by 6 x 1-min hill sprints with steady run back down	Rest	45-min easy run on flat plus 6 x 100m easy strides	120-150-min steady hill run – either a continuous climb or a sequence of up and down
2	45-75-min recovery run, flat or undulating	Steady 75-min run on flat	120-150-min hill tempo run with 45-min steady climb	Rest	Easy 60-min run, flat or incline, including 8 x 100m steady strides	Easy 45-min run on the flat	Race day OR steady 90-min hill run

COLD COMFORTS

Winter is no reason to lie about indoors under a duvet, as these 25 tips from runners and coaches will prove

1 SEEK SHELTER

"Find a good spot that's sheltered from the elements," says Dave Long of Coventry Godiva Harriers. "It's common for keen West Midlands runners to train underneath the M6 at Spaghetti Junction when it's icy underfoot elsewhere. You can run 1K reps on a dry surface, and there are hardly any cars above if you go early. If you haven't got access to a covered area, bus routes are a good bet – they are gritted, and the grit often spills onto the pavement."

2 MAKE A RAIN CHECK

Dress for the actual temperature. "It might feel cold, but you have to rely on numbers to know how you'll feel once you're actually out there – you will warm up," says Carmel Scales from Fareham. "Don't be influenced by national weather forecasts on the news. For hour-by-hour satellite images of your area, see bbc.co.uk/weather/ukweather. Instead of a raindrop over the south coast for the morning, for instance, you'll see that in fact it'll be dry from 5am until 7am, so you'll be fine. Likewise, if you see bad conditions approaching, you can prepare yourself by dressing in the appropriate clothing."

3 STRETCH YOUR WARM-UP

When it's cold outside, your ligaments, tendons and muscles take longer to loosen up, so it's good to extend your warm-up. "Try walking for five minutes, then alternate walking, brisk walking and jogging for six to 10 minutes before easing into your training pace," says cross-country coach Nick Anderson. "Or warm up indoors; start your run at the gym and then head out when you're ready, but before you start sweating."

4 INVEST IN MITTENS

"A cold-weather problem I have, which a number of others suffer from (especially women), is Raynaud's syndrome – very cold hands, especially the fingers. The pain can be excruciating," says Karen Hancock from Serpentine Running Club. "The solution that worked best for me is a pair of big pink ski mittens – in fact I am renowned for them at the club. Unlike gloves, mittens pool the heat from your fingers and are padded. They can be removed on the rare occasions I get too hot, and they have long, knitted cuffs so your wrists stay warm. I highly recommend them for long runs in the coldest months."

5 BEAT THE SNOW

What's the best strategy for ploughing on through snow? "Run in a short, relaxed stride, so that if you slip you can catch yourself," says Ian Williamson, endurance coach for the Shetland Amateur Athletics Club in Lerwick, which has the UK's highest annual snowfall. Your pace will slow, but short steps increase leg turnover. Wear trail-running shoes for traction.

6 HYDRATE

Don't overlook the importance of hydration in winter. "Because runners don't see their sweat losses in the winter, they're not as attentive to their drinking," says Dr Lawrence Armstrong, an exercise physiology expert from the University of Connecticut, USA. It's possible to sweat just as much as you do on a warm day – especially if you're layered up.

7 DO YOUR RESEARCH

"Take note of the course's elevation. As well as the temperature plummeting as you go up, there's the problem of exposure to the wind, which can be a killer," says Chris Fletcher from Serpentine Running Club. "Do your research, and dress accordingly. I did the Edale Skyline Fell Race, and the temperature at the bottom was about zero; I'd laughed at other runners with balaclavas and ski goggles – but they were the ones laughing at the top where it was more like -10°C."

8 EASE THE FREEZE

"Just knowing I've got a warm welcome home is enough to get me out the door every time," says Lesley Foster from Sunderland Strollers. "Before a run, I always fill a hot water bottle with piping-hot water and wrap it in a towel, then when I'm stripping down afterwards, I stand on it to warm me from the bottom up. And the last thing I want to do after a cold run is have to prepare and cook any food, so I'll put food in the slow cooker. Personally, I find it's better to eat hot food and then have a hot shower or bath, as you're heating yourself up from the inside first."

9 GO LONG

On the days when the mercury rises, and you don't have to trudge through slush and ice, make the most of it, says coach Jeff Galloway. "Whatever the distance of your longest run during the last two weeks, run up to two miles longer. Keep the pace very comfortable – at least two minutes per mile slower than 5K race pace. Add one to two miles every 14 days, as weather permits, until you hit 17 miles. At that distance you can maintain your endurance with one long run every 17 to 21 days."

10 FEEL THE BURN IN THE COLD

In need of extra motivation? Consider this: running in the cold burns calories like an oven. University of Kansas researchers found that cold-weather sessions cooked up to 12 per cent more calories, and 32 per cent more fat than the same sessions in warm weather. This is because your body needs to generate heat, which ramps up the burning of fatty deposits.

11 LEAVE THE SHORTS AT HOME

"I typically find my muscles and ligaments seize up in next to no time after cold-weather runs," says Matt Taylor from London. "As well as keeping me warm on those bitterly cold sessions, really snug compression tights also keep me warm afterwards and aid my recovery, pushing any lingering lactic acid

out of my muscles. If it's wet out, it's great to have a spare pair waiting for you, warming on the radiator. I also swear by my windproof fitted gilet, which allows free movement but also keeps my core warm. I've got reflective patches on the back for added safety."

12 TAKE A PIT-STOP

"It's easy to think that because it's cold you don't need as much hydration, but I find I sweat even more with the extra layers I wear in the cold," says Michael Morris from Morpeth Harriers. "The last thing I want when the temperature drops is a cold drink. I go for hot Ribena, before and after my runs. When I'm out, I leave a flask of it mid-route, or in my car if I'm doing loops, as a handy, warming pit-stop."

13 HANG TIGHT

It's not just your fingers that suffer the effects of being separated from your body, warns Dennis Murphy of Cardiff's Les Croupiers Running Club. "I've had runs before where I haven't adequately 'wrapped up' my nether regions and have suffered severe frost-nip. Gents should avoid underwear that allows air to circulate. I prefer tight pants rather than loose boxers. For extra warmth, invest in a pair of wool leggings."

14 PROTECT YOUR SKIN

"Your skin can take just as much of a battering in the cold as in the sun – and if it's cold and sunny, your face and hands are in for a tough time," says Paula Coates from Clapham Runners. "The cold really dries out your skin, which leaves it more vulnerable, as well as ageing. Hopefully in this day and age it's not just women who are worried about wrinkles! It's the thin skin around your eyes that really suffers, so I use Elizabeth Arden Eight Hour Cream before every run, but any good moisturiser should work. For your hands, go for something a bit hardier – I use Neutrogena hand cream. If it's good enough for Norwegian fishermen, it's good enough for me!"

15 CHOOSE NEW SHOES

A study at the Mayo Clinic in the USA looked at how temperature affects the cushioning of running shoes. "As temperatures get colder, the shock absorption of shoes decreases," says Dr Jay Smith. "A loss of shock absorption may result in a higher injury risk." When buying winter running shoes, go for a pair with extra EVA foam cushioning, the material least affected by cold temperatures according to the study. Got shoes with vents? Then insulate them with strips of duct tape.

16 GET FLEXIBLE

"Don't bank on sticking to your normal training schedule," says Williamson. Shetland winters are marked by periods of brief sunlight – less than six hours a day – so Shetland AAC runners adjust their schedules so they can run during the window of daylight. "If you're a morning or evening runner, consider switching to lunchtime, when it is warmest."

17 TAKE EXTRA CARE

"While it's great to run with friends, with really early morning runs it's not always possible – and if you're a woman, running on your own in the dark can be dangerous," says Susan Cuin from Colchester. "I always keep those runs to less than five miles and I leave a detailed note by the door of where I'm going to run and when I set off. I always carry a mobile with me, and I think it's a good idea to tape a 20p piece under

com), a three-day running festival culminating with a 10K. Or head for the Dubai Marathon and 10K, (22nd, dubaimarathon.org), the richest long-distance running event in history, with £500,000 prize money.

20 AIM HIGHER

"Dress for weather that's 20 degrees warmer than it feels outside," says Williamson. "After a minute or two of running, your body will warm up. It is just as uncomfortable to get overheated as it is to be too cold."

21 BUDDY UP

Winter is the time to make training more social. Think about joining a running club, or simply getting friends to join you. The benefits are twofold. Accidents are more likely in icy weather so there will be someone around to help if anything should go wrong and you'll be able to motivate each other through the freeze.

22 BEAT WINTER BLUES ON YOUR FEET

A run outdoors, especially at midday, can relieve Seasonal Affective Disorder (SAD), the deep depression that strikes 500,000 Brits – mostly women – every winter. Running stimulates the brain to release endorphins, neurochemicals credited with providing a mood-boost. Make yours a 5K or 10K; endorphin production usually begins around 15 to 20 minutes in and peaks after about 45 minutes.

23 STAY BELOW 60

How much running will compromise your immune system to the point of making you ill? For average runners, the line falls at 60 miles a week, says a study at the Human Performance Laboratory at Appalachian State University, in the USA.

24 SAVE FACE

Windburn occurs when cold temperatures and blustery conditions strip oil from your skin. Get heavy-duty protection from both a face cream and lip balm of SPF 30 or more.

25 KEEP MOVING

"To avoid getting too chilled after a run, keep your cool-down brief," says Anderson. "Slow down your pace for three to four minutes, then go inside. Take extra layers off and keep moving (walking on a treadmill or just around the house) for another five to 10 minutes before diving into the shower."

your laces in case the mobile packs in and you need to use a pay phone. Ignore any jibes, run facing the traffic and always use well-lit, popular routes. I find it comforting to take my dog – he'd be useless if I was in trouble, but any attacker doesn't know that!"

18 GET A LIFT

"It's extra tough to grind out the miles with the wind against you," says Williamson. "For a faster pace, ask someone to drop you off in a car and run back with the wind behind you." If you're running an out-and-back, begin by running into the wind, not with it, which will keep you from sweating too much. Sweat is bad news in winter; the moisture robs heat from your body up to 25 times faster than trapped air does.

19 GET AWAY

Overcome treadmill tedium and winter blues in one, by getting as close to the equator as you can in January. Try the Bermuda International Race Weekend (15th-17th 2010, bermudaraceweekend.

BEAT THE HEAT

Whether you're running at home or away in summertime, run sun-smart, focusing on hydration, clothing and your training schedule

The Great British Summer™: without a doubt the best time of year to lace up and hit the ground running. But whether we're treated to the full three-month quota of summer or the usual four days in July, it pays to run sun-smart for every second under the sun.

Without due care, soaring temperatures take their toll. Even in cooler temperatures, your body works double-time to shift excess heat. As the mercury rises, so does that cooling effort. And if your body struggles to keep up, you can suffer from dehydration or heat illnesses such as cramp and heat exhaustion. Luckily, you can make life easier for your body by practising sun-smart running – focusing on hydration, clothing and your training schedule.

TRAIN SMART

Factoring in the sun's effects on your body is good practice when planning sun-kissed training sessions. Is it absolutely necessary to go out on six-minute miles? Starting your run slowly can keep you going for longer on hot days. "The slower you start, the longer you'll keep your body heat from reaching a threshold," says Mike Gleeson, exercise physiologist at Loughborough University. For example, if you normally start out at seven-minute-mile pace, do your first mile at eight-minute pace, then speed up later on.

If you're planning to take your training regime on holiday, acclimatise in a gradual manner. "For the first three days or so, keep daytime sessions to 30 easy minutes," says coach Mike Gratton. When it comes to speed training, Gleeson advises running in the morning or evening. "Running in the hottest part of the day will put added strain on your cardio system. Your heart beats faster in warmer temperatures."

HYDRATION

With hydration, you shouldn't short-change your body at any time, let alone in the heat. Sweating – your body's cooling system – removes excess heat through evaporation. Physiologically, fluid losses reduce blood volume, which in turn reduces stroke volume in the heart. As a result, the heart is forced to work harder. Drinking to replace what you lose through sweat helps keep your blood volume constant. If your fluid levels dip too low, your blood volume will start to decrease. Sooner or later your body reaches a point where it says there's not enough blood to deliver to the muscles. "The body's response is to restrict blood flow to these less-essential areas," says Gleeson. "Your body will choose to save your life, and deliver blood to the vital organs and not the muscles. So you slow down." Just two per cent dehydration can cause a 20 per cent drop in performance.

Even worse, if fluid levels aren't topped up swiftly, you could suffer more serious problems, such as dizziness, cramps and vomiting. If dehydration strikes, head straight for a shaded area and fill up on water.

URINE TROUBLE?

How's your hydration? Check the colour of your urine against the shades on our chart

NORMAL	DEHYDRATED	SEVERELY DEHYDRATED

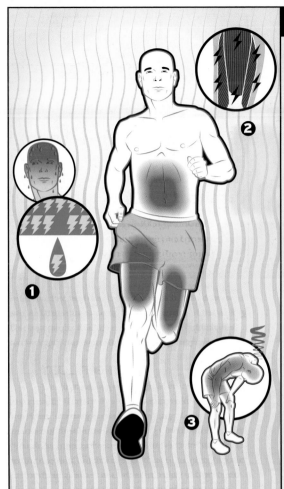

SYSTEM OVERLOAD

How to recognise the signs and symptoms of heat illness

❶ HEAT EXHAUSTION

CAUSE Failing to replace fluids and electrolytes when dehydration sets in.

SYMPTOMS A core body temperature of 102°F to 104°F, headache, fatigue, profuse sweating, nausea, clammy skin.

ACTION PLAN Apply a cold pack on the head and neck. Restore fluid and salt balance with foods and drinks that contain sodium.

❷ HEAT CRAMPS

CAUSE Loss of fluid and minerals (electrolytes) through respiration and sweat.

SYMPTOMS Severe abdominal cramps or large-muscle cramps (such as quads and glutes).

ACTION PLAN Restore fluid and salt balance with foods and drinks that contain sodium (salted snack foods, sports drinks).

❸ HEATSTROKE

CAUSE Extreme exertion, coupled with very hot, humid conditions and dehydration, impair your body's ability to maintain optimal temperature.

SYMPTOMS A core body temperature of 104°F or above, headache, nausea, vomiting, diarrhoea, rapid pulse, disorientation.

ACTION PLAN Emergency medical attention necessary.

But the best strategy is to avoid the problem altogether by keeping your fluid levels at optimum. To estimate your fluid needs, weigh yourself naked before and after a hard run, says Dr Neil Walsh, senior lecturer at the School of Sport Health and Exercise Science at Bangor University. "If you weigh one kilogram less after a run, you need to drink one litre of fluid." And checking the colour of your urine first thing each morning can give you a rough idea of your current hydration levels.

STAY-COOL KIT

Summer means vest time, right? Wrong. When it comes to keeping cool, the smart money's on loose-fitting clothing. The benefits are two-fold: you get more protection from the sun's energy-sapping heat,

plus looser garments allow you to take advantage of any breeze – including the one you make on your running travels. Fabric-wise, look for sports-specific synthetics, which stay drier and wick moisture better than natural fibres like cotton do. Colour-wise, the lighter the better, so you can reflect the sun's rays.

You lose a large proportion of your body's heat through your head. But if the sun is particularly strong, it's a good idea wear a loose-fitting cap. Choose one with a substantial peak that's constructed from technical fibres designed to help wick sweat away.

Finally, be sure to complete your get-up with a layer of sunscreen – with a minimum SPF of 15. Always opt for sweat-proof lotions, says Gleeson. "It's crucial that your sweat can evaporate, so you cool properly."

RAVE RUN

Peckforton Hills, Cheshire

IMAGE: KEVIN McGARRY

NATURAL SELECTION

What distance were you born to run: a fast 5K, a strong marathon or something in between? Here's how to figure out what kind of runner you really are – and realise your full potential

Success in some events comes more naturally than in others. In fact, few runners have the same potential to be outstanding at all distances. Some have the innate gift of speed, while others are natural-born long-distance runners. In the end, your physiology, temperament and priorities will determine your ideal racing distance.

You may be surprised to find out where your true strengths lie. "Everyone thinks the marathon is the Holy Grail, when a lot of people should really be doing the 5K," says Jason Karp, an exercise physiologist and running coach.

The physiology you're born with determines how well you'll perform your first time out, and how much improvement you'll be able to make in training. The good news is that with the appropriate training strategy, you can make the most of what you were born with.

So how do you determine whether you were meant to be a speed demon or a multiple marathon runner? You could turn to pricey lab tests, but that would probably be overkill. Your running habits reveal plenty about what distances you're most suited to excel at.

Read on to learn which physiological factors help shape your running identity. Then examine your training, racing history and tendencies to find out which distances are perfect for you. Finally, learn how to tweak your training routine and set realistic goals to better match your newfound specialty. Who knows? You might discover talents you didn't know you even possessed.

I
KNOW YOUR PHYSIOLOGY

II
IDENTIFY YOUR TRUE CALLING

III
TRAIN LIKE A SPECIALIST

IV
SET REACHABLE GOALS

THE RUNNER

THE SPEED RACER
These athletes are built to go fast – not long. Consequently, the 5K and 10K are ideal events to target.

THE MIDDLE-DISTANCE SPECIALIST
These people are best at sustaining a tough pace. So they're well suited to run strong 10-milers and half-marathons.

THE LONG-HAULER
These runners were really meant to go the distance. Though they may lack speed, their true calling is the marathon.

I KNOW YOUR PHYSIOLOGY

Each of these four qualities influences how fast and how far you can run – and which distance will suit you best

LACTATE THRESHOLD (LT)

pace is the fastest pace that you can sustain for an extended period (roughly 30 minutes or more) before lactate – a by-product of the fuel burned during hard exercise – starts building up in the blood. Marathon winners often have high lactate thresholds, which help them hold a strong pace for a long time. With targeted training – maintaining a certain intensity over a distance – you can raise your lactate threshold.

MUSCLES...

are made of slow- and fast-twitch fibres. An elite marathon runner's muscles might be 75 per cent slow-twitch; an Olympic sprinter probably has a high proportion of fast-twitch. Most runners are born with a modest mix of both. You can't change the muscle composition you inherit, but you can train your muscles for speed or to sustain steady paces over long distances.

VO2 MAX

measures the maximum amount of oxygen that can be consumed per minute while exercising. Runners with a naturally high VO2 max often find it easier to run faster because their hearts can deliver more oxygen to their muscles. There are many ways to boost VO2 max, including speedwork, which forces the heart to pump blood at a higher rate. Beginners can improve it by about 20 per cent. Fit runners can only fine-tune it.

RUNNING ECONOMY

measures the amount of oxygen you need to run at any pace. It reflects how efficiently you run. Other physical factors impact running economy – if you're overweight or have a sloppy gait, for instance, you're going to need more oxygen than a leaner person with a cleaner stride. As you run more, and improve factors like VO2 max, weight and biomechanics, you'll develop better running economy.

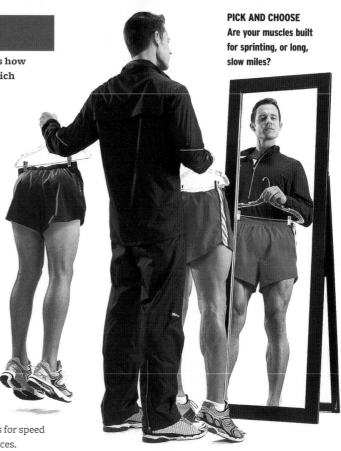

PICK AND CHOOSE
Are your muscles built for sprinting, or long, slow miles?

II IDENTIFY YOUR TRUE CALLING

Examine your own training and racing habits to learn what kind of running will give you the best performances

1 HOW MANY HOURS A WEEK CAN YOU DEVOTE TO TRAINING?

A. 2 to 3
B. 4 to 5
C. 6 or more

2 HOW WOULD YOU DESCRIBE THE PERFECT TRAINING RUN?

A. It brings a surge of adrenaline and power – like kicking into high gear.
B. Running right at the edge of your abilities – not backing off, but not pushing so much that you run out of steam.

C. It's getting into a meditative rhythm, where you can zone out or get absorbed in your thoughts, a conversation or your surroundings.

3 IF YOU COULD SKIP ANY SESSION EACH WEEK, WHAT WOULD IT BE?

A. Any run that takes more than an hour. It's just too exhausting and boring.
B. Workouts that don't feel long enough or fast enough.
C. Any run where there's pressure to hold a fast pace. It ceases to be enjoyable.

4 WHEN YOU'RE OUT ON A GROUP RUN, YOU STAND OUT FROM THE PACK BY:

A. Surging to the finish – no matter how hard the group has been running.
B. Managing to stick with the lead group, no matter how much they're pushing it.
C. Feeling pretty fresh at the end of a long run – no matter how far you've gone.

5 WHEN YOU GET INJURED, WHAT CAUSES THE PROBLEM?

A. Total mileage. Overdoing it always seems to trigger some ailment – like plantar fasciitis or a screaming IT band.
B. A muscle pull, a tendon tweak or something that got twisted or torn while trying to keep up or dash to the finish.
C. No major injuries.

6 HOW DO YOU FEEL ABOUT SPENDING MONEY ON RACING?

A. With all the races I do, it's hard to justify shelling out more than £20 on one.
B. Spending £35 or so on a race is okay, as long as there aren't a lot of other costs for travel and logistics.
C. No one likes to part with hard-earned cash, but for a few big events each year, it's not an issue to spend £70.

7 WHEN YOU'RE CHOOSING A RACE, WHAT MATTERS MOST?

A. Convenience. Running shouldn't take time away from family, work or other important commitments.
B. Getting a decent workout – and a good test – without having to deal with a lot of travel or race-day logistics.
C. It should feel like a big deal. Whether the race is a large, well-known event or is in a beautiful location, it

should be something to circle on the calendar and look forward to, and it should feel like a reward for all the hard work of training.

8 WHAT ARE THE RACE DISTANCES WHERE YOU HAD YOUR BEST FINISHING TIMES?

A. 5K
B. 10 miles or half-marathon
C. Marathon

ANSWER KEY
(Give yourself points as noted below)

❶	A=2	B=4	C=6
❷	A=1	B=2	C=3
❸	A=1	B=2	C=3
❹	A=1	B=2	C=0
❺	A=1	B=2	C=0
❻	A=2	B=4	C=6
❼	A=2	B=4	C=6
❽	A=2	B=4	C=6

INTERPRET YOUR SCORE

Your tally says a lot about you – your strengths, the distances you were born to run and your ideal training strategy.

10 TO 18 POINTS: YOU'RE A SPEED RACER

You may not have thought about 5Ks and 10Ks since you first started running, but as you seem to be able to pick up speed with ease, that may be the place to stand out. You can put your all into it without feeling like it compromises your life.

19 TO 26 POINTS: YOU'RE A MIDDLE-DISTANCE SPECIALIST

It may feel like the world revolves around the marathon, but you don't have to go that far: 10-milers and half-marathons could be for you. By running them, you'll find out how far and fast you can run. And as 13.1-milers become the most popular races, many have taken on the big-league feel of marathons.

27 TO 34 POINTS: YOU'RE A LONG-HAULER

While some people could never imagine 'looking forward' to a few hours of running, you savour the long, slow distances that let you spend long stretches of time outside. The marathon is your race. You may get left behind in a 5K, but that shouldn't matter.

III TRAIN LIKE A SPECIALIST

Target your strengths to maximise your training gains

Once you know your strong suit, you can develop the traits that will help you excel. Of course, with focused training, you can fulfill your potential at any distance. "Our bodies are remarkably adaptable," says exercise scientist Bill Pierce. Work out with purpose and, he says, and "you can reach your goals". Here's how…

BE A SPEED RACER
(RUN FAST 5Ks AND 10Ks)

➲ **YOUR GOAL** Improve VO2 max, fast-twitch muscles and running economy.

➲ **YOUR STRATEGY** Get lots of practice running fast. Intervals, which involve working near maximum heart rate, force the heart to move as much oxygen as it can to the muscles, which boosts VO2 max. The bursts of speed get your fast-twitch fibres firing. And as your legs and feet turn over at a quicker rate, you'll shed sloppiness and run more efficiently.

➲ **KEY WORKOUT** Speedwork. Run intervals about 10 seconds faster than 5K race pace, or the quickest pace you can sustain and repeat. At a track, run 400-1,600m intervals, or on the road, run fast for up to five minutes. Between intervals, jog for two minutes. Start with three intervals.

➲ **HOW TO IMPROVE** Work your legs. You'll need leg strength to make powerful strides and avoid injury. Twice a week, try moves like squats and lunges to strengthen your legs.

BE A MIDDLE-DISTANCE SPECIALIST
(RUN FAST 10-MILERS AND HALF-MARATHONS)

➲ **YOUR GOAL** Raise lactate threshold.

➲ **YOUR STRATEGY** Master the art of running comfortably hard. Hold an intense pace for 20 to 45 minutes – this delays the time it takes for lactate to start building up in the blood and for fatigue to set in. It also builds mental stamina; you'll have more confidence in the hardest moments of the race. Don't drop speedwork and long runs – they make tempo work feel more manageable.

➲ **KEY WORKOUT** Tempo run. Start with 15 to 20 minutes at a pace that's 15 to 45 seconds slower than

BE THE BEST
Know where your
strengths lie

your 5K pace. Build up to 30-to-45 minutes. As you get more comfortable, gradually increase the pace.

➲ **HOW TO IMPROVE** Learn to breathe and relax – even during maximum effort. When you're pushing your pace, it's natural to tense up, which steals energy your heart and legs need. Running on a treadmill in front of a mirror can help you evaluate your own form and identify any spots where you're tensing up.

BE A LONG-HAULER
(RUN A STRONG MARATHON)

➲ **YOUR GOAL** Improve running economy.

➲ **YOUR STRATEGY** Pile on the miles. The more you run, the more economical your form will become, and you'll feel stronger on your feet for longer. Also, your body will become more efficient at preserving energy for later in the race. Don't slack on the speedwork and tempo runs though – a strong heart and higher lactate threshold will help you stay strong for the final miles.

➲ **KEY WORKOUT** The long run. Start with a one-hour run and gradually build up to three hours. Aim to run about 30 seconds slower than your goal marathon pace. As you get more comfortable, work on picking up the pace in the middle miles. Then, try to shift into a higher gear in the last segment of the run.

➲ **HOW TO IMPROVE** Build a strong core, and your form will be less likely to fall apart when you're fatigued. Being at your ideal weight can help, too – the lighter you are, the less oxygen you'll need.

IV SET REACHABLE GOALS

Online tools help you find the right pace and best race

Runners have lots of questions. Is the marathon really for me? Is a 25-minute 5K realistic? Prediction calculators can provide some answers. These tools forecast how fast you can run one distance based on a time for another. Say you ran a 3:30 marathon, and the 5K time the calculator shows is five minutes faster than your PB. That's a sign that you'll perform better at long distances.

The predictions are based on algorithms that include factors such as race statistics and the natural tendency to run slower at longer distances. They're only accurate if you've trained for each distance.

Here are some good online prediction tools. Remember: they only predict potential.

THE BEST ONLINE PREDICTION TOOLS
At runnersworld.co.uk

Runnersworld.co.uk/calculators is loaded with resources that can help you gauge how fit and fast you are – and figure out how to make your mark. It also links to SmartCoach, a tool that lets you tailor a training plan to your ability and goals.

Race-time predictor This predicts how fast you could run 11 different distances based on your performance at one race distance, and suggests training paces based on your results.

Race-pace band This shows the pace you need to maintain at various distances to reach your goal. Then you can create your own marathon pace band listing your splits for race day.

TIME TRIAL
Work out your 5K pace for a general benchmark

ON OTHER SITES

Mcmillanrunning.com has a tool that converts any race time to equivalent distances.

Fetcheveryone.com allows you to build a portfolio of past and future races. The site calculates your PB times over a variety of distances.

Jeffgalloway.com has a calculator that's especially helpful for beginners or anyone who hasn't raced before. The site includes a 'Magic Mile' formula.

DON'T KNOW YOUR PACE?

Your 5K pace is a good benchmark to help you assess your fitness and set goals – whether you're running 3.1 miles or 26.2. If you haven't raced before (or for a while), this time trial, developed by exercise scientist Bill Pierce, will give you a good estimate.

1 At a track, run 3 x 1,600m (four laps) at a challenging pace, and time each segment. Jog for two minutes between intervals to recover. The goal is to run each segment at an even pace.

2 If the times of each of the three segments are similar (within 10 seconds of each other), work out your average pace per mile, then add 15 seconds. If not, try another day.

3 So if your segment times were 6:00, 6:04 and 6:08, your average pace is 6:04. Then add 15 seconds to get 6:19 – that time is a good estimate of your 5K pace per mile.

MILE IN A MONTH

The magic of the mile has enchanted runners for over a century, and it's a classic test of speed you should try too

Training for the mile is something you have probably never dreamed of doing, but the change of focus, even if you only do it for four weeks, and the variety, can be surprisingly enjoyable and may also reap benefits when you return to training for longer distance. Racing a mile – there is a variety of open events to try up and down the country – is also about as close as most of us will come to feeling like an elite athlete. These are a few key points to consider before you start your mile training.

1 QUALITY SESSIONS

Being of a shorter duration and a higher intensity, miling requires a greater amount of anaerobic work than races of 10K or longer. This means you need to train your body to cope with the rapid onset of fatigue, which results from faster anaerobic work. The best way to do this is to run interval sessions – preferably on grass, which is more forgiving than the track. The duration of the repetitions should be short, because you will be running at a speed equal to or faster than your mile time. Your session should be preceded by a good warm-up and some stretching exercises (it's preferable to stretch before an interval session rather than afterwards) and followed by a cool-down. It's best to build up to the pace at which you run the reps in successive sessions, rather than increasing the volume, because you are, after all, training your body to run faster.

2 FLEXIBILITY

Running speed is dictated by two factors: stride length and stride rate. Developing flexibility of the correct muscles will help you to increase your stride length without overtraining. Concentrate on stretching the muscles in the hamstrings, gluteals, calves, groin and quadriceps areas. Hold stretches for at least 30 seconds. Do the stretches before and after a session because the increased intensity of the exercise will lead to muscle tightening and stiffness. Self-massage will also help to counter this tightening.

3 DOWNHILL RUNNING

Increasing your stride rate will also help to boost your running speed. The most effective way to increase your stride rate is to do some downhill running, where you are almost forced to move your legs quicker. It is important that you do this in a safe manner to avoid the obvious injury problems. Find a suitable location that consists of a stretch of grass with a very gentle down slope. It makes sense to do this sort of workout when you are relatively fresh and warmed up; so following a 20-30 minute run will be better than after your longer Sunday effort. A good way to structure the run is to stretch, and then to do six to eight strides at a fast pace with a walk-back recovery. The emphasis should be on a fast pick-up of the legs.

4 STRENGTHENING

There is a strong association between muscle strength and speed, which is partly why most sprinters are bulky creatures and marathon runners are of a slighter build. Improving your strength will help to improve your miling but you need to work on the right muscles. As you will be on your toes more in the mile

MILE HIGH CLUB
This classic distance is a
great test of speed endurance

than in a long-distance race, it will help to strengthen the calves with a series of calf raises. You will also need driving quads, and half squats will strengthen those. Initially your body weight alone will provide sufficient resistance, but you may start holding weights when you want to progress.

5 THINK LIKE A MILER

Running, or indeed racing, on the track may be a completely different experience for you, but you have to think in a positive way and attack the track rather than being scared of it. It might be a refreshing change to have a bash at the mile, but your attitude must change to meet the new demand. Things happened very quickly – whatever the standard – in a race over this distance. You have to think about what you are doing. Decide in advance what pace you want to run at and calculate your desired 400m splits. Don't get carried away at the start if everyone else goes off a fast pace, be disciplined and run at the pace that suits you. That said, if you feel good with a lap to go, don't be afraid to take a risk and make a bold strike for home.

MILE PREDICTOR

The table below will give you a basic idea of what mile time you should be capable of on the basis of your best 10K performance. If you run much quicker than the predicted time, you clearly have talent for miling!

10K BEST	MILE PREDICTION
34:00	4:41
36:00	4:57
38:00	5:13
40:00	5:31
42:00	5:49
44:00	6:07
46:00	6:25
48:00	6:42
50:00	7:01
52:00	7:19
54:00	7:37
56:00	7:55
58:00	8:12
60:00	8:30

YOUR FIRST 5K

With the right advice, any runner can become a racer in just five weeks. How? Read on...

For one brief moment, probably while endorphins were still pumping through your body after a good run, you flirted with the idea of doing a marathon. Then the endorphins disappeared and the reality of training for four months and trying to squeeze in a handful of three- to four-hour-long runs set in. Fair enough. But how about a simple 5K instead?

It's a perfect distance: 3.1 miles require relatively little build-up, the training doesn't take over your life, and the race is over fairly quickly. And by logging only three or four runs per week, you can be ready to toe the line of a 5K in just five weeks.

Top coach Chris Carmichael (trainright.com) encourages all runners to try a 5K. "People run for a variety of reasons, but they get more out of it when they're working towards something specific," he says. "And a 5K race is an attainable goal for any runner." Plus, there's the 'fun factor', says US running guru Jeff Galloway, author of *Running: Getting Started*. "My favourite thing about 5K races is the atmosphere. Almost everyone there is in a good mood. How many other events in your life are like that?"

THE FIVE-WEEK PLAN

In the five weeks leading up to your first 5K, most coaches agree that you need to run three or four days a week. During one of those weekly runs, you should focus on increasing the amount you can run at one time until you build to at least the race distance, or the equivalent amount of time spent running. "I encourage runners, particularly beginners, to focus on time and effort, rather than becoming obsessed with miles and distance," says GB coach, Nick Anderson (fullpotential.co.uk). "Thinking in minutes is more gradual and self-paced and will help to make sure you don't get injured by doing too much too soon." Completing the equivalent of the 5K distance in training gives you the strength and confidence you need to finish the race. And if you increase your long run up to six miles (or twice the amount of time it should take you to cover the 5km), you'll run with even greater strength (or speed, if that's your thing).

Most of your running during the week should be at a comfortable pace. This is especially true for runners who simply want to finish the race. But because adding some faster training to your schedule is the best way to improve your speed and endurance, even novices should consider doing some quicker running. "Intervals are not reserved for elites," says Carmichael. "Running three one-mile intervals with recovery in between will do more to increase your sustainable running pace than running three miles at once."

> ## 'My favourite thing about 5K races is the atmosphere. Almost everyone there is in a good mood. How many other events in life are like that?'

5 WEEKS TO YOUR FIRST 5K

It's training time. New runners who need to build up to the distance should follow the Beginner Plan. Regular runners who've never raced a 5K can try the Intermediate Plan.

BEGINNER PLAN

WEEK	MON	TUES	WED	THURS	FRI	SAT	SUN
1	WALK/XT 20 min or day off	RUN 10 min	WALK/XT 20 min or day off	RUN 15 min	WALK/XT 20 min or day off	Rest	RUN 2 miles
2	WALK/XT 20 min or day off	RUN 15 min	WALK/XT 20 min or day off	RUN 20 min	WALK/XT 20 min or day off	Rest	RUN 2.5 miles
3	WALK/XT 30 min or day off	RUN 20 min	WALK/XT 30 min or day off	RUN 25 min	WALK/XT 30 min or day off	Rest	RUN 3 miles
4	WALK/XT 30 min or day off	RUN 25 min	WALK/XT 30 min or day off	RUN 30 min	WALK/XT 30 min or day off	Rest	RUN 3.5 miles
5	WALK/XT 30 min or day off	RUN 30 min	WALK/XT 30 min or day off	RUN 30 min	WALK/XT 30 min or day off	Rest	5K RACE

➔ **BEGINNER PLAN KEY** WALK/XT days: You can walk or cross-train (swim, bike, elliptical trainer, etc) at a moderate intensity for the stated amount of time, or take the day off. Weekday runs: All weekday runs should be at a steady, comfortable pace. Weekend long run: This is measured in miles, rather than minutes, to ensure you increase the distance you cover each week. Long-run pace should be two or three minutes per mile slower than the pace you can run one mile flat-out. Feel free to take walk breaks.

INTERMEDIATE PLAN

1	3 miles plus 5 x strides	Rest	4 miles plus 5 x strides	Rest	4 miles plus 5 x strides	2 to 3 miles; 15-min core workout	Rest
2	3 miles plus 5 x strides	Rest	4 miles with 2 x 5 min at SS intensity; 15-min core workout	Rest	3 miles plus 5 x strides	5 to 6 miles; 15-min core workout	Rest
3	3 miles plus 6 x strides	Rest	4 miles with 3 x 5 min at SS intensity; 15-min core workout	Rest	3 miles plus 6 x strides	6 miles with the last 15 min at SS intensity; 15-min core workout	Rest
4	3 miles plus 6 x strides	Rest	4 miles with 2 x 10 min at SS intensity; 15-min core workout	Rest	3 miles plus 5 x strides	6 miles with the last 15 min at SS intensity; 15-min core workout	Rest
5	3 miles plus 4 x strides	Rest	3 miles; 15-min core workout	Rest	2 miles	2 miles plus 3 x strides	5K RACE

➔ **INTERMEDIATE PLAN KEY** Weekly mileage: Except where noted, weekly mileage should be run at a perceived effort (PE) of six out of 10. Strides: After completing the run, run hard for 20 seconds and recover with easy jogging or walking for 45 seconds; repeat as instructed. Core workout: Do a series of basic exercises to strengthen core muscles and improve posture. SS intensity: Intervals at Steady State Intensity should be run at a PE of seven or eight. Do five minutes of easy running between SS intervals.

First-time racers can do some faster running one or two days a week, but these sessions don't have to be regimented. Anderson recommends adapting one session per week to include about 10 minutes of speedwork, made up of two five-minute runs at a faster pace, each framed by five minutes of jogging. Once this becomes easy, try one 10-minute interval at threshold pace – this is about 85 per cent of your maximum heart rate, where you can utter a few words but not hold a conversation. Always bookend harder runs with easy warm-up and cool-down jogs.

THE BIG DAY

The greatest challenge of running a 5K is finding the right pace, says Anderson. Start out too fast and you might struggle to finish. That's why Galloway recommends that all first-time racers (including veteran runners) get to the back of the pack at the starting line. This prevents an overzealous start and allows you to gradually build up speed, ideally running the final mile the fastest.

But how fast should you expect to run come race day? While Carmichael says the main goal should be to have fun, he tells experienced runners who are new to racing that they can expect to race about 30 seconds per mile faster than training pace. So, runners training at a nine-minute-per-mile pace should finish in around 26:25; those training at a 10-minute-mile pace should finish in 29:31; and those training at an 11-minute-mile pace should finish in around 32:39.

Galloway has a different way of predicting race times. Every two weeks, his clients run a mile on a track as fast as they can. Then he uses a pace calculator, like the one at runnersworld.co.uk, to predict their times for longer distances. In general, he finds that most runners slow down about 33 seconds per mile when they go from a one-mile run to 5K race.

However, most experts discourage first-timers from shooting for strict time goals. "Make it a race against yourself," says Carmichael, "because it's your progress that's most valuable to you." Galloway seconds that. "If you enjoy it, you'll do it again." And probably faster.

FIRST-TIME FIVER?

Run like a road-racing pro by avoiding these three common first-time mistakes

❶ TOO FAST, TOO SOON "Most first-time racers go out too fast and are miserable by the second mile," says Anderson. **EASY FIX** Start out at a comfortable pace with no huffing and puffing. Move up gradually through the gears in the second half of the race until you are running hard for the last half-mile.

❷ TOO MUCH FOOD Many first-timers eat too much before a race, particularly the night before. Most people have enough stored energy in their bodies to run a 5K without taking in any additional calories. **EASY FIX** "Eat normally before the race," says Anderson. Try small meals the day before. On race day, eat a carbohydrate breakfast, but the key is being hydrated. Have water and fruit juice or sports drink.

❸ TOO LITTLE WARM-UP/ COOL-DOWN Your body needs to warm up properly before it can run well at the higher intensity required to race a 5K. And a post-race cool-down helps you recover more quickly so that you'll feel better the day after the race. **EASY FIX** Include a 15-minute warm-up before the race, and a 15-minute cool-down after. For both, mix walking and jogging to help ease into and out of your race pace.

PIN DOWN A GOAL
You will get more out of your running if you work towards a race

THE ULTIMATE 10K PLAN

It's the nation's favourite distance – long enough to test your endurance, short enough for you to switch on the afterburners. Here's how to perfect your 10K

You'll be glad to hear that 10K training forms the ideal foundation of almost all types of running performance. That's because it includes ample amounts of the three core components of distance training: strength, stamina and speed. Obviously, you can use it to train for your goal 10K, but with certain adjustments you can also use it to prepare for everything from the 5K to the marathon. This is the classic distance, made famous by Ethiopian legends Haile Gebrselassie and Kenenisa Bekele. So read through the runner profiles below, and decide which of our six-week plans is best for you, but remember that these are not one-size-fits-all plans. If you can't complete a given session, you don't have to, and if you need to rearrange training days to fit your schedule, do so.

WHO AM I?

➔ **BEGINNER** You're a notch above novice. You've been running at least six months, and may have done a 5K or two. You run three to five miles, three or four days a week; have done a little fast running when you felt like it; and now you want to enter – and finish – what you consider to be a real distance race.

➔ **INTERMEDIATE** You've been running a year or more,

have done some 5Ks and maybe even a 10K, but you've always finished feeling as if you could or should have gone faster. You consider yourself mainly a recreational runner, but you still want to make a commitment, and see how fast you can go.

BEGINNER

If you are a beginner, your 10K goal should be less about achieving a personal best (PB) than an LDF (longest distance finished). You want to run the whole 6.2 miles, so your main aim is endurance, because it's likely to take you an hour to get there. "Basic aerobic strength is every runner's first need," says running coach Bud Baldaro, so you should aim to do most of your running at a steady, moderate pace.

However, we're also going to add a dash of pseudo-speedwork into your endurance stew for flavour. This will put some added spring into your step, give you a brief taste of what it feels like to run a little faster, and hasten your progression to the Intermediate level. So, every week, in addition to your steady running, you're going to do two extra things:
➔ **Aerobic Intervals (AI)** In these, you push the pace on a bit – until you breathe just a little harder

GREEN MEANS GO
The Manchester 10K is
one of the UK's most
popular races

than usual – followed by slow jogging until you feel rested enough to resume your regular speed, and you always, always stay well short of going anaerobic (simply stated that means squinty-eyed and gasping for breath). Treat these runs like play. When you do them, try to recreate that feeling you had as a child when you ran to the park and couldn't wait to get there.

➔ **Gentle Pick-ups (GP)** With pick-ups, you gradually increase your pace over 100 metres to about 90 per cent of all-out, hold it there for 10-20m then gradually decelerate. Walk to full recovery before you start the next one. Nothing big, nothing really stressful – just enough to let your body go.

(After a few AI/GP weeks, your normal pace should begin to feel more comfortable, and you'll get race fit more quickly this way.)

➔ **Race-Day Rules** Have something to drink and an energy bar or bagel two hours to 90 minutes before the race, and arrive early enough to make your way to the start without great stress. Walk around for about 10 minutes before the start; maybe even do a few minutes of slow jogging. Start off at a slower pace than you think you should, and work gradually into a comfortable and controlled pace. Let the race come to you. If there is a water station, stop to drink and relax for 10 seconds.

BEGINNER'S 10K SCHEDULE

WEEK	MON	TUES	WED	THURS	FRI	SAT	SUN	TOTAL
1	Rest	2 miles, 4 x 1 min AI, 2 miles	3 miles or rest	4 miles + 3 GP	Rest	5 miles	Rest	16-20 miles
2	Rest	2 miles	3 miles or rest	4 miles + 3 GP	Rest	5.5 miles	3.5 miles	18-21 miles
3	Rest	2 miles, 4 x 90 secs AI, 2 miles	3 miles or rest	4.5 miles + 3 GP	Rest	6 miles	4 miles	18.5-22 miles
4	Rest	2 miles, 6 x 90 secs AI, 2 miles	3 miles or rest	4.5 miles + 6 GP	Rest	6.5 miles	4.5 miles	20-24 miles
5	Rest	2 miles, 4 x 2 mins AI, 2 miles	3 miles or rest	5 miles + 6 GP	Rest	7 miles	5 miles	21.5-26 miles
TAPER	Rest	2 miles, 3 mins, 2 mins, 1 min AI, 2 miles	2 miles	2 miles + 2 GP	2 miles + 2 GP	Rest	10K Race	

INTERMEDIATE

Here's the two-pronged approach that will move you from recreational runner to the cusp of competitive athlete. First, you'll be adding miles to your endurance-building long run until it makes up 30 per cent of your weekly mileage. Second, you'll now be doing a substantial amount of tempo running aimed at elevating your anaerobic threshold, the speed above which blood lactate starts to accumulate in the system. You can avoid this unpleasantness with regular sustained sessions at just below 10K pace; that is, tempo-run pace. This will significantly improve your

endurance and running efficiency in just six weeks. So your training will include weekly 10-10 sessions (right) as tempo work (PI, below), along with a mix of intervals and uphill running, all of which strengthen running muscles, heart and related aerobic systems.

Oh, one more thing. Running fast requires effort and some discomfort. Even so, be conservative. If you can't maintain the same pace throughout a given session, or if your body really starts to complain, call it a day and think about adjusting your pace next time.

➔ **Pace Intervals (PI)** Run at target 10K pace to improve your efficiency and stamina, and to give you the feel of your race pace. For 10-minute/mile pace (a 1:02:06 10K), run 2:30 (for 400m), 5:00 (800m), 7:30 (1,200m). For nine-minute/mile pace (55:53), run 2:15 (400m), 4:30 (800m), 6:45 (1,200m). For eight-minute/mile pace (49:40), run 2:00 (400m), 4:00 (800m), 6:00 (1,200m). With pace and speed intervals (below), jog half the interval distance to recover.

➔ **Speed Intervals (SI)** Run these at 30 seconds-per-mile faster than race pace.

For 10-minute/mile pace: run 2:22 (for 400m), 4:44 (800m), 7:06 (1,200m).

For nine-minute/mile pace: 2:08 (400m), 4:16 (800m), 6:24 (1,200m).

For eight-minute/mile pace: 1:53 (400m), 3:45 (800m), 5:38 (1,200m).

10-10 10-minute tempo repetitions at 30 seconds per mile slower than 10K goal pace, with three- to five-minute slow jogs after each.

➔ **Total Uphill Time (TUT)** Run repetitions up the same hill, or work the uphill sections of a road or off-road course.

➔ **Strides (S)** Over 100m, gradually accelerate to about 90 per cent of all-out, hold it for five seconds, then smoothly decelerate. Walk to full recovery.

SEE THE SIGHTS
Just don't let them distract you from your goal time

➔ **Race-Day Rules** "Many intermediate runners run too fast in the first half of the race," says Baldaro. "That's just about as close as you can get to a guaranteed way of running a mediocre time. Even pace is best, which means the first half of the race should feel really easy." Divide the race into three two-mile sections: in-control pace for the first two, push a bit the middle two, then go hard the last two and, finally, sprint when you see the line.

INTERMEDIATE'S 10K SCHEDULE

WEEK	MON	TUES	WED	THURS	FRI	SAT	SUN	TOTAL
1	Rest	2 miles, 1-2 x 10-10, 2 miles	4 miles	400m, 800m, 1,200m, 800m , 400m PI	Rest	4 miles + 4 x 100m S	6-7 miles	24 miles
2	Rest	6 miles inc 6 mins TUT	4 miles	1,200m, 2 x 800m, 4 x 200m PI + 4 x 200m SI + 4 x 100m S	Rest	4.5 miles + 5 x 100m S	7-8 miles	26 miles
3	Rest	2 miles, 2-3 x 10-10, 2 miles	4 milest	800m, 1,200m, 800m PI + 2 x 400m, 4 x 100m S	Rest	5 miles + 6 x 100m S	7-8 miles	27.5 miles
4	Rest	6-7 miles inc 8 minutes TUT	4 miles	1,200m, 800m, 2 x 400m, 2 x 200m SI + 4 x 100m S	Rest	5 miles + 6 x 100m S	8-9 miles	29 miles
5	Rest	2 miles, 3-4 x 10-10, 2 miles	4 miles	800m, 4 x 400m, 4 x 200m, 800m SI, + 4 x 100m S	Rest	6 miles + 6 x 100m S	8-9 miles	31 miles
TAPER	Rest	800m, 2 x 200m, 400m, 2 x 200m SI + 6 x 100m S	4 miles	4 x 200m SI + 4 x 100m S	Rest	3 miles easy + 3 x 100m S	10K Race	

HALF TIME

Training for a half-marathon needn't be a slog – as these simple plans and success stories show

The half-marathon has something for everyone, whether you're a beginner looking to stretch yourself or a marathon runner looking to stay in tune. Training for a half is within reach, as our three-day-a-week beginner's and improver's schedules, devised by coach Nick Anderson (fullpotential.co.uk), go to show. And while you start to plan for your new PB, read how four runners, from beginner to elite, set their own.

The beginner's training schedule lets you run by time and effort, rather than counting miles. It's designed for those new to the half-marathon and builds from 30-minute run/walk sessions to race day over 12 weeks. The improver's programme is designed for runners who have run a few half-marathons, but are looking to improve on their best time. "You should certainly be looking at sub 1:50, but I've coached runners who have run under 1:30 for a half on a three-day-weekly schedule," says Anderson. Gauge your effort using your rate of perceived exertion or your maximum heart rate. There's more info on these with the training plans over the following pages...

THE BEGINNER'S STORY

JULIE DEADMAN
43, Knutsford

I've always enjoyed running, but I started to run more frequently as a way to relax while I was caring for my dad, who was unwell. After a long illness, he passed away but I had promised I'd run the Reading Half-Marathon for him – he was Reading born and bred, and a loyal supporter of Reading Football Club all his life.

My goal was to finish the race in under two hours. Ian Corless, my coach (fullpotential.co.uk), gave me structured weekly training plans that included speed and endurance work. On top of the support he gave me, learning how the various bits of the training jigsaw fitted together really helped me and increased my confidence in my own ability.

When the gun went off, I tried to stay patient and not charge for gaps. I kept to my goal pace and passed the 10K mark in 53 minutes – beating my 10K PB. I reached the 10-mile marker in 1:27. By then, I knew I would achieve my goal time and there was no greater feeling.

The finish is spectacular – you run into Reading FC's Madejski Stadium – and my emotions were sky high as I crossed the finish line in 1:55:12. I know my dad would have loved seeing me achieve my goal in his hometown.

BEGINNER'S HALF-MARATHON SCHEDULE

WEEK	MON	TUES	WED	THURS	FRI	SAT or SUN
1	Rest	30 mins: 5-min walk/ 5-min run, repeat 3 times 5/7	Rest	30 mins: 1-min walk/ 1-min easy jog/1-min run, repeat continuously 5/6/7	Rest	30 mins: 5-min walk/ 5-min run, repeat 3 times 5/7
2	Rest	30 mins: 4-min walk/6-min run, repeat 3 times 5/7	Rest	30 mins: 2-min walk/2-min easy jog/2-min run, repeat continuously 5/6/7	Rest	30 mins: 4-min walk/6-min run, repeat 3 times 5/7
3	Rest	30 mins: 2-min walk/8-min run, repeat 3 times 5/7	Rest	30 mins: 2-min walk/2-min easy jog/2-min run, repeat continuously 5/6/7	Rest	30 mins of 2-min walk/8-min run, repeat 3 times 5/7
4	Rest	30 mins: 2 x 10 mins of continuous easy running. Have a 5-min walk between blocks 5/7	Rest	45 mins: 3-min walk/3-min jog/3-min threshold run, repeat continuously 5/6-7/8	Rest	50 mins: 2-min walk/8-min run, repeat 4 times. Have a 5-min brisk walk warm-up & cool-down 5/7
5	Rest	20 mins continuous running with 5-min walk warm-up and cool-down 5/7	Rest	Repeat above session	Rest	60 mins: 3-min walk/12-min run, repeat 4 times 5/7
6	Rest	25 mins continuous running with 5-min walk warm-up and cool-down 5/7	Rest	5-min walk/5-min easy run/5-min threshold run, repeat 3 times 5/6-7/8	Rest	Repeat above session
7	Rest	30 mins easy-pace run with 5-min walk warm-up and cool-down 5/7	Rest	45 mins: 5 x 5-min threshold / 2-min walk & 5-min warm-up and cool-down 5/8	Rest	75 mins: 3-min walk/12-min run, repeat 5 times 5/7
8	Rest	40 mins easy pace with warm-up and cool-down walks 5/7	Rest	5-min threshold/5-min easy run, x 2 with warm-up walk/jog and cool-down 5/8	Rest	Repeat above session
9	Rest	45 mins easy pace with warm-up and cool-down walks 5/7	Rest	30 mins: 5-min easy/5-min threshold. Add a 5-min warm-up and cool-down jog 5/6-7/8	Rest	90 mins: 3-min walk/12-min run, repeat 6 times. 5/7
10	Rest	45 mins easy 6-7	Rest	40 mins: 5-min easy/5-min threshold. Add a 5-min warm-up and cool-down jog 5/6-7/8	Rest	100 mins: 18-min easy run/2-min walk, repeat 5 times 5/6-7
11	Rest	30 mins: 10 very easy jog/ 10 steady/10 threshold 6/7/8	Rest	40 mins easy pace: 2 x 10 mins threshold. Have 5-min jog between efforts 6/8	Rest	60 mins: 25 mins easy pace/5 min walk, repeat 2 times 5/6-7
12	Rest	30 mins: 5-min easy/5-min threshold, repeat 3 times 6/8	Rest	20 mins easy relaxed run 6-7	Rest	RACE DAY 15-20 mins easy pace/walk 5 mins. Take on your drinks while walking. 5/6-8

KEY TO PERCEIVED EFFORT

➔ **5 (OUT OF 10) OR 50% MAXIMUM HEART RATE (MAX HR)** A brisk walk.

➔ **6 (OUT OF 10) OR 60% MAX HR** Recovery running. This is a very easy running pace that allows you to maintain a conversation with no problems.

➔ **7 (OUT OF 10) OR 70% MAX HR** Steady running. A little harder than recovery pace, but you should still be able to hold a conversation.

➔ **8 (OUT OF 10) OR 80% MAX HR** Threshold running and target half-marathon pace. You should only be able to say a few words.

THE PRO'S STORY

**BRITISH ELITE RUNNER
JO PAVEY**
36, Devon

Moving up to the half-marathon is a natural progression for a distance track-runner with aspirations to run a full marathon – and that was my reason for entering the Great North Run in 2006.

Prior to that my career consisted almost solely of running up to 5,000m on the track, so the thought of a 13.1-mile road race was daunting. I needed to change the emphasis of my training. But with the race coming at the end of a long, low-mileage track season, the time available was far from ideal. I was anxious. However, having recently run a PB over 5,000m, I knew I was race fit – albeit for a much shorter distance.

Training went well. Long runs increased to 1:45 – they had been 1:20 during the summer; I did hill training for the climbs on the course; I reduced speedwork in favour of mile and 2K intervals and I added a 60-minute race-pace tempo run.

I didn't want to try anything too risky in my first outing, so my plan was simple: try to stay with the leader, then make a move during the last mile or so. I felt fine until we dropped down the final steep hill near the finish. I just fell apart. I managed to finish fourth. It was later found that my blood sugar levels, rather than falling, had gone abnormally high.

I learnt a lot from the experience. Crucially, I analysed how I could address this problem for the future, and I did better when I ran the race again in 2008, finishing third.

SIX PRO TIPS

**USA RECORD-HOLDER
RYAN HALL**, 27, on how to race your best half-marathon

❶ IN TRAINING...
Don't be afraid of mistakes. You're going to screw up sometimes. If I go out too hard on a tempo run, I think this is good practice for when I go out too fast in a race and have to regroup.

❷ SIMULATE RACE CONDITIONS
Want to run fast on the road? Do your intervals on the road.

❸ KNOW THE PURPOSE OF EACH WORKOUT
Make the hard runs hard and the recovery runs easy. Many runners make the mistake of running too hard on their easy days, which is counterproductive.

❹ AT THE RACE...
Inspect the course. Familiarise yourself with landmarks, so you have some mental breaks in addition to mile markers. Look for places to run the tangents if you're going for a PB.

❺ LET TERRAIN DICTATE YOUR PACE
If you want to average seven-minute miles, it's okay to run 7:10s up the hills and 6:50s down, rather than forcing yourself to stick to sevens the entire way.

❻ RUN THE MILE YOU'RE IN
I avoid thinking about how far I have to go early in the race, because that can be overwhelming. Late in the race I try to forget about how far I have gone, because that would give me an excuse to give in to fatigue.

CHART YOUR PROGRESS Proven training rules

Our friends at fetcheveryone.com have logged over 800,000 training sessions and 100,000 race times from UK runners. This chart shows how various finishers' training broke down between types of running in percentage terms. Notice how faster finishers do comparatively more warm-up and recovery runs, interval and tempo sessions than other runners. The long run also makes up less of their training schedule.

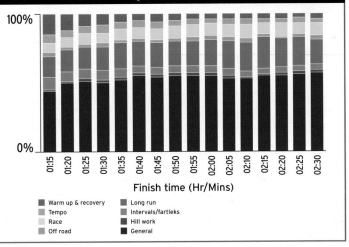

IMPROVER'S HALF-MARATHON SCHEDULE

WEEK	MON	TUES	WED	THURS	FRI	SAT or SUN
1	Rest	10 mins easy/8 mins @ threshold pace, repeat 2 times 6-7/8-8.5	Rest	10 mins easy, 2 x 5 mins of continuous hills (approx 45 secs up/45 secs down), 10 mins easy 6-7/8-8.5	Rest	60 mins easy 6-7
2	Rest	10 mins easy, 10 mins @ threshold pace, repeat 2 times 6-7/8-8.5	Rest	10 mins easy, 2 x 7 mins of continuous hills, 10 easy 6-7/8-8.5	Rest	70 mins easy 6-7
3	Rest	7 mins easy, 7 mins @ threshold pace, repeat 3 times 6-7/8-8.5	Rest	10 mins easy, 3 x 5 mins of continuous hills, 10 easy 6-7/8-8.5	Rest	75 mins easy 6-7
4	Rest	36 mins: 6 x 3 mins, with 3 mins easy in between Reps 1, 3 & 5 @ 6-7; reps 2, 4 & 6 @ 8-8.5	Rest	40-min hilly run. Easy but faster up hills 6 if easy, 7-8 if hilly run	Rest	60 mins easy or 10K race 6-7 or 8-9
5	Rest	45 mins relaxed 6-7	Rest	10 mins easy, 2 x 10 mins of continuous hills (approx 45 secs up/45 secs down), 10 easy 6-7/8-8.5	Rest	80 mins easy 6-7
6	Rest	5 mins easy, 2 x 12 mins @ threshold/HM race pace with 4 mins easy recovery, 5 mins easy 6-7/8-8.5	Rest	10 mins easy, 3 x 7 mins of continuous hills, 10 mins easy 6-7/8-8.5	Rest	80 mins with last 20 mins @ HM race pace 6-7/8
7	Rest	45 mins: 15 easy, 15 steady, 15 threshold 6/7/8	Rest	40 mins hilly run. Attack the hills, relax rest of run 6-7/8-8.5	Rest	60 mins easy 6-7
8	Rest	5 mins easy, 3 x 10 mins @ threshold/HM pace, 5 min easy 6-7/8-8.5	Rest	10 mins easy, 3 x 8 mins of continuous hills, 10 mins easy 6-7/8-8.5	Rest	90 mins easy with last 20 mins @ HM race pace 6-7/8
9	Rest	10 mins easy, 25 mins @ HM/threshold pace, 10 mins easy 6-7/8-8.5	Rest	10 mins easy, 2 x 6, 4, 2 mins @ HM, 10K, 5K pace with 2-min easy between sets, 10 easy 6-7/8-9	Rest	100-110 mins easy 6-7
10	Rest	10 mins easy, 5 x 2 mins hard/2 min easy, 10 min easy 6-7/8-9	Rest	45 mins hilly run or 40 mins easy if racing Sunday 6/7 or 8	Rest	75 mins easy OR 10K race 6-7 or 9
11	Rest	48 mins: 3-min threshold/3-min easy, repeat 8 times 6-7/8-8.5	Rest	15 mins easy, 5 x 3 mins @ 10K pace with 2-min easy recovery between each rep, 15 mins easy 6-7/9	Rest	60 mins easy 6-7
12	Rest	30 mins: 5 mins easy/5 mins @ threshold, repeat 3 times 6/7	Rest	20 mins easy 6	Rest	HALF-MARATHON RACE 8

KEY TO PERCEIVED EFFORT
➡ **6 (OUT OF 10) OR 60% MAXIMUM HEART RATE (MAX HR)** Recovery running. An easy pace that allows you to maintain a conversation.

➡ **7 (OUT OF 10) OR 70% MAX HR** Steady running. A little harder than recovery pace, but you should still be able to hold a conversation.
➡ **8-8.5 (OUT OF 10) OR**

80-85% MAX HR Threshold running and target half-marathon pace. It hurts, and you should only be able to speak a few words at a time.

➡ **8.5+ (OUT OF 10) OR 85%+ OF MAX HR** This is just below your maximum effort and you won't be able to speak. Use for short intervals and speedwork.

THE IMPROVER'S STORY

COLIN BAXTER
41, Leicester

I have been running for six years; I finished my first half-marathon in 1:54. Once you've got your first PB you have a new goal to beat next time.

Aspiration is key. A couple of years after joining Leicester Owls AC I started training with some of the faster guys at the club, which helped drop my PB to 1:38 in a year. Over the next year my PB dropped to 1:35, then 1:33. I then wanted to get under 1:30. I knew I could get there if i put in the extra work. Unfortunately, this came at a price – I fell and smashed my wrist. In hospital, waiting to go for an operation, I watched Paula Radcliffe cruise to victory in the New York Marathon – her post-pregnancy comeback race. I was out for five weeks. But I thought: "If Paula can do it, so can I!"

I thought the key to a sub-1:30 half was a sub-40-minute 10K. I introduced 2,000m reps to my training. When I first started I could only manage four reps and couldn't break eight minutes. But after a couple of weeks I could manage five, then started dipping under eight minutes.

After eight weekly sessions, I ran a 39:34 10K, and two weeks after that – in my first half-marathon since the accident – I ran 1:28:59 at the Belvoir Half-Marathon. Last April – a month after my 40th birthday – I ran 1:25:26 at the Belvoir Half. Sub-1:20 is at the back of my mind for now.

CHART YOUR PROGRESS Statistically proven training rules

Our friends at fetcheveryone.com have logged over 800,000 training sessions and 100,000 race times from UK runners. This chart shows a breakdown of training-session frequency and mileage for half-marathon finishers in times ranging from 1:15 to 2:30. There are no real secrets to running a fast time – the more you put in, the more you get out. A 1:15 half-marathon runner, for example, will typically run eight times a week, while a 1:30 finisher trains almost five times a week. But the chart also shows it's possible to run around three times a week and finish in well under two hours.

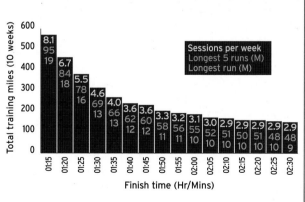

10 RULES OF MARATHON TRAINING

When it comes to marathon prep, there isn't one right plan. But these principles will help you figure out what works – for you

What's the best way to train for a marathon? Well, according to a recent report in the *International Journal of Sport Physiology and Performance*, there isn't one. A study of 93 elite marathoners found that there were no universal themes when it came to preparation for the 26.2-miler.

But it's not all bad. While marathon training hasn't been studied extensively, millions of runners have gone the distance. And when you look at the science and shared knowledge of marathon training, these overarching principles emerge.

1 RUN JUST ENOUGH

"Stay healthy" is the most important piece of training advice, and the most often ignored. It does you no good to train hard, and then get sick or injured. Better to be slightly under-trained, but feeling strong and eager, than to be overtrained. The trick, of course, is finding that fine line between the two.

2 BUILD YOUR TRAINING SLOWLY

Increase weekly mileage by just 10 per cent every week. Extend long runs by just one mile at a time up to 10 miles, then by two miles at a time if you want. Take recovery weeks as well as recovery days. Here's what eight weeks of training might look like, in terms of miles per week: 20-22-24-20-26-28-30-20.

3 RECOVER, RECOVER, RECOVER

You don't have to train hard seven days a week. You just have to train smart three or four days a week.

This was proven in a 1994 study at the University of Northern Iowa, where four-time-a-week runners performed just as well in a marathon as those training six times a week and covering 20 per cent more miles.

4 DO YOUR LONG RUNS

This is a no-brainer. The newer you are to marathon running, the more important your long runs. You simply have to become accustomed to being on your feet for three, four, or more hours. There's no magic length. Most experts recommend stopping at two-and-a-half to three hours, but you could try going further and include walk breaks. All systems work, as long as you get to the starting line healthy and strong.

5 PRACTISE YOUR MARATHON PACE

Makes sense, doesn't it? The key is adding 'Progressive Marathon-Pace' (MP) long runs to your programme. For example, try a two-mile warm-up, then do six miles at MP + 40 seconds, six more at MP + 20 and your final six at MP.

6 EXTEND YOUR TEMPO-RUN DISTANCE

Tempo runs were born as four-mile efforts, propounded by coach Dr Jack Daniels. Then another, Dr Joe Vigil, asked US elite runner Deena Kastor to hold the tempo pace longer – eventually up to 12 miles. He got another of his protégés, Meb Keflezighi, to 15. The result? Two Olympic marathon medals. Gradually extend your tempo runs, slowing by a few seconds per

IMAGE: GETTY

TRAIN TO GAIN
The right preparation can help
make those 26.2 miles fly by

mile from your four-mile pace. "The longer the tempo run workout you can sustain, the greater the dividends down the road," says Vigil.

7 EAT YOUR CARBS...

To stay healthy and recover well, you need to fuel your body efficiently. First, consume carbs – gel, sports drink and so on – during long, hard workouts to keep strong. Second, have a good helping of carbs as quickly as possible after workouts. This will replenish the glycogen (energy supply) in your depleted leg muscles. Add some protein for muscle repair.

8 ...AND PAY ATTENTION TO IRON

None of the marathon runners in the *International Journal of Sport Physiology and Performance* study identified themselves as "vegetarians". Running increases iron loss through sweating and pounding. You don't have to be a meat-eater to run a strong marathon, but you do have to consume enough iron. Consuming iron-rich foods with vitamin C, which increases the body's iron absorption, will help.

9 SIDESTEP INJURIES

If he were 22 years old again, two-time Olympic marathon runner Peter Pfitzinger, who competed in the 1984, and 1988 Games and is author of *Advanced Marathoning*, says he'd rest and/or cross-train for several days a week at the first hint of a problem. And that he'd include core training in his regime. "I'm convinced that core stability

helps runners maintain good running form and pace late in a race," says Pfitzinger.

10 TAPER FOR TWO TO THREE WEEKS

Many runners hate to taper. We are cursed with a sort of sublime obsessiveness – a big help when you're increasing your efforts, but an albatross when you're supposed to be cutting back. A new study from Ball State University, Indiana, showed a particular gain in Type IIa muscle-fibre strength – the so-called fast, aerobic muscles that can adapt to improve your performance – after a three-week taper.

KEY WORKOUTS FOR YOUR BEST 26.2

➔ MILE REPEATS

When it comes to marathon training, veteran 26.2-milers swear by this modified form of tempo training. You should run each mile repeat about 20 seconds faster than your predicted marathon goal pace, with a 400m recovery walk or jog. You'll get the best results if you can build up to 10 to 13 mile repeats.

➔ YASSO 800s

The goal, after several months of working up to it, is to run 10 x 800 metres in the same minutes:seconds as your goal time (in hours:minutes). If you want to run a 3:40 marathon, for example, you run your Yasso 800s in 3 minutes, 40 seconds. This workout isn't based on physiology; it's a good hard workout.

ULTIMATE CHALLENGE

Are you a marathon first-timer? Seeking a PB? Overworked or injury-prone? Luckily, there's a plan for all of us. So let's do a 26.2-miler together. We'll be with you every step of the way

As tough as it is, the marathon is alluring. Each year hundreds of thousands of runners take on the challenge of running 26.2 miles, but how best to train?

Most plans include long runs to build endurance, tempo runs or speedwork to strengthen the legs and lungs and rest days to recover from the hard work. But ability, experience, health and time constraints all come into the equation too. "You have to follow some general training principles when you run a marathon," says coach and exercise physiologist Greg McMillan (mcmillanrunning.com). "But adapting the plan for yourself is the most important factor." Sure, you've got to do some tough stuff. But training shouldn't be torture. "If it isn't fun, why do it?" says Bart Yasso, chief running officer of *Runner's World USA*, inventor of the Yasso 800s training session and all-round running guru.

A veteran of hundreds of marathons over 30 years, Yasso has a PB of 2:40 and has led dozens of marathon pace groups to sub-three-hour finishes. Over the page we publish Yasso's 16-week training plan, which has helped runners reach goals from 2:30 to "just finish". It's an intermediate plan for runners who've completed at least one marathon. If you are a first-timer, a PB seeker, an overworked or injury-prone runner, we tell you how to tweak it to your needs on the following pages. Or you can find beginner and advanced plans on our website (runnersworld.co.uk). You'll be in good company. Like you, the staff of *Runner's World* has diverse goals and challenges, and we're getting ready to run marathons ourselves this spring. So what do you say? Let's go long together.

GET RACE READY WITH RW!

Come run with the *Runner's World* pace groups
Runner's World staff and running friends have been helping runners hit their time targets since we first paced the London Marathon in 1998. The pace ranges from seven- to 11-minute miles (and run/walk groups at the London Marathon), so there's a group for everyone.

WHERE DO WE DO IT?

Our main pacing teams are geared towards the Virgin London Marathon on April 25, where we'll have six pairs of pace leaders. There's also the chance to run with us at these build-up half-marathons. All you need is a race number, so enter well in advance, then visit runnersworld.co.uk.

HOW DO THEY WORK?

We'll be there at the start, holding up a board with our respective paces on them. If you want to run at that pace, just run with us. It's that simple. You don't have to run with us all the way – if you want to speed up for the last few miles, or you need to fall back, that's fine.

RW SUPPORTERS AT THE LONDON MARATHON

Every year, members of the runnersworld.co.uk forum organise a support area at Mudchute, Docklands (mile 17). Volunteers hand out cheers, drinks and high-energy goodies throughout the day – simply make yourself known to them online in the weeks leading up to the race and you'll be allocated a personal

IMAGES: RW IMAGES

LONDON IS GO!
You may not be at the front of the start line, but you can reach the finish line

support crew. They're always on the lookout for more helpers too, so if you're not running but want to experience the buzz, get involved!

WHO ARE YOU? THE CHALLENGEE
Goal: Follow the plan to a strong finish. Coach Bart Yasso designed the plan over the page for someone who has been running for two or three years, gone through regular cycles of logging 30 miles a week, and finished a few half-marathons and at least one marathon. Here are some of his training philosophies:

➡ Hit the hills first Run on the hilliest route you can find during the first two months. The hills build leg and lung power, but don't subject your joints to the stress of speedwork. "You won't feel fast going up hills, but you'll feel strong," says Yasso.

➡ Hit the track later The speedwork – which builds your aerobic capacity – starts halfway through the programme. Why wait? "There are only so many times you can really lay it on the line," Yasso says. "If you do it week after week, you're going to dread it."

➡ Rehearse race pace The six- to 10-mile marathon-pace runs make your goal pace feel like your natural rhythm. "On race day, your body will just be in tune to it," says Yasso.

➡ Long runs The distance of your long run increases by two to three miles for two or three weeks, but then goes back down so that you can recover. Back in his younger days, Yasso used to run 23 miles every weekend. "I figured my body could handle it, but I paid for it later," he says. "Trust me. Whatever miles you don't do this week, you'll be able to run in 30 years."

➡ Go easy Easy days give you the energy you need to make the most of your hard workouts. When Yasso travelled to Africa's Rift Valley in the late 1990s, he was impressed with how some of the world's fastest runners would whip out four-minute miles in hard workouts, but on recovery runs, they'd chat, joke and laugh. "I swear they could read a newspaper and drink tea at the pace they were going," he says.

➡ Ramp up to the race During the final weeks leading up to the marathon, the weekly mileage falls by 10 to 30 per cent, but the intensity of the workouts remains high. Yasso calls it "Rest, don't rust". McMillan often sees runners taper too much. "Keep the hardness you've built," he says.

HERE'S THE PLAN

Bart Yasso's race-tested intermediate marathon-training programme

WEEK	MON	TUES	WED	THURS	FRI	SAT	SUN	TOTAL
	Rest	Easy	Hard Work: hills, speed	Rest	Easy or MP	Easy	long, slow distance LSD	MILES
1	Rest	Easy 4 miles	6 miles hills	Rest	Easy 4 miles	Easy 4 miles	7 miles LSD	25
2	Rest	Easy 4 miles	6 miles hills	Rest	Easy 5 miles	Easy 5 miles	9 miles LSD	28
3	Rest	Easy 3 miles	6 miles hills	Rest	Easy 5 miles	Easy 5 miles	12 miles LSD	30
4	Rest	Easy 4 miles	6 miles hills	Rest	Easy 4 miles	Easy 4 miles	10 miles LSD	28
5	Rest	Easy 4 miles	7 miles hills	Rest	Easy 4 miles	Easy 4 miles	13 miles LSD	32
6	Rest	Easy 7 miles	8 miles hills	Rest	Easy 6 miles	Easy 6 miles	2-mile warm-up, 5K race, 1-mile cool-down TOTAL: 6 miles	34
7	Rest	Easy 4 miles	7 miles hills	Rest	Easy 5 miles	Easy 5 miles	16 miles LSD	37
8	Rest	Easy 5 miles	HILL REPEATS: TOTAL: 8 miles	Rest	Easy 4 miles	Easy 4 miles	14 miles LSD	35
9	Rest	Easy 3 miles	MILE REPEATS 2-mile warm-up, 3 x 1 mile @ 10K pace, w/400-metre recovery, 2-mile cool-down TOTAL: 8 miles	Rest	1-mile warm-up, 7 miles @ MP, 1-mile cool-down TOTAL: 9 miles	Easy 3 miles	18 miles LSD	41

Week								Total
10	Rest	Easy 4 miles	YASSO 800s 2-mile warm-up, 6 x 800 metres w/ 400-metre recovery, 2-mile cool-down TOTAL: 9 miles	Rest	1-mile warm-up, 8 miles @ MP, 1-mile cool-down TOTAL: 10 miles	Easy 4 miles	20 miles LSD	42
11	Rest	Easy 4 miles	Easy 7 miles	Rest	1-mile warm-up, 8 miles @ MP, 1-mile cool-down TOTAL: 10 miles	Easy 4 miles	20 miles LSD	45
12	Rest	Easy 7 miles	MILE REPEATS 2-mile warm-up, 4 x 1 mile @ 10K pace, w/ 800-metre recovery, 2-mile cool-down TOTAL: 10 miles	Rest	Easy 7 miles	Easy 8 miles	15 miles LSD	47
13	Rest	Easy 6 miles	YASSO 800s 2-mile warm-up, 8 x 800 w/ 400-metre recovery, 2-mile cool-down TOTAL: 10 miles	Rest	Easy 6 miles	Easy 6 miles	22 miles LSD	48
14	Rest	Easy 8 miles	MILE REPEATS 2-mile warm-up, 3 x 1 mile @ 10K pace w/ 400-metre recovery, 2-mile cool-down TOTAL: 8 miles	Rest	Easy 7 miles	Easy 7 miles	15 miles LSD	45
15	Rest	Easy 5 miles	Easy 4 miles	Rest	Easy 6 miles	Easy 5 miles	12 miles LSD	32
16	Rest	Easy 5 miles	Rest	Easy 5 miles	Rest	Very easy 3 miles	Race day	13

➜ **KEY**

REST DAYS Ideally, don't exercise. At most cross-train with a no-impact activity like stretching, yoga or swimming.

EASY DAYS Run at a comfortable pace or cross-train with a sustained aerobic effort.

HILLS Run the mileage for the day on the hilliest route you can plot. These sessions build strength in the first seven weeks.

HILL REPEATS On week eight, find a hill that will take you at least two minutes to climb, and mark off a short repeat, halfway from the bottom, and a long repeat to the top. After a two-mile warm-up, run to the short mark three or four times, jogging back down to recover. Then run to the top three or four times, jogging back down to the short mark, then sprinting to the bottom. Finish with three or four sprints up to the short mark. Cool down with two miles of easy running.

SPEEDWORK (MILE REPEATS AND YASSO 800S) Warm up/cool down with two easy miles. For mile repeats, run a mile at your 10K pace, jog a lap for recovery and repeat three times. For the 800s, run 800m at a time equivalent to your marathon time. For example, if you're aiming for a 4:10 marathon, run each 800m in four minutes and 10 seconds. Jog 400m in betweens.

LSD Long, slow distance runs build endurance. These should be done at an easy pace, one to two minutes slower than your marathon goal pace.

MP Marathon goal pace – the speed you hope to hit in the race.

WHO ARE YOU? THE FIRST-TIMER
YOUR GOAL: Get comfortably across the finish line

RW FIRST-TIMER: ALICE PALMER, 23

Goal: To finish comfortably (but secretly hoping for sub-4:30)

"I'm excited and nervous about taking on my first marathon. I'm going to give the training my all – hopefully I can cross the line with a smile."

➔ **Are you ready?** Before signing up for 26.2 miles, ideally you should have a year of running in your log, by running or run/walking three to four times per week for four to six miles per run, says coach and exercise physiologist Jenny Hadfield, co-author of *Marathoning for Mortals* (Rodale). Too much too soon may set you up for injury and keep you from getting to the start line.

➔ **Run, Rest, and Relax** Every week, you should do three easy runs, one long run and rest on the other three days. To customise the plan on the previous page, ignore the hills, speedwork and marathon-pace runs, and do three to four easy miles on the road instead. Take a rest day every Saturday so you're fresh for your long run. "This will get you to the start line with enough of a base," says Yasso.

➔ **Focus on long** The long run is the most important part of your training because it helps you get used to spending time on your feet. Your long runs follow the same pattern as the ones in the plan on page 296 – adding two miles each week for three weeks, then cutting back by two miles for a week before building again – except since this is your first marathon, you won't run quite as far. Simply subtract two miles from each of the plan's Sunday long runs.

➔ **Drink and eat on the run** On long runs, take an energy gel every 45 minutes or 150 to 250 millilitres of sports drink (such as Lucozade, Gatorade or Powerade) every 15 to 20 minutes, even if you're not thirsty or hungry. This will restock your muscles with carbohydrates and keep your energy level from plummeting. Practise with the brand and flavour(s) that your target race will have at its water stations. Before each run, drink about 400-500ml of water. And throughout a typical day, whether running or not, try to drink at least one and a half litres of water.

➔ **Nervous newbie** Your goal is to make it to the finish line. "You'll have a PB," says Yasso.

WHO ARE YOU? THE INJURY-PRONE RUNNER
YOUR GOAL: Stay healthy throughout training

RW GEAR EDITOR: KERRY McCARTHY, 30
Goal: Run under four hours
"An ongoing hamstring problem has stopped me training properly for the last two years. I'm aiming to string together a decent chunk of uninterrupted training, which will enable me to ditch my current run/walk methodology and run under four hours at London."

Split Your Quality in Half Look at any two weeks of the training plan (page 296), and you'll see four to six "quality" workouts – hills or speed, marathon-pace work and the long run. If you are injury prone, you can cut the number of quality workouts in half, says McMillan – that is, doing two or three over the course of 14 days. That way you get more recovery between the hard efforts. You must, however, run long at least once every two weeks.

Cross-train But substitute intervals on the elliptical cross-trainer machine in the gym or aqua jogging for hard workouts every so often, McMillan says, to get a little relief from the impact. "You don't have to get your heart rate up to 200 to make up for not being on a run," says McMillan. "It's supposed to work with your running, not hurt you."

If it hurts, don't do it "Figure out what gets you injured, and cut it out," says Tim Hilden, physical therapist and biomechanics specialist at the Boulder Center for Sports Medicine in Colorado, USA. Your "orthopedic threshold", or what kind of training you can tolerate, is determined partly by genetics, injury history and your level of fitness. Don't do what hurts you. And heed twinges the first time you feel them. If you ignore the messages your pain is sending you, you'll end up making it worse, says Yasso.

Lube your joints Proper hydration helps ensure your joints are lubricated. Drink half a litre of water or sports drink before you run. And get plenty of Omega-3 fats, the kind in salmon, avocado and nuts, which help lower inflammation and repair muscle tissue.

Chill out Icy water post-run helps reduce inflammation.

WHO ARE YOU? THE TIME-PRESSED RUNNER
YOUR GOAL: Fit quality training into a busy work/life schedule

RW BUSY PERSON: JAMIE FRICKER, 22
Goal: To run sub-3:45
"I want to be able to hit this goal while fitting in training around my three-and-a-half hour round-trip commute and gym work."

➔ Focus on what counts The time-pressed runner has to make sure to get in quality workouts. Each week you should do: one long run, one speed session and a mid-distance, marathon-pace workout to get the endurance, speed and base fitness you'll need. Any other miles you log are extra credit. "You could cross-train or do nothing on the 'off' days as long as those three days are really quality," says Yasso.

➔ Do what you can, when you can If you have to move a long run to midweek, go ahead. But when you're rearranging your training week, keep these key principles in mind: take at least a day of rest in between hard or long efforts, and allow seven days in between long runs. If you get too caught up in making workouts you don't have time for, "you end up squeezing things in and you don't get enough recovery, and that just compresses the stress," McMillan says.

➔ Adjust expectations Many people start running when they're young and responsibility-free. But when they attempt it again while juggling training with kids, career and marriage, "they've forgotten to adjust their expectations to the way that their lives have changed," says Jeffrey Brown, a sports psychologist at Harvard Medical School. "You end up feeling like you're cheating on your marathon with your spouse," says Brown. "Take a long, hard look at the reasons you're running now. You're no longer competing to see who in your office is fastest. But you may be running for your kids, who'll be proud to have a healthy parent."

➔ Plan and pack food You're probably used to cramming every second of the day with activities; now work a nutrition plan into the equation. Getting healthy carbs within 30 minutes of a hard workout is critical to repairing muscle tissue so you can bounce back and give your all to your next workout (or your next meeting). You'll feel more satisfied if you eat real food.

➔ What next? Keep your kit in your car boot or desk drawer for between-appointment runs.

WHO ARE YOU? THE PB SEEKER
YOUR GOAL: Maximise training to run fast

RW PB-HUNTER: ALISON HAMLETT, 36

Goal: To set a personal best

"I set my marathon PB of 3:16 four years ago at the Mardi Gras Marathon in New Orleans. Since then I have completed around 10 marathons, but have always struggled to train properly and stick to a schedule."

> **Practise race pace** Run at your goal race pace most Fridays throughout training to get used to the feel of the pace. Start with four miles at goal pace for the first two weeks. On weeks three to seven, do six miles at goal pace. On weeks eight and nine, run seven miles at goal pace. Weeks 10 to 14, complete eight-milers at goal pace. Then back down for a six-miler two weeks before race day and a four-miler four days before the race. On each of these runs, add easy running to warm up and cool down.

> **Kick like Khannouchi** To prepare yourself for maintaining your pace through fatigue, finish the last three to four miles of your long runs at marathon goal pace or faster each week. Khalid Khannouchi, who was the first marathon runner to break 2:06, would finish long runs with four miles on the track and end up sprinting the last few laps.

> **Do what you love** You're a seasoned runner so you probably know which workouts charge you up. Do them to build confidence. "I did 5 x 1-mile repeats before a half-marathon and ran the race of my life," says Yasso. "So I'd do those for other races thinking I'd run well, and I did." It's as much about training your mind as it is about your body. "Do the workouts that, if you never did anything else, would make you feel like you're awesome," says McMillan.

> **Eat in stages** In the first month, as you build your mileage base, make sure you're getting a balanced diet. As you add hills and speedwork, pay extra attention to your protein intake to help your muscles recover. During the monster month of long runs (weeks eight to 12), make sure your carb intake is adequate. On days when you're not running long, at least 60 per cent of your calories should come from carbohydrates, to restock what you spent on hard training days.

> **Watch it** Don't be tempted to run faster paces than the plan dictates.

GETTING YOU TO 26.2

Ten marathon runners offer tips for being at your best on race day

1 TAKE NOTE

"For me the biggest thing in the early stages of marathon training was fear of the unknown," says Lina Martino from Tipton Harriers, West Midlands. "I'd only just taken up running and had no idea whether I was capable of running 26.2 miles and there were times I seriously doubted I could. Keeping a detailed training log so that I had a record of how I was progressing really helped. Seeing even the smallest progress in black and white really boosted my confidence. It also helped me keep things in perspective when I'd run an 18-miler slower than I'd hoped."

2 PRE-EMPT TO PREVENT

Pilates instructor Tim Hawes from the Momiji Tree clinic in North London found that pre-empting injuries helped him in his marathon battle. "I've always suffered from tight hamstrings and decided to try a technique called myofascial release," he says. "Standing, I'd put as much weight as was bearable on a tennis ball, then roll it around under the sole of my foot, getting into sore spots. Just two minutes a day on each foot had an amazing effect – I could stretch much better immediately afterwards and over the course of several days noticed how much deeper my stretch was."

3 CLOCK WATCHING

"Think of a long run in terms of X hours, not in terms of miles," says Susan Kennedy from Serpentine Running Club. "Just set off, and instead of worrying about how fast you're going, enjoy the run, knowing you can't make time pass more quickly. It takes all the anxiety and tedium out of it. The miles fly by with you hardly noticing. Time on your feet counts for twice as much as speed when you're tackling your first marathon – just getting used to the sensation of running for that amount of time is a big hurdle, and once you're mentally prepped for that it's all downhill!"

4 GET TOUGHER

Sometimes you need to prove to yourself that you're prepared to handle the worst that Mother Nature can throw at you before you're psychologically ready to tackle the arduous training, says Sarah Chapman from London. "I'd watch the weather forecast and make a point of scheduling training for truly horrid weather to help develop the determination and robustness required to cross the finish line," she says. "The only weather conditions that present a genuine excuse for skipping training are ice and hail storms combined with high winds. Everything else is simply a test of resolve."

5 MAKE A CONTRACT

For a spring marathon the early stages are in deepest winter, which for Andy Gwyther from Sevenoaks meant dark, cold, early-morning sessions. "Getting into a routine of consistency is key early on. I would write down what I was going to do before going to bed the night before as a way of making it non-negotiable in my mind when the alarm went off at 5:45am," he says. "It's easy to slack off when it gets tough so I repeat to myself that if I can't push on now, I'll bottle it in the actual race. I imagine the last five to 10 minutes is the end of the race to keep me strong."

6 TAKE BREAKS

When it came to increasing the length of long runs, Mary Wilkinson from Bingley Harriers in West Yorkshire struggled towards the end and was exhausted afterwards. "It's not easy to slow down when you're a naturally fast runner," she says. "I overcame this by starting at my normal long-run pace then walking for a minute after every 20 minutes I ran. Even if I felt great after 20 minutes, I made myself stop, which meant I was able to cope with much longer runs. As my training progressed, I lengthened the duration of the steady sections and was eventually able to do

the whole long run at my usual pace. Knowing there's a break approaching is far easier mentally."

7 PAY THE PROS

"One thing that really helped me in my first marathon was finding a chiropractor I trusted," says Garry Cochrane from Dragons Running Club in Leeds. "From day one I was plagued with a groin strain, but regular chiropractor sessions really helped me cope with the problem, giving me confidence. The advice meant I could continue to train, as I was reassured that nothing was going to snap or fall off and that it wouldn't get any worse. On race day there was no sign or feeling of the injury at all."

8 BE FLEXIBLE

Remember that any marathon training schedule is not cast in stone – it's just a route map, advises marathon veteran Peter Russell from Gravesend Road Runners in Kent. "It's to get you from where you are now to where you want to be, and nothing more," he says. "There are plenty of 'alternative routes' on the way. If you don't achieve one goal, or a week's planned runs, then take a diversion – we all have bad days/weeks and get lost on the way. It isn't the end of the world. Just adjust the schedule and relax. It's a strategy that's helped me tackle nine marathons and enjoy every one."

9 DISTRACTION TACTICS

"For me, the mental part is harder than the physical part – and the physical part is hard enough," says Johnny Christmas, London. "I found running alone really difficult and sometimes my heart sank knowing I would have to get out on a miserable day and do 18 miles plodding through mud on my own. Having an iPod was great – listening to podcasts (runningpodcasts.org) or music helped pass the time."

10 FIGHT THE FREEZE

The obvious problem of starting any training schedule in mid-winter isn't one you should take lightly, says Grant Wooler from Perth Road Runners in Scotland. "In the winter my hands get agonisingly cold – then I had a brainwave that I could combine my need for hydration on longer runs with keeping my hands warm. I'd fill my water bottle up with almost boiling water from the kettle, which would keep my hands warm for about eight miles, by which time my body was generating enough of its own heat. And by that time you need some hydration, when it is cool enough to drink."

ILLUSTRATION: DANNY ALLISON

HOW TO TAILOR YOUR TAPER

To race your best, you need to get enough rest beforehand.
But can you have too much of a good thing?

Tapering – scaling back your miles to allow your muscles to repair and your body to simply rest – is the critical last phase of training before a race. It's no less important to racing success than, say, long runs. But consider this: trimming your mileage right back abruptly might not be the best move. In fact, maintaining a higher volume during the taper period can give you a better chance of peaking on race day. "The problem with a big cut in mileage is that your body gets used to being on holiday," says exercise physiologist Greg McMillan. Top running coach Jack Daniels puts it more bluntly: "You can taper too much."

Just as you can add miles too quickly (and get injured), cutting them drastically can lead to a sluggish or sickly feeling. It's not uncommon even for elite athletes to come down with a stinking cold the week before a big race. One possible reason: a major mileage cut can signal to the immune system that it's okay to ease up. But by maintaining volume, your immune response remains constant.

McMillan not only maintains more of his runners' miles in the days leading up to a race, he also shortens the taper (two weeks for a marathon, seven to 10 days for a half). He says today's recreational runners simply don't need as much rest as those of 30 years ago. That's because they log 30- to 40-mile weeks instead of 70, making a heavy taper unnecessary. In addition, he says, "we understand the recovery cycle better." Today's training programmes have rest and recovery built into them, so runners are less likely to overtrain.

So what's the key to a successful taper? Some cutback in total mileage combined with a little quality work. McMillan recommends reducing volume by 10 to 40 per cent, depending on race distance and your fatigue level. A 5K, of course, requires less of a reduction and a shorter taper than a marathon (see 'Necessary Cutbacks', right). Similarly, low-mileage runners need less taper time than long-haulers.

It's best to reduce volume by eliminating miles from each of your weekly runs. Do a shorter long run, fewer miles on easy days, and less higher-intensity work (instead of eight 800s, run four; instead of four tempo miles, do two). Just don't cut out quality altogether – multiple studies suggest that some fast-paced running is critical to keeping your lungs and legs sharp.

And keep in mind that every athlete is an "experiment of one," says Daniels. Percentages and time lines are guidelines – use them as a place to start, and adjust according to how you feel. Test your fatigue level a week or two before your taper by doing a two- to six-mile run at race pace. If you feel sluggish or just don't run the time you want, you might need to extend your taper by a few days or reduce your mileage by another five to 10 per cent. Do what feels comfortable for you. "Part of a taper is physiological; part is psychological," says Daniels. "If it doesn't settle in your mind, it interferes with the benefits come race day."

TAPER YOUR DIET

Tweaking your food intake is an essential part of your pre-race preparation. For a marathon, begin seven days before the race; for a 5K or 10K, start four days before.

➲ 7 DAYS BEFORE
Reduce your intake by 100 calories for every mile you knock off your training.

➲ 4 DAYS BEFORE
Start carbohydrate-loading. Aim for around 500g per day. Wholegrain pasta or bread is ideal.

➲ 2 DAYS BEFORE
Start fluid loading.

Sports drinks are good.

➲ THE NIGHT BEFORE
Eat a high-carb meal of 800-1,000 calories. Stick to what you know rather than risk surprising your stomach on race day.

➲ RACE DAY
Eat 800 calories of low-fat carbs up to two hours before.

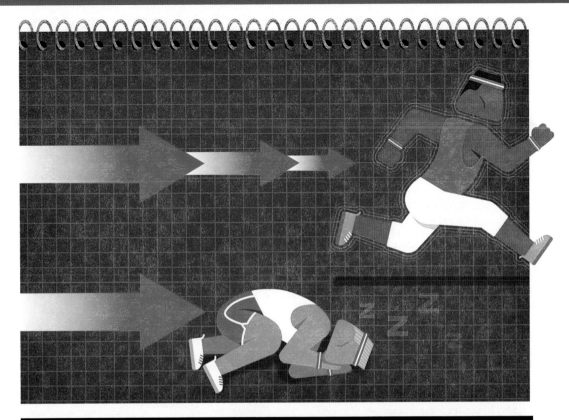

NECESSARY CUTBACKS

Tapering correctly is critical. Rest too much and you might feel sluggish on race day; scale back too little and you may be tired. Use these guidelines developed by coach Greg McMillan before you toe the line. (Add easy days according to your schedule.)

	7 days before		4		2 OR 1	
5K OR 10K	Reduce weekly mileage by 10 to 20%; 3 to 5 x 3 minutes at goal 5K or 10K pace, one-minute rest		Rest or run according to your schedule		Rest or run according to your schedule	

	10 days before	7	4	2 OR 1
1/2 MARATHON	Reduce weekly mileage by 10 to 20%	10 miles, with the last 2 to 3 at half-marathon pace	5 x 3 mins at half-marathon pace, 1-minute rest	Rest or run according to your schedule

	14 days before	12	10	7	4	2 OR 1
MARATHON	Reduce weekly mileage by 10 to 20%	10 x 400m at 5K pace, 1-min rests	3 x 2K at 10K pace, 2 to 3-min rests	Reduce mileage by another 10 to 20% 12-mile run with last 6 at race pace	4 x 3 minutes at 10K pace, 1-min rests	Rest or run according to your schedule

RUN A PERFECT RACE

The alarm clock rings... now what? Here's how to navigate any course correctly

To race well, you need to train well – that much is obvious. But there are also race-day logistics to master. Even if training has gone like a dream, you can still blow everything by tearing around on race morning in a manic panic in search of safety pins; finding yourself at the starting line with a jumble of jingling keys; or getting held-up mid-race trying to pass an iPod-wearing runner. So, to make sure your hard training doesn't go to waste, we've compiled all the advice you need to successfully navigate race day. Our tips start before the start, finish after the finish, and – if employed properly – will guarantee a glitch-free race (and maybe even a PB).

McMillan Running (mcmillanrunning.com). With the race start still half a day away, you can think clearly about all the things you want with you on the morning itself.

TRAVEL LIGHT

You could save yourself the post-race hassle of retrieving your belongings by not checking anything into the baggage hold area. Wear an old sweatshirt and jogging pants over your racing outfit that you can toss at the start (most races donate the clothes). "Only 50 out of 37,000 runners might not get back what they left at the start," says Dave Bedford, race director of the London Marathon. If you need to check your bag in, don't put anything in your sack that you can't live without (such as your keys; see 'Secure your key', below).

SHOW YOUR NUMBER

Even though most races time with chips, you still have to wear a number. "Bib numbers show race officials that you are a registered runner," says Bedford. "They should be visible at all times." Pin your bib on the front of your racing outfit with four safety pins to keep it from flapping around.

SECURE YOUR KEY

Find somewhere to stash your car key (note: singular), but not where someone might find it, like in the petrol cap or on top of a tyre. If the key is not too bulky, slide it into a zip-up pocket or lace it into your shoe. You could also hand your keys to a spectator friend – as long as he has a nicer car than yours.

STASH SOME CASH

If you have money with you for an emergency, you won't need it. If you don't, you will. So pin a £10 note – inside a freezer bag to prevent it from going soggy – inside your vest or put it in the pocket of your shorts, just in case.

BAG YOURSELF

They're not stylish, but plastic bin bags do keep you warm and dry if it's cold and raining. "Cut a hole for just your head, and tuck your arms inside," recommends Bedford.

WARM UP WISELY

If possible, warm up by running the first mile or so of the race course to get the lie of the land. If you can't

BEFORE THE GUN

Your pre-race goal should be to arrive at the starting line relaxed and ready to run. Here's how to do it

LAY IT OUT

"The night before your race, lay out everything you'll need on the day on an extra bed or the floor," says Greg McMillan, running coach and director of

GO AS A RUNNER

If you must dress up in a costume, "make sure it doesn't interfere with other runners", says Chris Sumner, race director of the Robin Hood Festival of Running. "Always show consideration towards others. For your own safety, make sure you can run in the outfit if it's heavy, and practise beforehand."

do that, warm up on a nearby road or pavement, not in a grassy field – early morning dew can soak through your shoes and socks.

LINE UP ON TIME

Don't get there first, because the extra wait will only make you anxious. Instead, watch the clock and keep an eye on runners as they fill in behind the start. Then join in. Many races have signs showing you where to stand according to your predicted pace. What if your race doesn't have markers? If you're hoping to run a four-hour (or longer) marathon, don't line up within 100 yards of a Kenyan.

AND YOU'RE OFF!

Once the race starts, there's more to think about than just putting one foot in front of the other

WAIT!

"Don't start your watch at the gun," recommends McMillan. It's hard to resist when you're keen to get going, but starting your watch immediately after the starting gun will yield a depressing finishing time, because it might take several minutes to cross the starting line. Turn your watch face inside your wrist to avoid an accidental bump that might activate the stopwatch, then hit the start button when you reach the start line. This will synchronise your chip time and your watch time, so you can accurately calculate your pace.

LOOK FOR ROOM

As you ramp up to race pace, try to achieve 'daylight' between you and other runners, which is basically two full stride lengths.

BE PATIENT

Don't bob and weave through the starting pack. You'll waste energy without getting very far. Instead, jog or walk with your arms slightly out to help you keep your balance. And be sure not to follow the guy with the headband who has jumped onto the curb and is sprinting ahead. The race gods will, without question, make him trip.

DRINK SECOND

The first water stop in larger races often resembles a crowded underground station at rush hour. As long as you're not thirsty, skip it. "If you don't need the water, then don't get involved for the sake of it," says Sumner. "Try to avoid the crush and focus on getting to the next water station." If you need to, start with a water bottle, drink along the way and discard it when you're done. You can refuel at later drink stations once the field has thinned out.

PASS WITH CAUTION

Runners listening to MP3 players are in a world of their own and can't hear you behind them, so they probably don't know that you're approaching. "If you do come across someone wearing headphones," advises Sumner, "slow down slightly, concentrate on the whole picture around you and take a wide berth while making sure not to interfere with anyone else."

RACE-READY CHECKLIST What to pack on the big day

1 Baseball cap and/or sunglasses: either will be helpful if you'll be running into the sun (research this beforehand) or rain.

2 Vest: at the very least you'll feel faster.

3 Bib number: take four safety pins and secure one to each corner – any fewer will cause floppage.

4 Digital stopwatch: so you can be your own clock.

5 Emergency cash: a tenner pinned to vest or in pocket of shorts.

6 Cotton gloves: cheap, they'll keep your hands warm and they double as a hankie for mid-race nose or face wiping.

7 Throwaway shirt and/or bin bag: the shirt will keep you warm before the start; the bag will keep you warm and dry.

8 Running shorts: your favourite, comfiest, speediest pair. Now is not the time to try anything brand new.

9 Socks: ankle-high or lower, no cotton (to reduce blister risk).

10 Running shoes: see number 8.

11 Timing chip: fasten to your shoe with the secure tie (no lacing required).

12 Car key: lace into the shoe that doesn't have the timing chip.

13 Sunscreen: be smart – you might be out there a while.

14 Vaseline or some other sports lubricant: apply the lubricant to your inner thighs, armpits, and, ahem, other spots where you're likely to chafe.

15 Roll of toilet paper: in case the Portaloos come up empty.

DON'T CUT CORNERS

"The quickest way to take a corner is actually to slow down going into it," says Sumner. "The most important thing is not to cut corners. You might think you're saving time by cutting on the inside but if you jump the kerb or mount a grass verge at speed, you're asking to have an accident. Slow down and take a slightly wider curve going into the corner, then move to the inside and accelerate away."

SAVE SOME STRIDES

If you run along the outside of a curve, you will run more distance than if you take the tangent, which is a straight line between the beginning and end of the curve. "Tangents are the shortest distance between two points – and that's how the course was measured," says McMillan. "So running the tangents doesn't make the course shorter. But it doesn't make it longer."

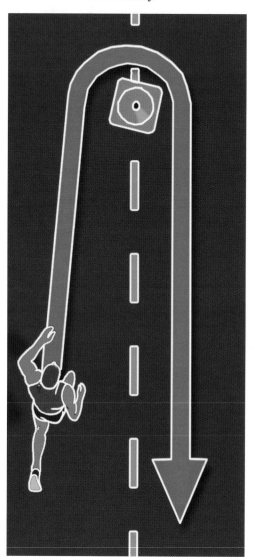

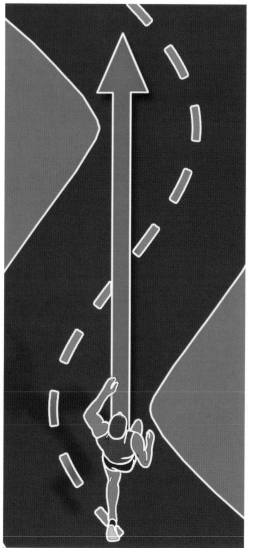

HAPPY ENDINGS

As you cross the finish line, you're not quite done yet: the finishing funnel stretches ahead

TAKE THE WRAP

Worn like a cape, mylar blankets keep the heat in. And if you're offered a sticker or piece of tape with the cape, use it to secure the blanket at the neck so that you can keep your hands free. Note: it doesn't matter which side of the blanket is in and which is out. It traps your body heat either way.

DITCH THE CHIP

If you've used one of those secure plastic ties to attach your chip to your shoe, it takes the volunteers about two seconds to get it off. "Another efficient way is to lace the chip into the shoe just below the knot so all you have to do is untie your shoe to get it off," says Mike Burns, president of ChampionChip. "If the chip is laced further down, below the eyelets and along the tongue, you'll have to unlace the shoe to remove it."

DRINK UP

Even though you are no longer running, you need fluids to rehydrate and recover. Take some and keep moving. Don't stop now, or you risk being knocked around by fellow disoriented competitors.

FIND YOUR FAMILY

Have a prearranged spot to meet up with your family and friends after the race. Anything solid and immovable is best, such as a tree or the front steps of a building. Don't suggest something like the middle of a field, which could be jam-packed with runners come race day. Next, make sure you spot your group before they see you. Now start limping (cue the sympathy violins). But do so with a huge smile on your face.

PHOTO FINISH How to get a mantel-worthy finish-line picture

3:28:56

DON'T
- Look down
- Obscure your bib number
- Fumble for your watch
- Drag your feet

DO
- Run under the clock
- Lift your arms and head, and smile
- Make sure your number is visible
- Finish with a few strong strides

426

ROAD TO RECOVERY

So you've completed your first marathon. How you recover from it is just as important as how you trained for it – so read on

Congratulations: marathon done! But running 26.2 miles places high demands on the body and you're likely to end up with depleted fuel stores, fluid in the muscles, dehydration and perhaps some damaged muscle tissue. So, not surprisingly, you will be susceptible to injury and infection after the race. You may also be feeling disorientated, or even depressed, in the come-down after achieving such a significant goal.

There's no formula for calculating how long your body will take to recover. A seasoned marathon runner can expect to bounce back quicker than a marathon novice, for example. What you can do though, is make sure you know exactly what your body needs. Here's how to deal with the most common post-marathon ailments, how to combat the blues and, of course, top advice on when and how to resume running.

HEALTH AND NUTRITION

Delayed onset muscle soreness (DOMS) can begin eight or more hours after the race and may linger for up to a week after the marathon. For the first 24 hours after the race, apply ice (wrapped in a cloth) frequently to any painful parts of your legs, keeping it on for about 12 minutes at a time. Elevate your feet and legs for at least an hour after the marathon and for 30 minutes a day for a week.

In the days following the race, take ibuprofen or aspirin to calm muscle inflammation and ease pain. Rub salicylate anti-inflammatory creams into skin over aching joints or throbbing tendons – these ointments penetrate deeply enough to limit discomfort.

BLISTERS

The best advice for dealing with blisters is leave them be. If they've broken open during the race, your main concern should be preventing infection. Twice a day, soak your feet for up to 20 minutes in water containing iodine solution. Gently dry your feet, and cover the blistered area with a sterile gauze or plaster. Continue this process until the blister no longer oozes.

COLDS AND FLU

The stress of running a marathon can depress your immune system, leaving you susceptible to colds, flu and other infections in the days immediately following the race. Self-care is the best way to reduce your risk of contracting a virus, so make sure you get plenty of sleep, eat well-balanced meals and drink lots of water. You might also want to try herbal remedies such as echinacea, or nutritional supplements such as zinc and vitamin C.

LACK OF ENERGY

A general lack of energy in the week following a marathon is perfectly usual. Try to eat meals comprising 50-60 per cent carbohydrate to replenish your glycogen reserves, and foods rich in protein to assist your body in repairing muscle and tissue. Indulge any cravings you might have – these could be your body's way of telling you what it needs.

Eat foods rich in iron – including meat, spinach, beans, peaches, parsley and peas – and promote iron absorption by drinking orange juice or consume other rich sources of vitamin C.

WEIGHT GAIN

Some runners complain of weight gain immediately after a marathon. This is most likely due to water retention as your muscles repair and rebuild. Don't be tempted to diet – your body requires a full complement of nutrients to recover from the stress of the race. If you're still gaining weight after the first week, adjust your calorie intake to suit your new activity levels.

ILLUSTRATION: EMILIANO PONZI

FIGHTING THE POST-MARATHON BLUES

You've spent several months training hard and thinking about little else but your marathon, and now it's all over. And you're depressed. Luckily there are plenty of ways to combat the post-marathon blues.

Set new running goals and try shorter distances, or join a club for some company. Try something new, such as cross-training. Most importantly, give yourself a treat such as a holiday. You've earned it!

HOW TO RESUME TRAINING

Now the big question: how do you pick up your training afterwards? For many years, exercise scientists have debated whether it is best to rest completely or jog lightly during the days that follow a marathon. The argument could go either way: light jogging should stimulate blood flow to the muscles, reduce tightness and preserve fitness. On the other hand, total rest allows the leg muscles to devote all their energies to the rebuilding process.

To gauge the relative values of rest and running, scientists in the USA recently studied a large group of marathon runners. About half of the marathon runners refrained from running for a week following a marathon, while the other group jogged lightly for 30 minutes each day. Both sets of runners were stiff and sore during the week after the race, but the resting runners recovered much more quickly. Leg-muscle endurance returned to normal after three days for the inactive runners, but was still below par after seven days for the light joggers. So take a one-week rest from training after your marathon. You deserve the break, and your muscles will return to normal more quickly.

During this one-week respite, you can do some light walking to burn off a few calories, keep your leg muscles loose and satisfy your desire for exercise. Once you're ready to get back to your favourite sport, prudence is the word. Remember that it takes four weeks for your muscles to really return to normal, so run only 30-60 per cent of your usual mileage.

Heart-rate monitoring is another good way of gauging when you are ready to resume training. A resting heart rate of 10 beats per minute or more above your pre-race rate is a sign that your body has yet to fully recover. So listen to it, and take it steady.

TIME TO UNWIND

Essential advice from runners and readers on how to recover

1 DRINK UP
The last thing many runners want immediately after crossing the finish line is solid food – so think liquid nourishment instead. "50:50 orange juice and Coke really hits the spot," says Rich Shardlow from Bromsgrove & Redditch AC. "It was introduced to me as a post-rugby drink, and I guess the sugar, caffeine and vitamin C all work together to give you a boost."

2 WARM DOWN
Recovery starts the moment you finish the race. "Keep walking for a few minutes to help your body warm down," says Adrian Stott from Sri Chinmoy AC in Edinburgh. Vicki Thompson from Jarrow & Hebburn AC says: "I follow a walk with a slow 10-minute jog – it gives you time to analyse your race and 'feel' which parts of the body are hurting for attention later on."

3 FEEL THE STRETCH
Those waste products, such as lactic acid, will make an unwelcome reappearance if you don't take action. "Straight after warming down, I do punch squats to get blood flowing through my body and stretch out areas like the back and glutes that get missed from just 'walking it off'," says Rob Codling from Bristol. "Find something to lean against, lower yourself down, pause, breathe, and as you rise up, punch one arm in the air." Clare Naden from Clapham Chasers lies on her stomach and pushes herself up on her hands, pressing her hips into the ground to work the lower back and hamstrings.

4 FEEL THE RUB
A post-race massage can be a wonderful thing. "I always carry a foam roller with me and work on my IT band and calves, focusing on tight or knotted areas," says David Watson from Up & Running in Nottingham. Katie Bretherick from Abbey Runners in Leeds rubs up using Better You Magnesium Oil sports spray to get the blood flowing. "It's got all sorts of essential oils, which are absorbed through the skin and draw the lactic acid and other toxins out – it feels like you've had a professional massage."

5 COOL IT
The thought of an ice bath after hard runs is enough to make most runners wince. Rather than the full monty, Wendi Witton from Brighton stands in a waist-high water butt in her back garden with a mug of tea. "At training camps in the Algarve we'd stand in the sea after long runs." Gillian Wasson from Springwell RC has a warm shower then showers from the hips down with cold water. "It's what they do to horses after races to speed recovery," she notes.

6 HAVE A BANQUET
Once you can stomach solids, advice from readers overflows. "A ready-salted crisp sandwich washed down with cola replaces all the minerals you sweated out," says Tufat Nladi from Black Pear Joggers. A post-race meal at a favourite eatery is the perfect incentive for Phil Sanders from Kent AC. "Knowing you've got a roast dinner and pudding waiting for you is enough to keep any runner's spirits up." Lorna Gold from Centurion Running Club opts for "a mixed grill containing half a farmyard. I noticed it's what the winners of the Abingdon Marathon ate."

7 GET CHANGED
You might want to wear your racing vest as a badge of honour, but it may not be the best option. "We often forget just how low our defences are after

a race, so I immediately throw on layers," says Tessa Dollar from Shropshire. Adrian Stott, meanwhile, always has a pair of fresh socks and sports sandals to slip into, which "let my swollen feet recover in half the time". David Phillips from Birmingham pulls on a pair of compression tights and keeps them on overnight to squeeze the lactic acid out.

8 BACK TO FORM

How long should you leave it before you start training for a new race target? "As a rule of thumb, it takes a day per mile of distance raced to fully recover," says George Gandy, director of Athletics at Loughborough University. "I always take a complete week off after marathons, followed by gradual tapering back to full training for three weeks – it's done my PBs a world of good." Andy Knowles from Faversham goes down the cross-training route. "I alternate days of swimming, cycling, rowing and core work – you return to running much stronger as a result."

9 SLEEP MATTERS

Kicking back with a DVD after you've stretched, iced and eaten might seem like the perfect option – but not for Toby Pearson from Thames Hare and Hounds Club in London. "It's sleep or nothing," he says. "Listen to your body and if you're tired – which you should be – have a nap, and go to bed early. Your body doesn't recover half as quickly sitting on a sofa." James Garner from Carlisle ups the ante: "I need three extra hours' sleep a night for at least five days after a big race or I'll get ill." Susan Kennedy from Serpentine Running Club in London says sleep should take precedence. "I agreed to see my husband sing on the Monday night after a marathon, went to bed late and came down with a terrible cold. The lesson is to be selfish – put yourself first when you're recovering from a serious race."

10 MIND GAMES

It's not just your muscles that will need some R&R. "When I first started racing, I'd suffer Post-Race Apathy Syndrome – that empty feeling after months of building up to a race," says Adrian Stott. "Book yourself in to do a shorter race a few weeks after your 'big race' – it'll tell you where you are in your body's recovery process." Lee Maynard from Egham swears by putting pen to paper. "Draw up a timetable of when you can start running again – stick it up on your fridge and it'll make you really look forward to getting back out there without slipping up."

Subscribe to TRIATHLETE'S WORLD

ONLY £3
for the first 3 issues*

SAVE £8.97 ON YOUR FIRST 3 ISSUES

Triathlete's World offers health, fitness and nutrition advice around a core of easy-to-follow training programmes, product buying guides and event information.

Subscribe securely online at
www.qualitymagazines.co.uk/tw/SA17

Or call today and quote offer code SA17
0844 848 1601†

Order lines open 8am-9.30pm (Mon-Fri), 8am-4pm (Sat)

†BT landline calls to 0844 numbers will cost no more than 5p per minute; calls made from mobiles and other networks usually cost more.

Classified

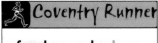

Classified

Runner's Rescue

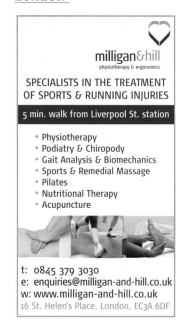
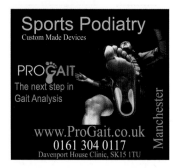
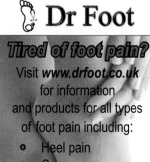
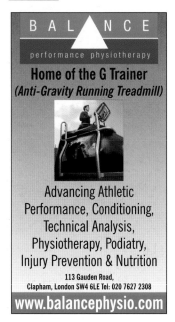
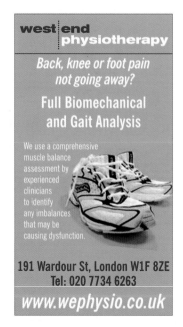

Travel

Midlands

Notts/Yorkshire

Travel

Northamptonshire

Surrey